The Chains of Black America

Also by Michael Holzman

Lukács's Road to God

Writing as Social Action (with Marilyn Cooper)

James Jesus Angleton: The C.I.A., and the Craft of
Counterintelligence

Transgressions (novel)

Guy Burgess: Revolutionary in an Old School Tie

The Black Poverty Cycle and How to End It

Minority Students and Public Education:
A Resource Book (Two Volumes)

Donald and Melinda Maclean: Idealism and Espionage

The Chains of Black America

The Hammer of the Police

The Anvil of the Schools

Michael Holzman

Chelmsford Press   Briarcliff Manor, New York

 Chelmsford Press
Briarcliff Manor, New York

ISBN-13: 978-0692369319
ISBN-10: 0692369317

The "dark ghetto's invisible walls have been erected by the white society, by those who have power, both to confine those who have no power and to perpetuate their powerlessness . . . Their inhabitants are subject peoples, victims of the greed, cruelty, insensitivity, guilt and fear of their masters." *Kenneth B. Clark. Dark Ghetto: Dilemmas of Social Power. New York: Harper and Row, 1965, p. 11.*

For Jane

Acknowledgments

Rosa Smith and Phillip Jackson have been inspirations for this work.

I also wish to acknowledge the help of Kristen Balonek, RiShawn Biddle, John Caniglia, Jing Che, the late Marco Mcmillian, Evangeline Monroe, Susan Plum, Anthony Simmons, Elspeth Stuckey Smith, and Steve Van Dine.

Errors are, of course, my own. I would be grateful to have them brought to my attention so that they might be corrected.

Table of Contents

Introduction

Melvin C. High is Sheriff of Prince George's County, Maryland. The younger of two sons of a share cropper and a school teacher in Union County, Mississippi, High attended Tennessee State University, receiving a Bachelor's of Science degree, taught high school, served in the Marine Corps in Vietnam, and then began a career in policing. His daughter, Tracy Richelle High, attended Yale University and Harvard Law School. She is Deputy Managing Partner of the Litigation Group at Sullivan and Cromwell, where her "practice focuses on representing financial institutions and other corporations in complex civil litigation, including shareholder derivative and class action suits, regulatory enforcement proceedings, corporate internal investigations, and labor and employment matters . . ."[1]

The biographies of Sheriff High and his daughter sum up the American dream: from a farm in rural Mississippi to a "white shoe" Wall Street law firm in two generations. Unfortunately, their story is all too unusual for African-Americans. This book is a description of how two great institutions of American government—the education and criminal justice systems—often hinder, rather than enable, the achievement of equal opportunities for the descendants of enslaved Africans. The book is about the situation of African Americans, rather than about "people of color," or impoverished Americans, because of the specific history of African Americans and the way in which their oppression affects others. It is perhaps not too much to say that until descent from enslaved Africans is no longer a cause for lack of equality of opportunity, the United States will never be a just society.

Each chapter, beginning with a national survey in Chapter One, includes demographic, health, income, wealth, and economic mobility data, followed by sections on the criminal justice and education systems and concluding with attempts at modeling a more equitable society. This modeling is extended nationally in a final chapter. In addition to the national overview in Chapter One, there are chapters on eight cities: Chicago, Cleveland, Memphis, Milwaukee, New Orleans, New York City, Philadelphia, and Rochester, New York. Each of these has a significant, highly segregated, African American population. In each, African American incarceration rates are many times higher than those of White, non-Hispanics, and educational outcomes are much less favorable for African American than for White, non-Hispanic, students. There are many other cities where these conditions prevail, such as Minneapolis, Buffalo, Montgomery and Miami, but eight examples should suffice. There is also a chapter on Sheriff High's Prince George's County, a predominately African American, middle class, suburban area. The county is not without its problems, but those problems do not include institutionalized racism. The lives of the descendants of enslaved Africans now living in Prince George's county do not greatly differ from those of White, non-Hispanic, residents of neighboring suburban counties. They differ dramatically from those of African Americans in the dark ghettos of cities where their manacles are forged by blows of the hammers of racist criminal justice systems on the anvils of racist school systems.

The institutionalized racism of much of America's education and criminal justice systems can be ended at any time by the actions of those individuals occupying positions of authority in those institutions: police chiefs, district attorneys, judges, mayors, members of school boards, school district superintendents, school principals. It should not be all that difficult for them to do the right thing. It is, as a matter of fact, their duty to do so.

Notes: Introduction

[1] http://www.sullcrom.com/lawyers/TracyRichelle-High. The schools in Union County, Mississippi, underwent an unusually peaceful and thorough integration in the 1960s. "When the process of integration completed in 1970, African American students comprised 29 percent of the school district's students and 20 percent of the schools' faculty." Mississippi Civil Rights Project, History County-by-County. School Desegregation in Union County. http://mscivilrightsproject.org/index.php?option=com_content&view =article&id=192:school-desegregation-in-union-county&Itemid=81

The Chains of Black America

The Hammer of the Police

The Anvil of the Schools

Chapter One: The National Picture

American society has a dual socio-economic structure.[1] There is the *class* structure in which most Americans live, characterized by a certain lingering mobility of income and wealth, with differentials that are, in turn, traceable to differences in education and to an increasing extent to differences in inherited wealth, and there is what has been called the *caste* status of the American descendants of enslaved Africans, characterized by generally low incomes and little or no wealth or mobility. Many recent discussions of American society have focused on class: income and wealth, the levels of each, inequality and mobility. But research about income and wealth groupings and mobility in the United States is of limited use if it does not factor in the caste effects of racism.

Despite the fact that from a scientific point of view there is no such thing as race, racism is real on the level of a belief, an ideology, that can, and usually does, strongly affect the actions of racist members of the dominant race and the institutions they control. It can be generalized, "xenophobia," or it can be focused on a specific group. In the United States that group, for obvious historical reasons, is composed of the descendants of enslaved Africans.

Racism ensures that caste status almost always trumps class for African Americans.

The Demographics of Caste

Racism is fundamental in America. It is visible in age and gender population distributions, longevity and health as well as wealth and income. To begin with its effects on life itself: Among the 232 million residents of this country whom the Bureau of the Census designates as "White alone" the percentage of females exceeds males by only 1.2%. On the other hand, the 39.6 million "Black alone" Americans have a gender gap that is three times as great: over 4%. Nearly three percent of male African Americans are "missing." There are also age differentials. The Black population of America is considerably younger than that of White America. The median age of the White population is 40.2 years, that of the Black population just 32.9 years. This is a function both of a larger percentage of young people among African Americans than among White, non-Hispanic, Americans and a smaller percentage of the elderly in the African American community in comparison to the White community.

When we look more closely at these statistics, we find that there is a larger proportion of Black than White Americans at every age cohort until age 44, at which point the distribution reverses, until for the age cohorts 75 and over, fully 7% of White Americans have reached that milestone, while only 4% of the African American population survives more than ten years beyond retirement age. The male African American population, in particular, shows a disproportionate decline in numbers with increasing age. This decline begins as early as age 18 and continues until, by age 65, there are only two African American men for every three African American women. As a consequence, there are nearly 700,000 fewer African American men over the age of 18 than there would be if the age and gender ratios of African Americans were the same as those of White Americans.[2]

Life expectancy at birth, another crucial measure of human development, tells the same story. An African American man can expect to die five years earlier than a White, non-Hispanic, American man; an African American woman can expect to die three years earlier than a White American woman.[3] White Americans have life expectancies at the European Union average; Black Americans have life expectancies similar to those of people in Serbia, Sri Lanka and Oman.[4] *Male* African Americans have life expectancies similar to those of people living in Guatemala (world rank number 143).

African Americans in general have shorter lives than White Americans; African American men have much shorter lives.[*]

Why is this? One factor is health. According to the Kaiser Family Foundation, while 8.5% of White men report being "in only fair or poor health," 13.3% of Black men do so. Just 3.5% of White men, but 6.3% of Black men, have diabetes. The disparities in statistics for women are similar. While 9% of White women report being "in only fair or poor health," nearly twice as many, 17%, of Black women do so. Just 3% of White women, but more than twice

---

[*] For African American females life expectancy at birth is 78 years, for Black males 72 years, while for White females it is 81 years, for White males 77 years.

that, 7.3%, of Black women, have diabetes. The rate of deaths per thousand live births is another crucial public health indicator. There are 5.5 deaths per thousand live births for White, non-Hispanic, Americans, more than twice that, 13 per thousand, for Black Americans. Infant mortality rates for African Americans are worse than those for most of the world's developed countries.[5] Sara Wakefield and Christopher Wildeman have pointed out that "The black infant mortality rate in the United States is roughly in line with the infant mortality rates of Belarus, Sri Lanka, and Uruguay . . ."[6] Sri Lanka, a country with vital statistics comparable to many of those of African Americans, ranks 164th in the world for its death rate, 147th for its infant mortality rate, 83rd for life expectancy at birth, according to the CIA's World Fact Book. We can note in passing that for many years everyday life for much of Sri Lanka's population has been characterized by the violence of civil war.

A key factor in the relative poor health and shorter lives of African Americans is the unusual American healthcare system. Unlike those of many developed countries, it is by and large a business, a way for corporations and individuals to profit from the health needs of the general population. As such, its benefits are distributed by income, and as income varies by race, African Americans have been among the least able to receive equal access to healthcare. While just 15% of Adult White Americans were uninsured in 2011, nearly twice that percentage, 26%, of Black American adults were uninsured.[7] (This does appear to be improving since the passing of the Affordable Healthcare Act, but there is as yet a long way to go.[8])

These demographic and health indicators are consequences of the interrelated burdens of poverty, high incarceration rates and poor educational opportunities of the American descendants of enslaved Africans. They are basic signs that African Americans, in general, live under markedly different conditions from those in which many White Americans enjoy "the American way of life."

Income

Class itself is a contested term. Its roots are in the medieval European division of people among landless workers, owners of the land (and often owners of the workers themselves as well), clergy and what became a gradually growing group of merchants and others not bound to the soil. In the nineteenth- and early-twentieth centuries European and American classes were generally assumed to be just three: people who worked with their hands; people who worked with their minds, and people who lived off incomes produced by the other two groups without themselves needing to work: coal miners, for example and, say, lawyers and "aristocrats." Long defined in this way by how people obtained the means for survival, class has gradually became associated with the amount of those means. Over the last century, especially in the United States, a division by income has come into common use, with classes measured from a median, usually in tenths (deciles) or fifths (quintiles), without regard to the sources of that income.[9]

When we focus on the contemporary income divisions of class, we find that generalizations about the distribution of American incomes are highly misleading if not disaggregated by race. According to the Bureau of the Census, in 2013, while median *household* income of White, non-Hispanics, was $58,270, Black Americans, whose household incomes have changed little over the past thirty years,[10] reported to the Census in 2013 household incomes with a median of $34,598, just two-thirds of the White level.[11] Nearly half of Black households have incomes below 130 percent of the poverty level and 47% of those are "food insecure," according to the United States Department of Agriculture.[12]

Individual per capita income for White Americans is $30,077 and $18,102 for African Americans, just 60% of the White per capita income. Internationally, for individual per capita income, White America would rank with Switzerland, at third; Black America would be far down the list, around 23rd or 24th, between Spain and Greece. The Pew Charitable Trusts 2012 report *Pursuing the American Dream*, found that "Just over two-thirds of blacks were raised at the bottom of the income ladder compared with only 11 percent of whites."[13] This is not a continuum between rich and poor, the latter of whom are often "coincidentally" Black. As with the demographic data, it is a token of the existence of two separate economies, two separate ways of life.

We can more closely examine income distribution differentials by considering the percentages and numbers of African American and White American households at discrete income levels. There are higher percentages of Black than White households at each income level up to $50,000 per year, then the distribution reverses.[14] Thirty-seven percent of those at the lowest income level, $10,000 and below, are Black: more than twice the Black share in the general population. At each successively higher income level the number of Black households as a percentage of the number of White households declines. The middle 50% of White household incomes ranges from $35,000 to $100,000. The middle 50% of Black household incomes ranges from $15,000 to about $55,000. In other words, a large proportion of the middle 50% of Black household incomes are below the poverty line and if they were White they would not make it into the middle class grouping by income. At the other end of the scale, approximately one-quarter of White households have incomes over $100,000, as compared to just 10% of Black households. At the highest level reported by the Census, incomes over $200,000, the number of Black households is just 4% of the number of White households. Only 1% of Black households have incomes equivalent to those of the top 5% of White household incomes.

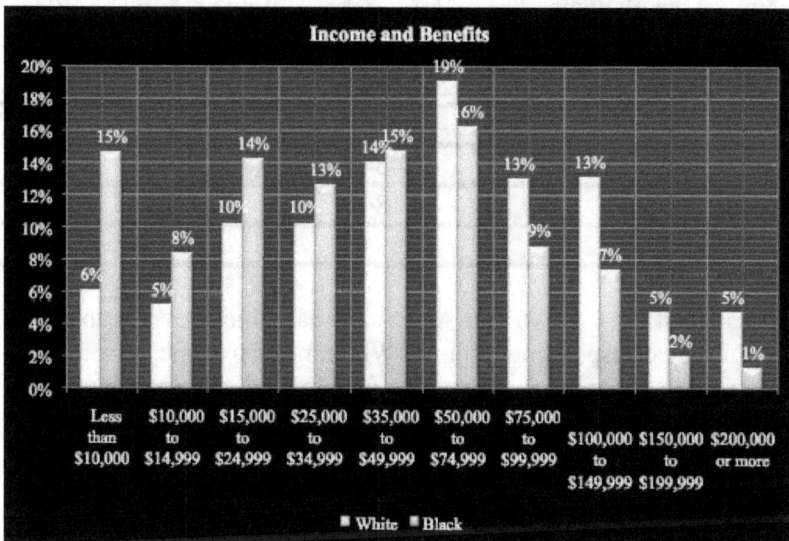

Income disparities are customarily measured in quintiles: groups of 20% of the population.[15] The following table gives the upper limit of each of the lower four quintiles and the lower limit of the top 5%

for the United States as a whole and for White, non-Hispanic, Americans and African Americans (2012).

Family Income Quintiles	U.S.	White	Black
Lower Limit of Top 5%	$210,000	224,000	145,000
Fourth (upper limit)	119,000	130,000	84,000
Third (Middle)	76,500	86,000	51,000
Second	50,000	58,000	31,000
Lowest	28,000	34,000	16,000

Nationally, median family income is quite close to the mean figure for the middle quintile. However, the top 5% received about 20% of the aggregate income of each group in 2012, the top quintile half, and the lowest quintile 3% of total group aggregate income. Because of this, upper quintile mean incomes are characteristically much higher than median incomes.

Family Mean Income	U.S.	White	U.S. Black
Top 5%	$352,338	384,794	226,811
Highest Fifth	209,559	219,769	138,371
Fourth	95,474	105,512	66,597
Third (Middle)	62,464	71,589	40,843
Second	38,184	45,781	23,525
Lowest	15,534	20,371	8,190

The poorest 20% of African Americans have incomes less than half that of the corresponding group of White, non-Hispanic, Americans.

Income for most working age people is determined by wages. Wages for Black workers are lower than those for White workers at every wage percentile. And the gap is getting wider. The recent Economic Policy Institute study, *Raising America's Pay,* found that in 1979 at the 50th wage percentile, Black wages were 83% of White wages.[16] By 2013 they had declined to 77%. The higher up the income ladder, the greater the gap between Black and White wages. This trend is also increasing. For the lowest paid jobs, between 1979 and 2013, Black wages fell from 95% of White wages to 91%. For wages at the 95th percentile, the highest paid workers, Black wages fell from 79% of White wages in 1979 to 70% in 2013. In 1979 the gap between hourly wages for Black and White workers at the lowest end of the pay scale (the 10th percentile) was $1.59 (2013 dollars). By 2013 this had narrowed to just $0.81. But at the highest percentile, the 95th, the gap widened between 1979 and 2013 from $9.68 to $17.18, nearly doubling. A consequence of this is that while wages at the 95th percentile for White workers are six times those at the 10th percentile, the multiple for Black workers is just five. The "tilt" of earnings toward the highest group is significantly less for Black workers. From one point of view this Black wage distribution is a good thing: the Black community is less inequitable than the White community. From another point of view this is simply one more indication that the American descendants of enslaved Africans do not fully participate in the general American economy. African Americans are, in practice, locked out of the highest paid jobs.

Wealth

Wealth and income are often conflated. A banker with an income of a million dollars a year may be referred to as wealthy, whether or not she has significant assets. (She could, after all, spend her entire income on rent and vacations, or give most of it to charity.) Others may have significant wealth, investments, for example, or greatly appreciated property, without particularly high incomes from the interest on those assets. It is important to keep the distinction between income and wealth in mind as economic status is as, if not more, dependent on wealth than on income. A crucial finding of Thomas Piketty's *Capital in the Twenty-First Century* is that "In the United States . . . the top decile own 72 percent of America's wealth, while the bottom half claim just 2 percent." (He goes on to note "that this source, like most surveys in which wealth is self-reported, underestimates the largest fortunes.")[17] It is now generally accepted that the wealthier members of the population are capturing increasing shares of the growth in wealth. (Effectively countering the "grow a larger pie" theory of how to achieve income equity. In fact, it is now the case that the larger the pie, the greater are the number of slices consumed by the very wealthy.) Between 1983 and 2010 the bottom fifth of the population experienced a 3% *decline* in its share of the growth of wealth, while the top 1% increased its share by nearly 40%.[18] Of course, the top 1% is nearly entirely White.

In general, it is rather odd to talk about Black wealth: there is too little to make much difference. According to a Bureau of the Census study, in 2011 the median net worth of White, non-Hispanic, households was $110,500, $33,408 without home equity. The median net worth of African American households was $6,314; just $2,124 without home equity: only 6% of that of non-Hispanic White American households.[19] While sixteen percent of White households have zero or negative net worth, including home equity, twice that percentage, one-third of Black households, are "broke," with zero or negative net worth (three to six times Piketty's estimate of 5% to 10% of households in all developed countries at this level). The Pew "Pursuing the American Dream" researchers found that "for family wealth . . . 57 percent of blacks were raised at the bottom, but only 14 percent of whites were.

At the other end of the income and wealth ladders, almost one-quarter (23 percent) of whites were raised at the top [quintile] versus only 2 percent of blacks. *In fact, the percentage of black families at the top two rungs of the family income and wealth ladders is so small that median and absolute mobility estimates cannot be calculated with statistical certainty"* [20] (emphasis added).

The Pew researchers estimate that just 9% of African Americans are born into families in the national fourth or fifth quintile of income and just 8% into the fourth or fifth quintile of wealth, as compared with nearly half of White Americans by each measure.[21] At the other end of the scale, 36% of those in the bottom quintile of wealth are Black, even though African Americans are only 13% of the total population.

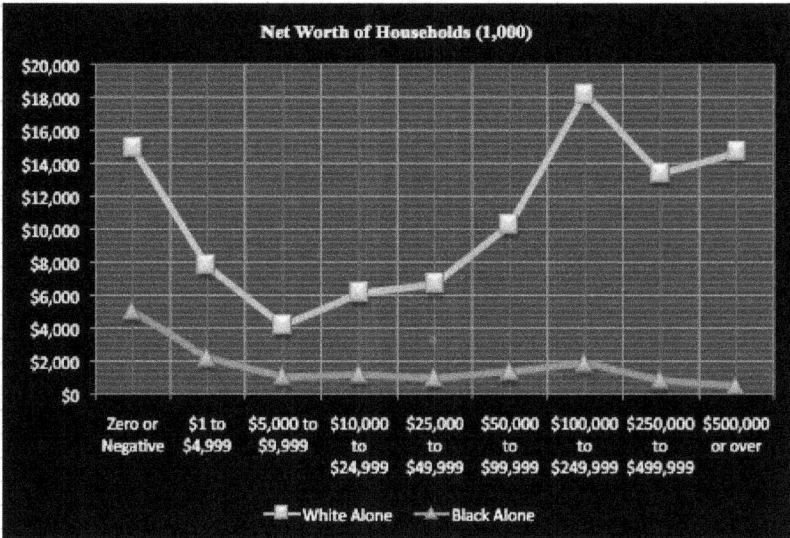

Net Worth of Households (1,000)

We can estimate that the total wealth of African American households, including home equity, is not more than 4% of White, non-Hispanic, household net worth.[22] Only 3% of Black households, as compared to 15% of White households, have net worth of half a million dollars or more. There is only one African American billionaire, Oprah Winfrey. Her net assets are estimated at $3 billion. The next wealthiest African Americans are a cluster of half a dozen entertainers and athletes each with net worth in the $450-$550 million range.[23] There are probably 1,000 White Americans at that level, many of whom do not work at all, but live on unearned incomes, much of which is from inherited wealth.

As the recent report *Beyond Broke* puts it, "race is a stronger predictor of wealth than class."[24]

Poverty

The vast, and rather peculiar, literature about poverty in America begins with the early-modern European assumption that the poor, to adapt Fitzgerald's phrase, are different from you and me. There is an insistence that people living in poverty are a special group, quite apart from, well, you and me, ignoring the fact that for most of human history the poor, say those experiencing life-long "food insecurity," not knowing where their next meal was coming from, have been most of us. We were poor because the number of seeds saved from one harvest were barely sufficient to produce another harvest of a similar size and because any surplus beyond that needed for life itself was appropriated by the very small group monopolizing the force to do so. With the coming of the industrial revolution a hitherto peripheral aspect of poverty, unemployment, came to the attention of those with the leisure to write about poverty. Subsistence farmers and hereditary farm laborers were brought to the new factories, first in the English Midlands, then as far afield as New England and India. The business cycle, periods of prosperity followed seemingly inexplicably by periods of economic collapse, resulted in their periodic unemployment, vastly increasing the numbers of wanderers on the roads and dwellers in the misery of workhouses.

Poverty began to be associated with that unemployment, which was as often as not viewed, by those who had no need to work for their bread, as voluntary and thus a failing of "character." Some years ago Richard Herrenstein wrote that "the tendency to be unemployed may run in the genes of a family about as certainly as bad teeth do now."[25] Herrenstein apparently believed that unemployment is somehow intrinsic to individuals, presumably a typical 6 percent of those in comparatively good times in developed countries, rising to 25 percent during severe economic contractions. It is difficult to make sense of this. Why should "the tendency to be unemployed" just happen to correlate with business cycles? There are more fruitful ways to look at the issue. Mark Robert Rank, having observed that "For much of our recent history, we have looked at poverty as the domain of the individual . . . [T]he causes of poverty have been routinely reduced to individual inadequacies, and the impact of such poverty has been localized to the individual's household or perhaps the immediate neighborhood," makes a further, crucial, observation: "This viewpoint has helped to maintain the status quo of severe economic deprivation in America . . ."[26] Which, of course, is why it is so stubbornly supported by those benefitting from the status quo.

Rank elsewhere states something that at first sight appears similar to Herrenstein's assertion: "Those with working class or lower-class parents are likely to remain working or lower-class themselves. Similarly, those whose parents are affluent are likely to remain affluent . . ." But he goes on to point to obvious extrinsic matters: "The . . . parents' class differences result in significant differences in the resources and opportunities available to their children.

> These differences in turn affect children's future life chances and outcomes, including the accumulation of skills and education . . . Differences in income and social class transmitted from one generation to the next are critical in explaining the differences in human capital and skill that exist in today's society."[27]

Expanding on this, Rank explains: "Essential to an initial understanding of poverty is the concept of economic vulnerability and an awareness of the importance of the lack of human capital in accentuating such vulnerability . . .

> Those who do well in the labor market often do so as a result of the human capital they have acquired . . . As a result, they are in greater demand by employers and enjoy brighter job and earnings prospects . . . On the other hand, those who face an elevated risk of poverty tend to have acquired less valuable human capital. Their educations may be truncated or of an inferior quality, while their job experience and skills may be less marketable . . . Additional attributes can also limit their ability to compete effectively in the labor market. Households that reside in inner cities or in remote rural areas often face diminished job prospects. Single mothers with young children experience reduced flexibility in their ability to take a job as a result of having to arrange child care. In addition, employers may use factors such as race and gender to screen and/or limit the promotion of potential employees.[28]

This explanation begins to shift from a focus on the characterological deficits of individuals to an analysis of social structures, which Rank summarized as follows: "U.S. poverty is largely the result of structural failings at the economic, political, and social levels."[29] He concludes: "It is one thing for a country to be mired in poverty but to lack the resources to change the conditions. It is quite another to have the capital and assets but consistently fail to do much about it. It is the latter that characterizes the United States."[30] We might observe that structures that repeatedly fail, but are maintained, in the long run are better understood as succeeding in achieving goals other than those professed.

The center of this mystery is that it is not the country that is mired in poverty; it is the country's comparatively powerless groups, in particular, the caste of African Americans.

The association of poverty with the descendants of enslaved Africans is a comparatively recent phenomenon. Until Emancipation it made little sense to describe enslaved Africans as "poor," poor being a comparative term, while slaves were absolutely (one might say definitionally), destitute. Under Jim Crow, the wide-spread debt peonage of their descendants, and their concentration in the South, continued to set African Americans apart. In these circumstances the "clinical" attitude toward impoverished people, of which Herrenstein's is a somewhat belated example, was race-neutral, as it were, as African Americans were out of consideration. In the early twentieth century the poor were often conceptualized as White immigrant urban slum dwellers: first Irish, then Slavic, "Russian" (i.e., Jewish) and Italian, with an occasional glance toward Appalachia. Impoverished African Americans became visible to academic observers and policy makers with the Great Migration. After the Second World War, the White middle (and lower middle) class was encouraged to move to Levittown and their former inner city residences became available to Black first generation immigrants from the rural South. Poverty, and to a lesser extent, unemployment, became Black phenomena, situations in need of an explanation for African Americans themselves as much as for academics and policy makers. For a certain strand of thought within the African American community (associated, possibly inaccurately, with Malcolm X), Black poverty in America was similar to the poverty of areas colonized by European states: "Applied to America, the colonial model was straightforward: Ghettos export their unskilled labor and import consumer goods . . . Unable to import capital, ghettos neither produce the material needed for their subsistence nor accumulate the capital essential to development"[31] However, Michael Katz has found that others, "Thomas Sowell, for one, traced black disadvantage to discrimination rather than exploitation . . . Nor were black people robbed of very much by white America: 'The real problem is that deliberate discrimination, unconscious racism and general neglect have left black people too poor to be robbed of anything that would make a difference on a national scale.'"[32]

It was thought, or it was claimed, that the rising tide (or bigger apple pie) of the post-war American economy would expand the middle class (however defined) to include everyone in the United States. However, as a Johnson Administration's Council of Economic Advisors report "argued . . . economic growth by itself would not eliminate poverty in America.

[The report] anchored poverty in income distribution, employment discrimination, and inadequate transfer payments by government, and it proposed a comprehensive program for its reduction. "By the poor," asserted the report, "we mean those who are not now maintaining a decent standard of living—those whose basic needs exceed their means to satisfy them." It also firmly rejected explanations based on character or heredity: "The idea that the bulk of the poor are condemned to that condition because of innate deficiencies of character or intelligence has not withstood intensive analysis." On the contrary, those living in poverty simply lack "the earned income, property income and savings, and transfer payments to meet their minimum needs."[33]

The oft-maligned "war on poverty" did much good, among other things supporting large numbers of lower middle class jobs in programs like CETA. The later Earned Income Tax Credit (EITC) initiative has also "proved effective at moving huge numbers of families over the poverty line—although only families close to the poverty line to begin with and those having some income from work. In 2010 the EITC lifted 6.3 million people, of whom 3.3 million were children, out of poverty. Without it, child poverty would have been 25 percent higher."[34] These programs met " . . . the criterion [John Rawls] applied to social policies and institutions: They are to be judged by the degree to which they improved the circumstances of 'the least advantaged members of society.'"[35] However, since the Nixon Administration's adoption of its "Southern Strategy," the creation of a base for the Republican Party in the former Confederacy, and the highly successful tactic of the Reagan Administration associating poverty with African Americans (e.g., "welfare queens"), efforts to alleviate, much less eliminate, poverty in the United States have slowed.

Mark Robert Rank's influential book, *One Nation, Underprivileged: Why American Poverty Affects Us All,* attempts to change the terms of the debate with its reiterated claims that most

Americans go through periods of poverty and "most spells of poverty are of fairly modest length. The typical pattern is that households are impoverished for one or two years and then manage to get above the poverty line . . . In contrast, a much smaller number of households experience chronic poverty for years at a time . . . [such as] minorities living in inner-city areas."[36] Rank takes poverty seriously as a tragedy both for those who are poor and for the country as a whole: "Poverty leads to rising health care expenditures, a less effective work force, and scores of other direct and indirect costs that affect us all. Our current path of apathy is a far more expensive road to take than one that aggressively reduces the extent of poverty."[37] Rank's otherwise impressive, and impressively compassionate, work nonetheless reifies poverty: it is a thing, a condition in which people, seemingly at random, somehow become involved. He works hard to reduce the identification of poverty with African Americans, not without some statistical sleight of hand. Most Americans may go through spells of poverty, if among the "most" African Americans are included, while it may be that a smaller number of all households experience chronic poverty, but a much larger percentage of African Americans do so.

Rank makes the situation of the poor vividly present to those reading his book by detailing the household economics of everyday life at the poverty level. He begins by describing how the poverty level for incomes was set at three times the income needed for an adequate diet. Then, writing in 2005, Rank says: "To illustrate what these numbers mean in a day-to-day sense, let us take the poverty level for a family of four—$18,392.

Using the one-third/two-thirds split, our hypothetical family would have $6,131 available for food during the year. This comes out to $118 a week, $16.86 a day, or $4.22 a day for each member of that family. Assuming that family members eat three meals per day, this works out to $1.41 per person per meal per day. Taking the remaining two-thirds of the poverty line's threshold--$12,261—provides our family with $236 per week for other expenses. For example, the average fair-market rent for a two-bedroom apartment (which would represent fairly tight quarters for such a family) across 130 major metropolitan areas was around $600, or $150 per week . . . This leaves our family of four with $86 a week for all other expenses, including transportation, clothing, child care, utilities, medical costs, and the various additional expenditures that a family might have."[38] Rank emphasizes that this is at the top of the poverty range. On the other hand, "Forty-one percent of poor individuals have incomes less than one-half of the poverty line. For a family of four this would be $9,052, or 14 percent of the national median income."[39]

To bring Rank's work up to date, in 2014 a Big Mac Meal, for example, costs $5.69; a Dollar Breakfast Menu costs $1.00 for a Sausage McMuffin, but milk is another dollar, orange juice $1.39. Three dollars and thirty-nine cents, then, for breakfast, another $6.69 for lunch and that again for dinner: $16.77 for meals for a day at what is probably a minimal level, more than ten times Rank's calculation of the budget for three meals a day at the poverty line in 2005. (Three meals at MacDonald's every day may be problematic in many ways, but it is probably close to the minimal cost of sustenance.) Average fair market rent for two bedroom housing in Alameda County, California is now $1,578; in Allegheny County, Pennsylvania, $789.[40] Taking a mid-point of those, we might make a rough estimate of a cost of living in poverty as nearly double Rank's 2005 figure, further increasing the pressure on a family living at or below the poverty line.

Civilized life does not consist only of survival-level rations and housing. Even a person living in poverty may wish from time to time to go to a concert or to a museum. Admission to the Art Institute of Chicago is $18 for city residents. The least expensive seats for the Chicago Symphony are about $30. The least expensive seats for the Philadelphia Orchestra are about $45. Admission to the Philadelphia Museum of Art is $20. A monthly visit to a museum and the symphony in these cities for our family of four, with children's discounts, would cost about as much as a week of groceries. As there is little or no surplus in their budget, it would come down to a choice: a monthly visit to the symphony and art museum or a week's worth of meals. Choose one.

This consideration of poverty, its history and experience, is essential for understanding the condition of Black America as exceptionally large numbers of African Americans live in poverty. A quarter of all African American families have incomes below the poverty level, as compared to 11% of White Americans. Twenty-nine percent of Black families with children, as compared to 12% of

White families with children, have incomes below the poverty line and, crucially, 43% of single Black mothers (women with children and no husband present) have incomes below the poverty line. As a result, more than one-third, 35%, of African American children (compared to 14% of White children), live below the poverty line.

Rank calculated the cumulative percentages of Black and White Americans who have spent one or more of their adult years living below the poverty line. "By age 28 . . . the black population will have exceeded the cumulative level of lifetime poverty that the white population reaches by age 75. In other words, blacks have experienced in nine years the same risk of poverty that whites face in fifty-six years."[41] A bare majority of White Americans experience poverty at some point in their lives, often briefly. Nearly all African Americans do so, a large number not at all briefly. Or as Rank somewhat cautiously concludes, "being black appears to be a unique disadvantage when it comes to experiencing poverty across the adult life course."[42]

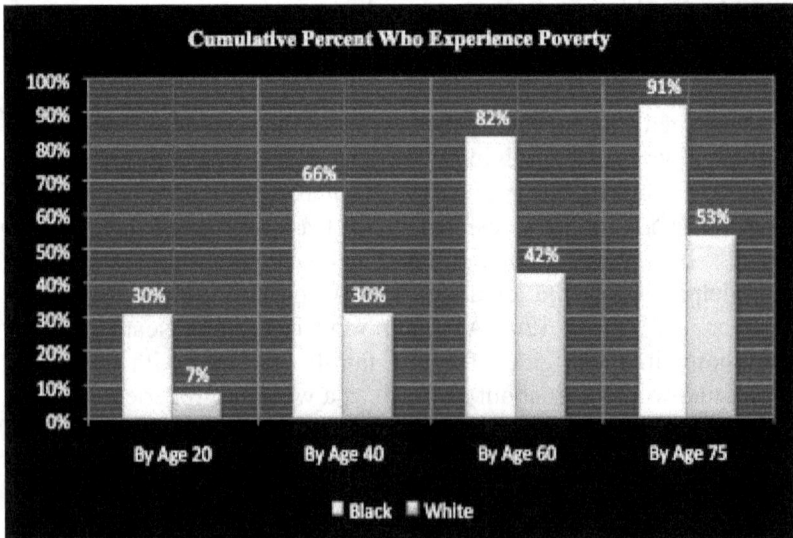

Cumulative Percent Who Experience Poverty

Since the financial crisis of 2007 economic matters have become worse for most Americans and particularly for African-Americans. To identify a single, telling, example, while nearly 90% of White, non-Hispanic, Americans were "food secure" in 2013, just 74% of

African-Americans households reached that most basic threshold. Of the 26% of African-American households that were "food insecure" (sometimes not knowing where their next meal was coming from), 16% had low food security and 10% were in a situation of very low food security (not having enough to eat). These were the worst statistics for any of the major U.S. racial/ethnic groups.[43] They are unknown in any other developed country.

The Black Ghetto, or Hypersegregation

Why is it that although some progress has been made in terms of the incomes of Black households, the accumulated wealth of African Americans is insignificant, their poverty rates so high? In their *Black Wealth/White Wealth: A New Perspective on Racial Inequality* Melvin Oliver and Thomas Shapiro express no doubts on this score: "We cannot help but conclude that factors related to race are central to the racial wealth gap and that something like a racial wealth tax is at work."[44] They, along with others, including Michelle Alexander[45] and Douglas Blackmon,[46] not to mention Gunnar Myrdal and W. E. B. DuBois, trace the racial wealth gap to slavery and the largely successful efforts of White Americans of the former Confederacy to defeat and undo Reconstruction.

Oliver and Shapiro differ from their colleagues and predecessors in defining an active role of the state, not just the Southern states, but the American state itself, in preventing the acquisition of wealth by African Americans. "Our first concept, 'racialization of state policy,' refers to how state policy has impaired the ability of many black Americans to accumulate wealth—and discouraged them from doing so—from the beginning of slavery throughout American history . . . The modern welfare state has racialized citizenship, social organization, and economic status while consigning blacks to a relentlessly impoverished and subordinate position within it."[47] They begin this story with the failure of the national government to fulfill the implied promise of land ownership, "forty acres and a mule," despite some efforts in that direction by the Union Army. This was followed by the epoch of debt peonage in the South, during the period of Jim Crow, as described by Blackmon, when the law was used to force many African Americans into a perpetual cycle of debt to White landowners. Alexander brings this picture up to date with her examination of mass incarceration, a subject to which we will return frequently in the following pages. In between, Oliver and Shapiro and many others point to the mid-twentieth-century Federal Housing Authority's policies of suburbanization, and "redlining" during and after the Great Migration from Southern farms to northern factories, as minimizing home ownership by African Americans and subsidizing it for White Americans, for many of whom it became the chief instrument for wealth creation.[48]

The National Housing Act of 1934 established a federal mortgage guarantee program administered through the Federal Housing Administration (FHA). FHA loans were used to create the first suburbs for White veterans returning from World War II. Those houses were affordable but were solely for White families, as the program explicitly reserved them for "the race for which they are intended." The deeds in one of the largest suburban developments, Levittown, explicitly forbade occupancy by "any person other than members of the Caucasian race." Despite the Supreme Court's 1949 ruling finding the FHA restrictive covenants unconstitutional, private restrictions remained in legal effect until the Civil Rights Act of 1968. "Official government policy supported the prejudiced attitudes of private finance companies, realtors, appraisers, and a white public resistant to sharing social space with blacks."[49] Since then, segregation has been imposed and maintained by realtors, banks and other non-governmental actors, working more or less informally with local officials. As a result, "racial segregation became a permanent structural feature of the spatial organization of American cities in the years after World War II."[50]

Segregation is a significant factor limiting wealth in the African American community. As a matter of fact, Douglas Massey and Nancy Denton argued in *American Apartheid: Segregation and the Making of the Underclass,* that segregation is the *determining* factor in the continuing disadvantaged status of the descendants of enslaved Africans: "Our fundamental argument is that racial segregation—and its characteristic institutional form, the black ghetto—are the key structural factors responsible for the perpetuation of black poverty in the United States."[51] They find that "Black segregation is not comparable to the limited and transient segregation experienced by other racial and ethnic groups, now or in the past . . .

This extreme racial isolation did not just happen: it was manufactured by whites through a series of self-conscious

actions and purposeful institutional arrangements that continue today. Not only is the depth of black segregation unprecedented and utterly unique compared with that of other groups, but it shows little sign of change with the passage of time or improvements in socioeconomic status."[52]
They quote the powerful summary of their teacher, Kenneth Clark: "the dark ghetto's invisible walls have been erected by the white society, by those who have power, both to confine those who have no power and to perpetuate their powerlessness . . . Their inhabitants are subject peoples, victims of the greed, cruelty, insensitivity, guilt and fear of their masters."[53] Massey and Denton agree with critics of the family dysfunction theorists that the situation of African Americans is not a matter of individual character traits or individual actions: "The effect of segregation on black well-being is structural, not individual. Residential segregation lies beyond the ability of any individual to change; it constrains black life chances irrespective of personal traits, individual motivations, or private achievements." [54]

Massey and Denton conceptualize segregation as *the* cause of the disadvantaged situation of African Americans. "If the black ghetto was deliberately constructed by whites through a series of private decisions and institutional practices,

> if racial discrimination persists at remarkably high levels in U.S. housing markets, if intensive residential segregation continues to be imposed on blacks by virtue of their skin color, and if segregation concentrates poverty to build a self-perpetuating spiral of decay into black neighborhoods, then a variety of deleterious consequences automatically follow for individual African Americans . . . In a segregated world, the deck is stacked against black socio-economic progress, political empowerment, and full participation in the mainstream of American life.[55]

At the turn of the twenty-first century the housing boom resulted in extraordinary increases in house prices even in the urban ghettos, such as Bedford-Stuyvesant in New York City, bringing paper wealth to some Black homeowners. But then those homeowners were specifically targeted by the speculators, realtors and banks who initiated the sub-prime mortgage crisis, liquidating their new-found equity and in many cases forcing them into foreclosure.[56] The difficulties experienced by African Americans in purchasing homes, the ease with which they have been displaced, and the restrictions on where they might buy houses, have left each generation of African Americans with little or no inherited wealth. To a great extent, each generation starts from, and all too often returns to, zero.

Mobility

Health statistics, relative incomes, poverty and wealth data make it clear that the descendants of enslaved Africans remain today in their traditional place at the bottom of American society. Evidence that that place is not merely on the lowest rung of the class structure, but caste-like, not on the ladder at all, can be found in studies of economic mobility. Oliver and Shapiro analyzed mobility between places in the hierarchy of the occupations of successive American generations (white collar/blue collar: a proxy for income). For the American population in general, their "results indicate a strikingly high degree of occupational inheritance for those at the top of the status hierarchy.

For respondents with upper-white-collar parents, occupational status is maintained nearly 60 percent of the time. By the same token, only one in eight of those with upper-white-collar backgrounds find themselves in the lowest ranking group. At the other end of the occupational range nearly one-third, like their parents, are in low-skilled occupations. Thus two-thirds of those from lower-blue-collar backgrounds achieved mobility. Those from lower-white-collar backgrounds experience a noteworthy amount of upward mobility; over half secure upper-white-collar professional and technical positions.

This is one version of the American dream. Immigrants arrive in New York, Los Angeles or Chicago, working at first in "low-skilled" occupations, rising themselves or helping their children to rise through the various occupational groups to high status occupations: the children of maids and taxi cab drivers earning law and medical degrees. This is the view from 30,000 feet. Drawing closer, Raj Chetty and his associates have found that intergenerational income mobility varies strikingly by geographical area. Dividing the country into "commuting zones" (CZs) they find that their data shows that: "Some CZs in the U.S. have relative mobility comparable to the highest mobility countries in the world, such as Canada and Denmark, while others have lower levels of mobility than any developed country for which data are available . . . the probability that a child reaches the top fifth of the income distribution conditional on having parents in the bottom fifth is 4.4% in Charlotte, compared with 10.8% in Salt Lake City and 12.9% in San Jose . . ."[57] It is perhaps suggestive that Salt Lake County has only 16,000 African American residents out of close to a million residents; San Jose has 30,000 out of approximately half a million; Charlotte is 40% Black.

Indeed, when Oliver and Shapiro disaggregate their data by race, their results "reveal a tale of 'two mobilities.'

> For whites the mobility figures for the general population are reproduced with a sharper emphasis on achievement and upward mobility . . . with slightly over 60 percent of those from upper-white-collar backgrounds maintaining their lofty status. Over 70 percent of those from lower-blue-collar origins achieve higher-ranking occupations . . ."

On the other hand, "only a little over one-third of the black parents from upper-white-collar backgrounds successfully transmit their status to their children . . .

> twice as many blacks . . . as white . . . from upper-white-collar backgrounds fall all the way to lower-blue-collar positions . . . nearly two out of five blacks from lower-blue-collar backgrounds remain stuck in unskilled, and, for the most part, poorly paid jobs . . . rates of "long distance" upward mobility for [blacks] are substantially lower . . . than for whites . . ."[58]

Oliver and Shapiro attribute this lack of intergenerational mobility of African Americans to a lack of accumulated wealth: the correlation between occupational status and net worth that is found in the White community is not found in the Black community. "No matter how high up the ladder blacks climb, they accumulate very few assets . . . Asset poverty is passed on from one generation to the next, no matter how much occupational attainment or mobility blacks achieve."[59]

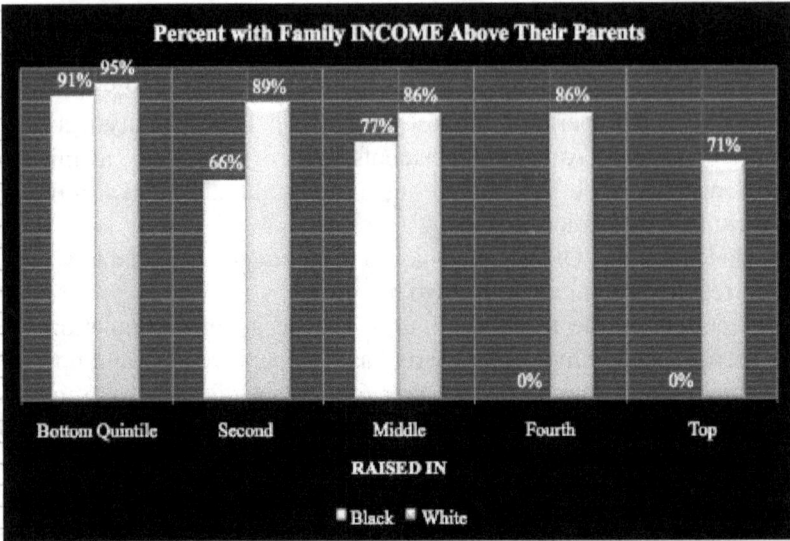

Percent with Family INCOME Above Their Parents

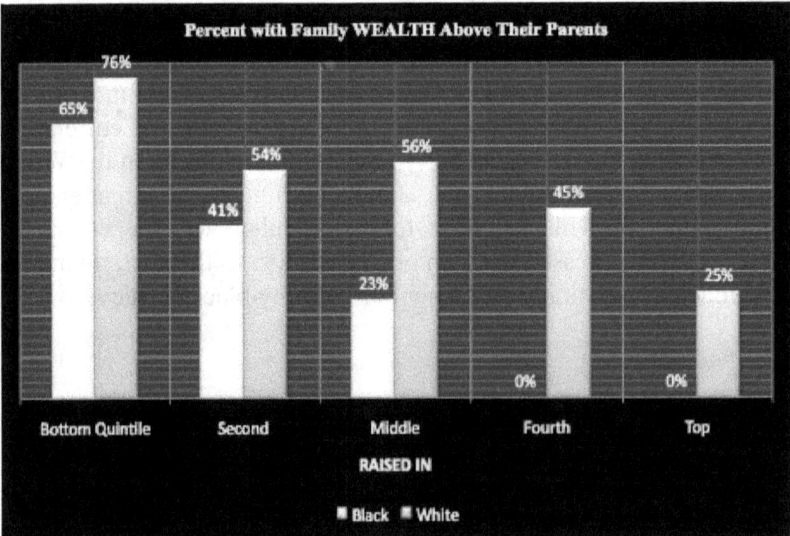

Percent with Family WEALTH Above Their Parents

The mobility study by the Pew Charitable Trusts cited earlier concurs with these findings: African Americans are much less likely than White Americans to better either the income or wealth of their parents. "For family income, a majority of all Americans exceed their parents; however, blacks have lower absolute [income] mobility gains than whites." The gap is 4% for those raised in the bottom quintile, 23% for those raised in the second quintile, 11% for those raised in the middle quintile. (The gap for the top two income quintiles cannot be calculated for lack of significant numbers of Black incomes at those levels.) Wealth mobility, or the lack thereof, is even more of a problem than intergenerational income mobility for African Americans: "only 23 percent of blacks raised in the middle exceed their parents' wealth compared with 56 percent of whites. Only in the bottom [quintile] do a majority of blacks surpass their parents' wealth, but a black-white gap of 8 percentage points still exists."[60]

At each of the lower three quintiles a higher percentage of White Americans exceed their parental income and wealth than the percentages of African Americans who do so. Further, the percentage of African Americans who exceed their parents' wealth diminishes from the bottom to the middle quintile: 65%, 41%, 23%, while for White Americans, those raised in the middle three quintiles all have about a 50:50 chance of exceeding their parents' wealth. The difference between the Black and White communities in the percentage of those who are not upwardly mobile in each is also striking. "More than half of black adults (53 percent for family income and 50 percent for family wealth) raised at the bottom remain stuck there as adults, but only a third of whites [33 percent for both income and wealth] do." It is not surprising then that the Pew researchers found that "Blacks also are more *downwardly* mobile than whites. For family income, over half (56 percent) raised in the middle fall to the bottom or second rung as adults, compared with almost a third (32 percent) of whites. For family wealth, more than two-thirds (68 percent) of blacks raised in the middle fall to the bottom or second rung as adults, compared with just under a third (30 percent) of whites" (emphasis added).[61]

An earlier study, by Julia B. Isaacs of the Brookings Institution, also funded by the Pew Charitable Trusts, concluded that "Economic success in the parental generation—at least as measured by family income—does not appear to protect black children from future economic adversity the same way it protects white children."[62] Like other researchers, Isaacs and her colleagues found that there were too few African Americans in the highest income quintile to analyze mobility in that group. However, they did find that two-thirds of African Americans who were the children of families with incomes in the fourth (second highest) quintile had lower incomes than their parents, as did 69% of those born into the middle quintile. White families, on the other hand, had significant intergenerational upward mobility in every quintile and an astonishing 38% of White Americans born into the highest income quintile remaining there.

A Federal Reserve Bank of Chicago study by Bhashkar Mazumder has also found that "About 60 percent of blacks whose parents were in the top half of the income distribution fall below the 50th percentile in the subsequent generation. The analogous figure for whites is 36 percent." At the opposite end of the income distribution, "more than 50 percent of blacks who start in the bottom quintile in the parent generation remain there in the child generation, but only 26 percent of whites remain in the bottom quintile in both generations." He concludes, alarmingly that "assuming that these specific probabilities are a permanent feature of the U.S. economy, they can be used to calculate an implied steady-state distribution . . .

> [I]n the steady state, 39 percent of blacks would occupy the bottom quintile of the income distribution and only 8 percent would be in the top quintile. This finding suggests that rather than convergence, blacks will remain perpetually disadvantaged in American society if mobility patterns continue to evolve as they have . . . [63]

This is the definition of caste.

Although the exact figures given in these studies differ, they agree that there is no significant intergenerational upward mobility for Black Americans in either income or wealth. The Black community is a caste in which two-thirds of the children are born into the bottom national quintile in income and nearly as large a proportion are born into the bottom quintile in wealth. Even those in the second highest income quintile have family incomes virtually identical to those in the bottom quintile, averaging $25,500 across the two quintiles (as compared to $38,000 and $46,000 for White Americans). Nearly one-third of Black Americans are at the poverty level in income with little wealth and little hope of improving their situation. Racial caste in America trumps class.

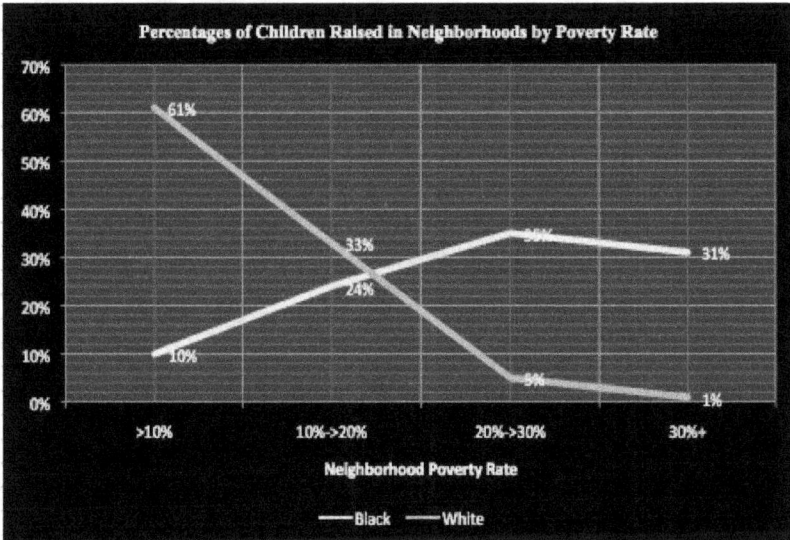

Percentages of Children Raised in Neighborhoods by Poverty Rate

Why is this? Some explanations are static: This is how things are. The causes for the continuing poverty of the African American community, in this view, are to be found in the nature of that community, the structure of the Black family or the attitudes and clothing choices of Black teenagers. Patrick Sharkey has taken a close look at the mobility issue from a slightly different angle, focusing on the influence of the types of neighborhoods in which children grow up. He has found that for the cohort born between 1985 and 2000 (as with both earlier and later cohorts), Black and White children were raised in radically different environments. Two-thirds of those Black children grew up in neighborhoods with poverty rates over (usually far over) 20%. In comparison, just 6% of White children grow up in high poverty neighborhoods; nearly two-thirds grow up in very low poverty neighborhoods.[64] "Examining downward mobility within neighborhood poverty categories, there are extremely high rates of downward mobility among blacks raised in neighborhoods [both] with more than 10 percent poverty and more than 20 percent poverty . . ."[65] Given that 90% of Black children grow up in neighborhoods with more than 10% poverty, Sharkey's findings would indicate, in line with the data reviewed above, that the vast majority of Black children grow up to experience downward economic mobility. It is not then unexpected that the percentages of Black children living in higher poverty neighborhoods actually increased over the course of the second half of the twentieth century. Mark Robert Rank points to the nature of the living conditions of the descendants of enslaved Africans in America, mentioning what will be taken here as one of the two crucial factors enforcing caste: " . . . race exerts a powerful effect upon the life chances of children apart from social class . . . patterns of racial residential segregation ensure that *more black children find themselves in schools that are severely segregated and that lack resources than do white children from similar social class backgrounds*"[66] (emphasis added).

Sharkey's "main conclusion from these results is that neighborhood poverty appears to be an important part of the reason why blacks experience more downward relative economic mobility than whites,

> a finding that is consistent with the idea that the impoverished social environments surrounding the relatively few advantaged African Americans may make it difficult for those families to preserve their advantaged position in the income distribution and to transmit these advantages to their children. When white families advance in the income distribution they are able to translate this economic advantage into spatial advantage in ways that African Americans are not, by buying into communities that provide quality schools and healthy environments for children. These results suggest that one consequence of this pattern is that middle-class status is particularly precarious for blacks, and downward mobility is more common as a result.[67]

Or as Massey and Denton put it: "the persistence of racial segregation in the housing market has meant that middle-class blacks are less able to isolate themselves from the poor than the middle classes of other groups.

> As a result, middle-class blacks live in much poorer neighborhoods than do middle-class whites, Hispanics, or Asians . . . Segregation . . . is directly responsible for the creation of a harsh and uniquely disadvantaged black residential environment, making it quite likely that individual blacks themselves will fail, no matter what their socioeconomic characteristics or family

background. Racial segregation is the institutional nexus that enables the transmission of poverty from person to person and generation to generation . . .[68]

As an explanation, however partial, this is a dynamic, rather than static, picture of the position of the descendants of enslaved Africans, as a group, in American society. While White Americans can, and do, find housing in "communities that provide quality schools and healthy environments for children," if they can afford it, many even relatively advantaged African Americans cannot and do not and instead are confined with their impoverished peers to communities with low quality schools and unhealthy environments. This extraordinary restriction of African Americans to particular neighborhoods has been called "hypersegregation." Wilkes and Iceland define hypersegregation as existing when "a group is so segregated that its members have little chance of contact with outsiders . . ."[69] They calculated that in 2000, 38.5% of the African American population lived in hypersegregated metropolitan areas. If we add the non-metropolitan Black population in Southern states, it is clear that the majority of African Americans are hypersegregated. Unsurprisingly, Wilkes and Iceland believe that the effects of this are highly deleterious. "Hypersegregation increases the isolation of African Americans from other members of society. It concentrates African Americans in neighborhoods [and rural areas] that often have a host of issues associated with poverty, including exposure to crime, poorer access to health care, inadequate access to public transit, poor policing, dilapidated and substandard housing, and poor schools with few resources." The hypersegregated metropolitan areas that Wilkes and Iceland list, from Atlanta to Washington, D.C., have, for example, high school graduation rates for African American male students on average well below 50%.

The research of Sharkey, Wilkes and Iceland, Massey and Denton points to continuing, if not increasing, segregation as a factor in what Oliver and Shapiro call the "sedimentation" of African Americans at the bottom—or below the bottom—of the American class system.[70] The American descendants of enslaved Africans have incomes far below those of White Americans. Their "wealth" is far below that of White Americans. Their intergenerational mobility is for all practical purposes completely unlike that of White Americans, a matter of churning, rather than progress from one generation to the next. These disadvantages form and maintain the lived experience of the caste of the descendants of enslaved Africans in America.

The Anvil of Caste: Public Education

The preceding pages have described how in terms of life expectancy, health, incomes, wealth and economic mobility the vast majority of the American descendants of enslaved Africans live outside the American mainstream, outside the class system itself in a caste from which relatively few escape. We turn now to causation: how this caste system is enforced and reproduced for generation after generation. Massey and Denton gave a careful account of the mechanisms and some of the effects of residential segregation. Wilkes and Iceland agree about the causes of segregation, observing that the "hypersegregation of African Americans in so many U.S. metropolitan areas is largely the result of racism and discrimination by whites."[71] That is, hypersegregation and the other markers of caste are enforced by the actions of White Americans, not, by and large, by the wishes and actions of the American descendants of enslaved Africans, but by the actions of institutions historically controlled by White Americans, such as the Federal Housing Administration (FHA), municipal and county zoning authorities, banks and real estate businesses. Massey and Denton wrote in *American Apartheid* that "By the late 1960s, virtually all American cities with significant black populations had come to house large ghettos characterized by extreme segregation and spatial isolation. Whereas before 1940 no racial or ethnic group in American history had ever experienced an isolation index above 60%, by 1970 this level was normal for blacks in large American cities."[72] They then specify that "These conditions came about because of decisions taken by whites to deny blacks access to urban housing markets and to exclude them from white neighborhoods."

What is it about neighborhood segregation, as an instrument for enforcing caste boundaries that helps create and perpetuate the caste status of African Americans? After all, it could be the case, and sometimes is the case, that African Americans choose to live in highly segregated neighborhoods (as in predominately Black middle class Prince George's County, Maryland). Sharkey cites education as the catalyst that converts hypersegregation into inter-generational poverty: "The fact that public schools are typically organized and partially funded by residential districts, for instance, means that the quality of educational opportunities depends directly on where one lives."[73] And although education is a good thing in itself, it is also the main factor in the economic status of the working population.

Thomas Piketty advises that "The best way to increase wages and reduce wage inequalities in the long run is to invest in education and skills."[74] This is not a novel observation. Bureau of Labor Statistics data show dramatic increases in wages and salaries from degree attainment at the high school, college and graduate levels.

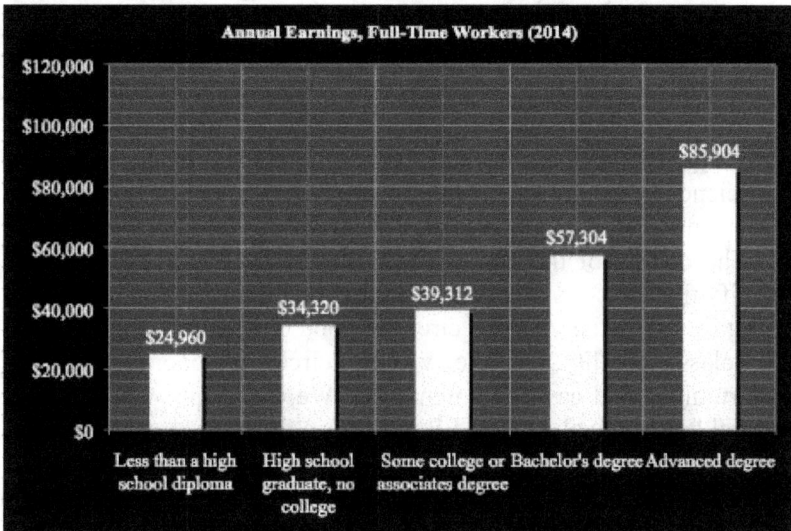

Annual Earnings, Full-Time Workers (2014)

Education level	Annual Earnings
Less than a high school diploma	$24,960
High school graduate, no college	$34,320
Some college or associates degree	$39,312
Bachelor's degree	$57,304
Advanced degree	$85,904

The wage gaps between workers with various levels of education have increased over the past generation, the size of those gaps growing greater at the highest education levels. The wage gap between workers with high school educations, as compared to those without a diploma, has grown from 21% to 28%. But that between workers with a college degree or more and those without a college education has grown from 29% to 53% and that between holders of advanced degrees and those with just a high school education has grown from 32% to 71%.[75]

Chetty and his colleagues find that the difference in college attendance rates between children in the lowest income homes and those in the highest is 67.5 percentage points and that the quality of the K-12 school system is "positively correlated with mobility."[76]

Income, then, correlates with education, especially higher education, and economic mobility correlates with the quality of the K-12 schools available. (As do college attendance and completion rates.) This is a virtuous circle for many White families, a vicious circle for most Black families with their lower incomes and fewer high quality schools available to them in their hypersegregated neighborhoods.

Elementary and Secondary Education

The U.S. Department of Education's National Assessment of Educational Progress (NAEP) periodically measures literacy skills at grades 4, 8 and 12. The results are reported at four levels: below expectations at grade level (at Basic and below Basic) and at or above expected grade level performance (Proficient and Advanced). As reading is the basis for all other education, and as by grade 8 schooling has had ample time to be effective, grade 8 reading proficiency can be taken as a good indicator of educational achievement and the opportunities necessary for that achievement.

The quality of the data made available by NAEP allows us to identify those factors most significant in determining whether a child will grow up in the virtuous circle of good educational opportunities and class mobility, or the vicious circle of poor educational opportunities and caste sedimentation. We can begin with the most general level of analysis. NAEP provides a description of the relative status of Black and White student literacy skills at grade 8. In 2013, 40% of White students read at the Proficient level and 6% read at the Advanced level. In 2013 16% of Black students read at the Proficient level in grade 8 and 1% read at the Advanced level. This can be interpreted to mean that nearly half of White students now have reading skills at or above those expected at grade 8 while 83% of African American students at grade 8 still read below the level expected. According to U.S. Department of Education data for the 2011-12 school year, the most recent available, there were nearly 600,000 Black public school students in eighth grade. Therefore, there were approximately 100,00 Black students reading at or above grade level in grade 8, which is one-third the number that would be expected if Black students had educational opportunities and outcomes equal to those of White students. Or, to put this another way, there were nearly half a million Black students in grade 8 who were not reading at grade level, with little chance for the type of success in school that would lead to later success in life. That is the problem and the challenge.

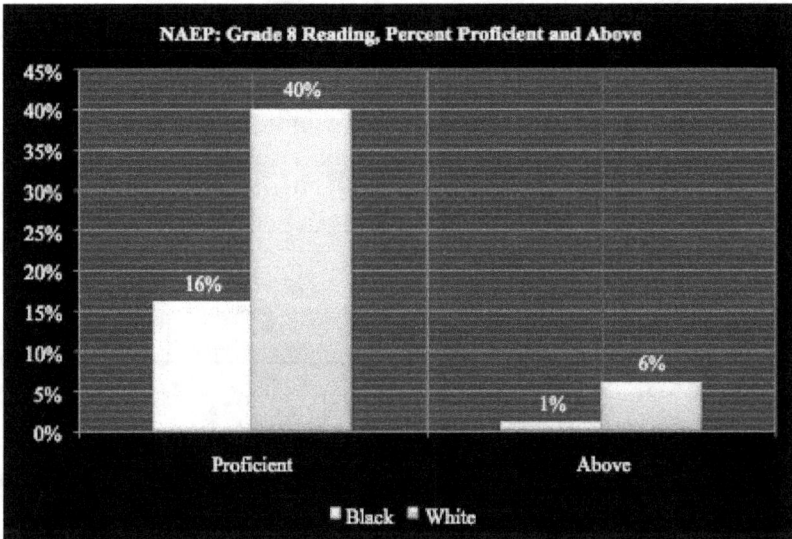

NAEP: Grade 8 Reading, Percent Proficient and Above

■ Black ■ White

What are the primary factors affecting educational outcomes? NAEP allows refinements in analysis that may contribute to an answer to this question. We can, for example, look at results within races by income, parental education and school location and we can cross-tabulate these. By doing so we can examine the crucial variables that influence the disparate learning outcomes just outlined. First we will look at family income as an influence on Black student learning.

Family Income and Learning Outcomes

Kornrich and Furstenberg have found "that the [growing] gap in parental investment [in education] between the top and bottom of the income distribution matches recent findings . . . that the gap in test scores between children of parents at the 90th percentile of the income distribution and those at the 10th percentile has grown over time."[77] Wealthy families invest in more education for their children. Poorer families cannot invest in more education for their children: they haven't the money.

NAEP uses eligibility for the National Lunch Program (free and reduced cost meals) as an income indicator. Eligibility for the National Lunch Program, which is set at 185% of the poverty level, varies by family size. For a family of three (e.g., a single parent and two children) an income of $36,131 or less qualifies for reduced price meals. More than 43% of Black families have incomes below this amount, as do just 22% of White families. We should keep in mind the fact that a Black family eligible for the National Lunch Program is a nearly average Black family, in terms of income, while a White family eligible for the National Lunch Program is fairly atypical.

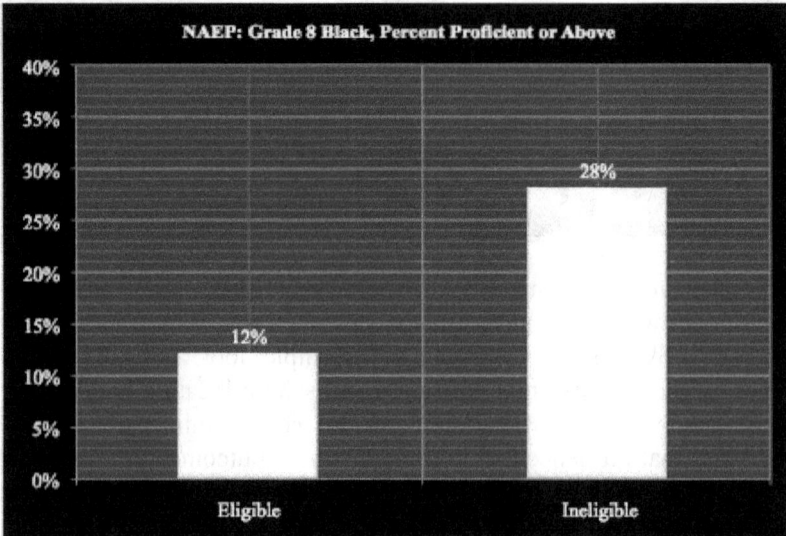

NAEP: Grade 8 Black, Percent Proficient or Above

	Eligible	Ineligible
	12%	28%

In 2013, 12% of Black students from families eligible for the National Lunch Program, those with incomes of $36,000 or less, scored at or above grade level in 2013. Twenty-eight percent of ineligible, less poor, Black students scored at or above grade level. The gap between these two groups has widened by 7 percentage points since the beginning of the century. Other things being equal, below average family income appears to account for a difference of 16 percentage points for Black students in grade 8 reading. It is between two and three times more likely that Black students in grade 8 will read at or above grade level if their families are in the upper than if their families are in the lower half of the Black income distribution.

Parental Education and Learning Outcomes

On the basis of student reports, NAEP records parental education (highest level for either parent) as "Did not finish high school," "Graduated high school," "Some education after high school" or "Graduated College." It is not clear how accurate these student reports are, but they are probably fair approximations, particularly at the extremes. Black students who reported that neither of their parents had finished high school scored at Proficient or above 8% of the time in 2013. Black students who reported that a parent had graduated from high school were at or above grade level 9% of the time in 2013, while for Black students who said that at least one of their parents had some education after high school, 21% were at Proficient or above in reading at grade 8. The Black children of college graduates were at or above grade level in 22% of the time.

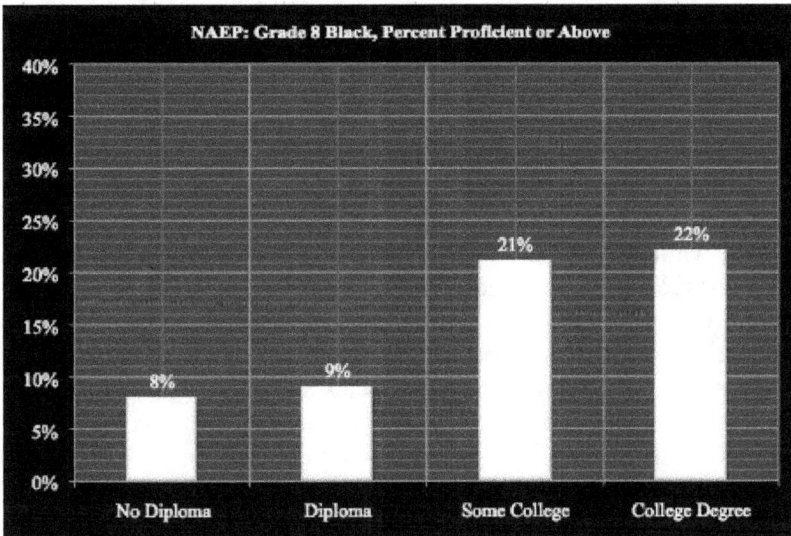

NAEP: Grade 8 Black, Percent Proficient or Above

Looking just at reported parental education, the difference between the scores in grade 8 reading of students reporting parents as having educational attainment at the "no high school diploma" level and those reporting parents as having educational attainment at the "college degree" level is 14 percentage points for Black students. Increasing parental education from the lowest to the highest category nearly triples the percentage of students at or above grade level for Black students. The effect of increasing parental education for Black students is approximately the same as that from higher family income, which is not very surprising, given the correlation between educational attainment and income.

We can look at this another way by calculating the *numbers* of students reading at grade level (Proficient and above) with parents at various reported educational attainment levels by aligning NAEP and Census data. Seventeen percent of Black adults over 25 years reported to the Census that they had less than a high school diploma, equivalent to NAEP's "Did not finish high school."[78] Thirty-one percent of Black adults said that they were high school graduates with a diploma or its equivalent, which correlates with NAEP's "Graduated high school." Thirty-three percent of African Americans reported some college or associate's degree, equivalent to "Some education after high school" and 19% of African Americans reported attaining a Bachelor's degree or higher: "Graduated College."

Since 8% of grade 8 Black students reporting no parent with a diploma read at grade level or above, and 17% of Black adults report that they did not graduate from high school, we can estimate that just 1% (8% of 17%) of grade 8 Black students read at grade level in spite of having parents who did not finish high school. Three percent of Black students report that one of their parents completed high school while they themselves read at grade level. Seven percent of Black students read at grade level in grade 8 and have at least one parent who had some college. And 4% of Black students at grade 8 read at grade level and report that at least one of their parents has a college degree. (The percentage of Black students in grade 8 reading at grade level who are the children of college graduates is lower than that of those whose parents have "some college" because there are fewer adult Black college graduates.) Or to assign numbers of students to those percentages, just under 8,000 Black students in grade 8 whose parents did not complete high school read at or above grade level. Just under 41,000, five times as many, whose parents had some college, read at grade level.

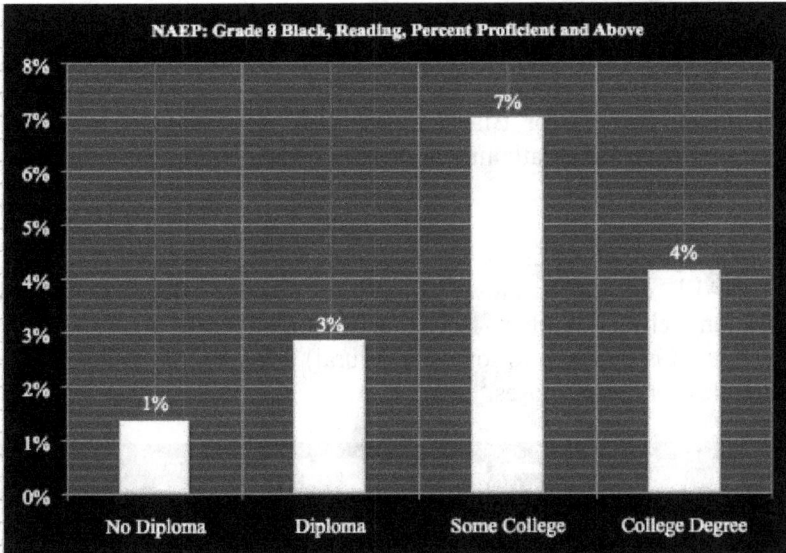

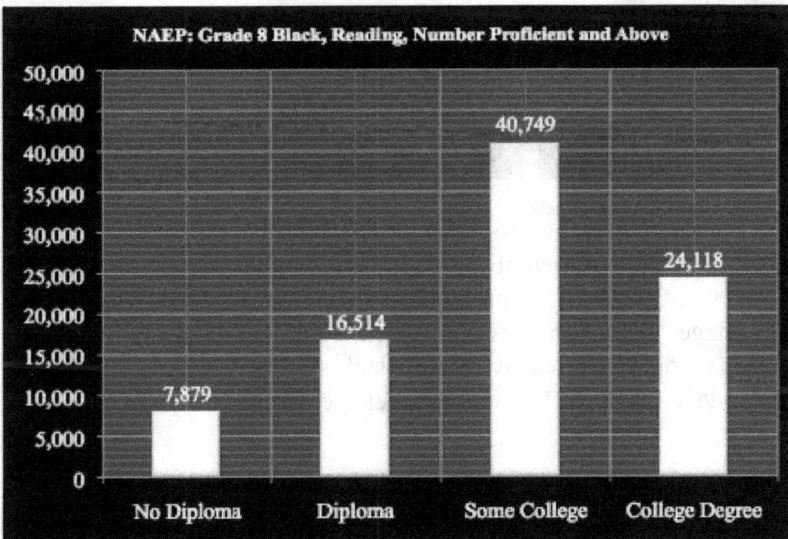

Of the grade 8 Black students reading at or above grade level, two-thirds have college-educated parents. Parental education attainment matters for Black students, as well as for others, and levels of educational attainment are reproduced from one generation to the next.

School Location and Learning Outcomes
NAEP data also allows us to test for the effects of school location: city, suburban, town and rural.[79] City and suburban locations (as opposed to towns and rural) appear to be the effective variables for our purposes.[80]

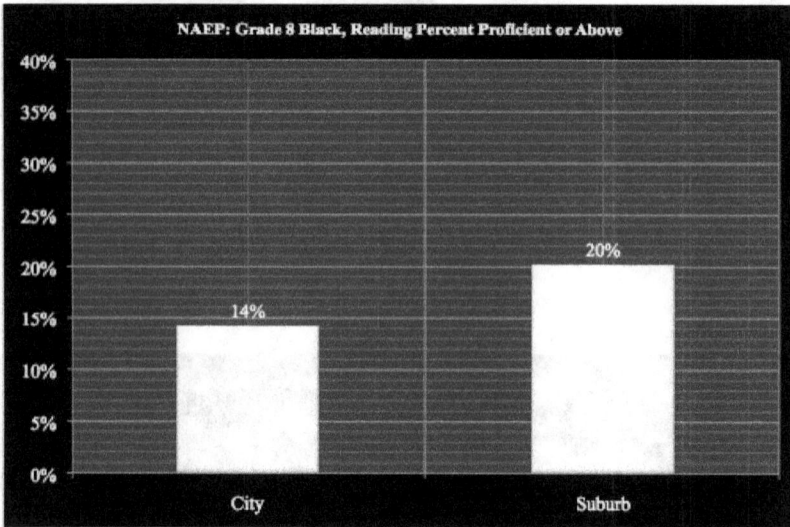

NAEP: Grade 8 Black, Reading Percent Proficient or Above

Fourteen percent (36,700) of Black grade 8 students in city schools in 2013 scored at the Proficient or above levels, while 20% (35,700) of those in suburban schools did so, nearly a fifty percent advantage in percentages for Black suburban students, who are, however, outnumbered by urban Black students 262,000 to 178,000 at grade 8.[†] The difference between percentages of students at or

---

[†] There is a complication with the classification of school location, in that "suburban" schools include those in small cities that have become part of a

above Proficient in grade 8 reading in city schools and those in suburban schools is 6 percentage points for Black students. Moving from city to suburban schools increases the percentage of students at or above grade level for Black students by nearly 50%.

Family Income, Parental Education and School Location

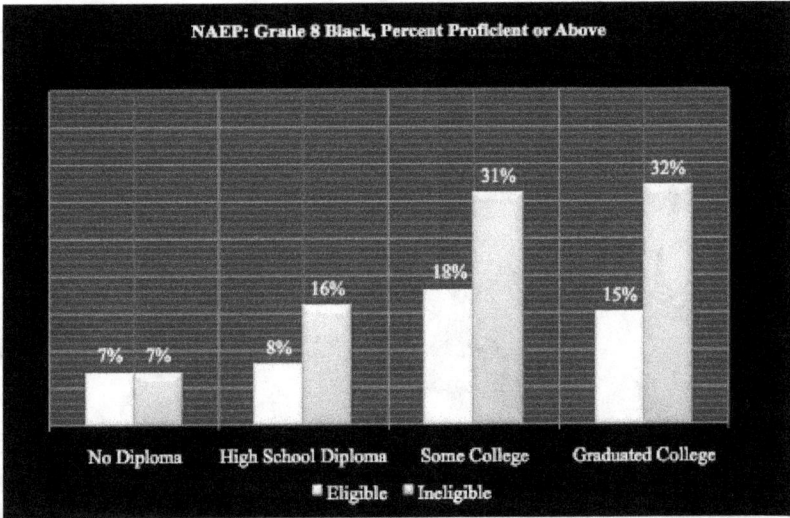

NAEP: Grade 8 Black, Percent Proficient or Above

Cross-tabulating *parental education* and *National Lunch Program eligibility,* that is, income, we find that for Black students whose parents did not graduate from high school there is no difference by family income category in the low percentage of students scoring at or above Proficient: each is 7%. On the other hand, Black students reporting that at least one of their parents graduated from college have great differences in reading proficiency related to family income. Fifteen percent of those from the poorer families, those eligible for the National Lunch Program, and 32% of those from the less poor families, ineligible for the National Lunch Program, read at the Proficient or above levels, the latter percentage being nearly twice the over-all percentage (17%) of Black students reaching the Proficient or above levels.

---

larger urban area. Schools in Camden, New Jersey, for example, are "suburban" in relation to Philadelphia.

Cross-tabulating *school location* and National Lunch Program eligibility, we find that 11% of the poorer Black students in city schools, those who were eligible for the National Lunch Program in 2013, scored at the Proficient or above levels, as did 25% of those from less poor families, those with incomes over $36,000. Fifteen percent of Black students in suburban schools from poorer families scored at the Proficient or above levels, as did 30% of those from families with incomes over $36,000, who were ineligible.

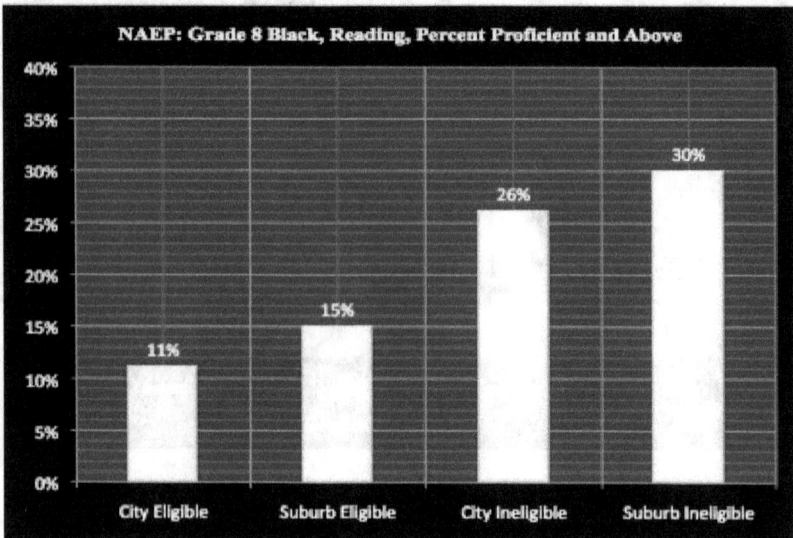

NAEP: Grade 8 Black, Reading, Percent Proficient and Above

Category	Percent
City Eligible	11%
Suburb Eligible	15%
City Ineligible	26%
Suburb Ineligible	30%

Attending suburban schools approximately doubles the percentages of Black students scoring Proficient or above in grade 8 reading, for each family income group. *The combined effect of higher family income and suburban school location nearly triples the percentage of Black students reading at or above grade level.*

Forty-six percent of White, non-Hispanic, students in grade 8 score at grade level in the grade 8 NAEP assessment of reading. The highest achievement level for a sub-group of Black students, those from less poor families ineligible for the National Lunch Program with a college-educated parent, is 32%, still a fourteen point gap.

The NAEP assessments allow us to look at students, by race and family income, that is, eligibility for the National Lunch Program, who attend schools in a selection of large cities. When we do so we find that there is an 18-point gap between the national average achievement level of all *White,* non-Hispanic, students and the percentage from poorer families scoring Proficient or above who attend schools in large cities. This is the penalty for attending urban public schools serving students whose families have incomes below 185% of the poverty level, regardless of whether the student is Black or White.

One-third of White, non-Hispanic, Americans live in suburbs, but only a few more than one-fifth of Black Americans do so. As Mark Robert Rank has observed: "the vast differences in educational quality according to residence and income illuminate the magnitude of these opportunity differences."[81] And as "Shapiro and Jonson note, 'By accessing quality school systems parents ensure specific kinds of schooling for their children and in this way help to pass their own social position along to the next generation.'"[82] Kornrich and Furstenberg have added to this their research into the effects of parental investments in education beyond buying homes in suburban school districts. "Parents invest in their children's outcomes in many ways . . .

> In the race to the top, higher-income children are at an ever greater advantage because their parents can and do spend more on child care, preschool, and the growing costs of postsecondary education. The costs borne by the family impose a growing burden on low- and moderate-income families, whose incomes have stagnated over the past several decades. It seems evident that unless constraints on less-advantaged households are reduced, the children of low- and moderate-income families will continue to lose ground. Thus, contemporary increases in inequality may lead to even greater increases in inequality in the future as advantage and disadvantage are passed across the generations through investment.[83]

There is at least one other factor affecting learning outcomes: disparities in school discipline. The harsher treatment of Black children begins in pre-kindergarten. "Black children represent 18% of preschool enrollment, but 48% of preschool children receiving more than one out-of-school suspension; in comparison, white students represent 43% of preschool enrollment but 26% of preschool children receiving more than one out-of-school suspension."[84] If these statistics are taken at face value we would have to believe that Black three-year-olds are apparently four or five times more prone to disrupting a preschool classroom than White three-year-olds and teachers seem to know no way to deal with a disruptive (by any definition) three-year-old than to bar (usually him) from school, an action that will have a profoundly disruptive effect on the child's educational prospects and his or her family arrangements.

This use of school discipline procedures to disproportionately interrupt the educations of Black children continues throughout elementary and secondary school. During elementary and secondary school, "Black students are suspended and expelled at a rate three times greater than white students. On average, 5% of white students are suspended, compared to 16% of black students . . . Black girls are suspended at higher rates (12%) than girls of any race or ethnicity and most boys."[85] And, as a quick route into the school-to-prison pipeline, Black students are nearly twice as likely to be referred to law enforcement or subjected to school related arrests as White, non-Hispanic, students.

Factors Affecting Learning Outcomes: Summary

The baseline for lack of privilege in this country is the situation of a Black student in grade 8 of an urban school, whose low family income makes them eligible for the National Lunch Program and whose parents do not have high school diplomas. The chances of this student being taught to read at or above grade level are 99 to 1 against (and probably worse for those whose families are at or below the poverty line). From there, parental educational attainment strongly influences student achievement. Family income does as well. The remaining difference in student achievement, the 14% between the highest achieving Black subgroup at grade 8 and the White average, is arguably attributable to the difference in the quality of schools they attend and such factors as disparate application of school discipline practices, teacher experience and skill, quality of curriculum and the condition of buildings and equipment.

Massey and Denton found that "because poverty is associated with poor educational performance segregation also concentrates educational disadvantage."[86] Further, "Because of segregation, the same income buys black and white families educational environments that are of vastly different quality."[87] Because of segregation, relatively high income Black families (i.e., those with college-educated adults with incomes over the $36,000 level of eligibilty for the National Lunch Program) more frequently than their White income peers live in areas where the schools are poorly funded. Massey and Denton modeled this effect for various segregation levels. "As the level of racial segregation increases . . . educational disadvantage is concentrated along with poverty. Given complete segregation between blacks and whites and a 20% rate of black poverty, our simulation predicts that children will attend high schools where 47% of the students score below the 15th percentile on the CAT; and raising the rate of black poverty to 30% increases the percentage of low-scoring students to 58%."[88] The inequitable distribution of educational opportunities in the United States is a principal way in which "sedimenation," caste status, comes about.

School Funding

But why is it that schools in hypersegregated Black communities offer fewer educational opportunities, have worst results, than those in suburban (and urban) predominately White communities?

School finance laws and practices, seemingly race neutral, restrict educational opportunities for Black students. In almost every state (Vermont and Hawaii are exceptions) schools are organized into districts with differing resources. The tradition of financing most of school expenses by local, district-specific, property taxes and the practice of providing less experienced, less effective, teachers to schools serving more impoverished students, ensures that schools serving the children of higher income families have greater resources than those serving the children of lower income families. The NAEP results described above illustrate the effects of these disparities in funding between districts and the related within-district diversions of resources from schools and classrooms in which Black children struggle to learn to those catering to White children from more prosperous families. Mark Robert Rank makes this argument, observing that "as a result of the way that public education is funded at the primary and secondary levels, the quality of that education varies widely depending on the wealth of the community in which one resides.

The bulk of U.S. school funding for elementary, middle, and high schools comes from the local tax base, primarily property taxes. School districts with a well-endowed property tax base generally have ample funding to operate quality public schools. This involves paying teachers competitive salaries, keeping student/teacher ratios relatively low, purchasing the necessary educational resources such as books for libraries or computer equipment for instruction, and so on . . . On the other hand, schools in poor communities with diminished tax bases often are financially strapped. Teachers are frequently underpaid and overstressed, the physical facilities may be severely deteriorated and outdated, class sizes are often quite large, as well as many other disadvantages. Students in these schools . . . wind up being denied a quality education as a result.[89]

These disparities in school funding have a long and explicit history of intentional limitation of educational opportunities for the descendants of enslaved Africans. Before Emancipation, literacy among enslaved Africans and their enslaved descendants was often forbidden and severely punished. During Reconstruction, schooling was promoted by the Freedmen's Bureau and the new constitutions of the former slave states. After Reconstruction, those constitutions were replaced and support for the new schools for Black children was reduced to a fraction of that for the schools for White children. In many places in the United States today the predominant race of the students is immediately apparent from the facilities and condition of the school: the wide lawns, corridors displaying art-work, impressive science laboratories of schools catering to White students; dirt or asphalt playing fields, battered steel doors, bare corridor walls and deteriorating or absent science facilities of schools where most of the students are the descendants of enslaved Africans.

The concentration of Black students in hypersegregated urban areas has given rise to the common "donut" effect of school quality: a Black student need only walk across an urban district boundary to find a school that provides twice or more the level of educational opportunities found in that student's neighborhood school. Hence it is no surprise that urban Black women have attempted to register their children in suburban schools, and unfortunately also not surprising that they have been arrested and charged with felonies for doing so: charged with attempted theft of education. Rank points out the obvious: "It is blatantly wrong that some American children, simply by virtue of their parents' economic standing, must settle for a substandard educational experience, while others receive a well-rounded education. All are American children, and all are entitled to a quality education."[90]

One aspect of this situation—within state, inter-district funding disparities—has improved. A 2008 paper by Kim Rueben and Sheila Murray found declines in funding disparities as a consequence of court decisions, with most of the remaining inequality attributable to differences between states.[91] Within states, they found that district-by-district expenditures for Black students were, in general, slightly higher than those for White students, but lower than those for Asian students, with a Black/White spending ratio of 1.08. This appears to be an artifact of federal, and occasionally state, additional funding for students with "special needs," such as poverty. Reuben and Murray noted, however, that "although spending differences have lessened between districts, it is unclear whether inequities are lessened at the school level." They cite studies that identified "large disparities in school funding within districts, with schools serving high-poverty students receiving substantially less district funding." The devil being in the details, they find that a "significant part of the disparities found in spending and staffing across districts is related to staffing rules and the right to transfer and fill jobs district-wide based on seniority or tenure within a district.

> Districts often allocate a certain number of staff to a school, rather than giving schools a per student amount for staff compensation. As teachers gain experience, they often take advantage of seniority rules to move to more affluent schools where students are perceived as easier to teach . . . This can lead to more experienced teachers clustering at low-poverty schools with vacancies at schools serving underserved populations filled by new teachers. As a result, new teachers (who have much lower salaries than experienced teachers) work disproportionately in schools in the poorest neighborhoods. Because of the large range in staff pay, schools with the highest needs within a district often receive substantially less funding because they employ the least experienced teachers.[92]

Reuben and Murray also find that the age of school buildings increases with the percentage of students eligible for the National Lunch Program and teacher career stability *decreases* as the percentage of students who are Black increases.

According to a widely-cited 2011 U. S. Department of Education study of Title I schools (i.e., those serving high percentages of students from impoverished families) by Ruth Heuer and Stephanie Stullich: "42 percent to 46 percent of Title I schools (depending on school grade level) had per-pupil personnel expenditure levels that were below their district's average for non–Title I schools at the same grade level, and from 19 percent to 24 percent were more than 10 percent below the non–Title I school average."[93] In other words, within districts, nearly half the schools serving students from impoverished households received *less* funding from their district than those serving students from more prosperous households and nearly a quarter of those had per-student-expenditures significantly lower. "Similar patterns were found when comparing higher-poverty and lower-poverty schools within districts . . .

> Other expenditure categories examined in this study showed an increase in the percentage of Title I schools with below-average expenditure levels, compared with total non-personnel expenditures. At the elementary level, for example, the percentage of Title I schools that had per-pupil expenditures below their district's average for non–Title I schools at the same grade level was 46 percent for total personnel expenditures, 49 percent for instructional staff expenditures, 50 percent for teacher salary expenditures, and 54 percent for non-personnel expenditures.

The authors of the study conclude with the observation that "It is worth noting that in some districts, a higher level of state and local resources were directed to Title I and higher-poverty schools relative to more advantaged schools in those districts. The example of these districts suggests that directing a higher level of state and local resources to high-need schools is an achievable goal." Or to put it another way, the decision to relatively underfund schools serving students living in poverty is discretionary: all too many district administrations and boards of education simply choose to do so.

The work of Heuer and Stullich was followed by a Center for American Progress paper by Ary Spatig-Amerikaner *(Unequal Education: Federal Loophole Enables Lower Spending on Students of Color)*, in which Spatig-Amerikaner used a database of actual state and local spending on school-level personnel and non-personnel resources. She found that "schools with 90 percent or more students of color spend a full $733 less per student per year than schools with 90 percent or more white students . . ."[94] Like Reuben and Murray, Spatig-Amerikaner attributed these differences in per pupil instructional spending to "maldistribution of resources at the district level . . . Districts have teacher assignment practices that place the least-experienced teachers in high-minority, high-poverty schools. Because novice teachers earn so much less in salary, the total spending at these high-needs schools is likely to be lower than spending at schools in wealthier neighborhoods that employ veteran teachers."[95]

Heuer and Stullich found that there is an inverse relationship between the district percentage of Title I eligible schools and funding. Spatig-Amerikaner showed that there is a direct relationship between the racial composition of schools and instructional expenditures holding both between districts and within districts. The relationship, unsurprisingly, is that as Black student enrollment rises, instructional expenditures decline.

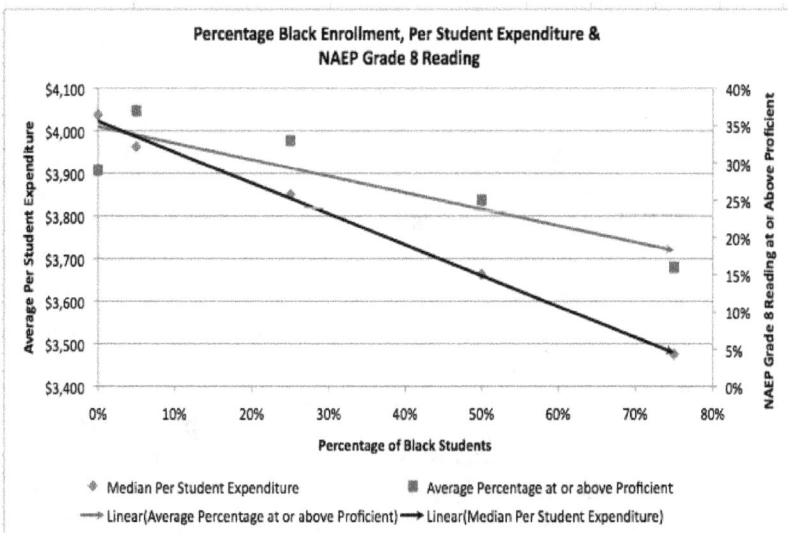

Percentage Black Enrollment, Per Student Expenditure &
NAEP Grade 8 Reading

◆ Median Per Student Expenditure   ■ Average Percentage at or above Proficient
→ Linear(Average Percentage at or above Proficient) → Linear(Median Per Student Expenditure)

Using Spatig-Amerikaner's national data we can measure average per-student-expenditure against the percentage of Black students in schools. The accompanying chart adds to that data the percentage of Black students scoring at or above Proficient on the NAEP Grade 8 Reading test. As the percentage of Black students (horizontal scale) rises, the per-student expenditure decreases, as does the percentage of Black students scoring at or above Proficient on the NAEP grade 8 Reading test.

The level of per-student-expenditures is an indication of the opportunity to learn from more highly experienced, better-educated teachers, with predictable results.

The findings of Reuben and Murray, Heuer and Stullich, Spatig-Amerikaner, the Schott Foundation and others demonstrate that, by and large, intra-district school funding in the United States is radically unfair: higher for the children of higher income, especially White, non-Hispanic, families and lower for the children of lower income, especially Black, families. Or, to summarize, the families of most African-American children are poor. Because they are poor and Black they are likely to live in neighborhoods of concentrated poverty. High poverty neighborhood schools are likely to be disproportionately staffed by inexperienced, less-well-educated teachers. Student educational achievement in such schools is less that that of students in low-poverty schools, without regard to the income level of any given student's family.

It is against this background that New Jersey's Education Law Center has established a set of core "fairness principles" for school funding. These include:

- Varying levels of funding are required to provide equal educational opportunities to children with different needs.
- The level of funding should increase relative to the level of concentrated student poverty. That is, state finance systems should provide more funding to districts serving larger shares of students in poverty . . .
- Student poverty — especially concentrated student poverty — is the most critical variable affecting funding levels. . . . State finance systems should deliver greater levels of funding to higher-poverty versus lower-poverty settings, while controlling for differences in other cost factors.[96]

Bringing the quality of K-12 education available to median income Black suburban families to Black families living in cities would most likely double the percentage of Black children reading at grade level in grade 8. That, in turn, would greatly increase the chances of those children graduating career and college ready from high school, increasing their chances of higher adult incomes and lower incarceration rates for the young men.

Inequities in Postsecondary Education

The progress of students from high school graduation to college attendance is related to the percentage of minority and low-income students in the high schools they attend. The college attendance rate of 2006-07 high school graduates at 4-year institutions in the 2007-08 year was 47% for students from high schools with less than 5% minority enrollment and 31% for students from high schools with 50% or more minority enrollment. As this data from the National Center for Education Statistics counts as minorities Asian students, who typically have higher graduation and college attendance rates than White, non-Hispanic, students, the differentials are no doubt greater when "minorities" are defined as Black, Hispanic and American Indian students alone.

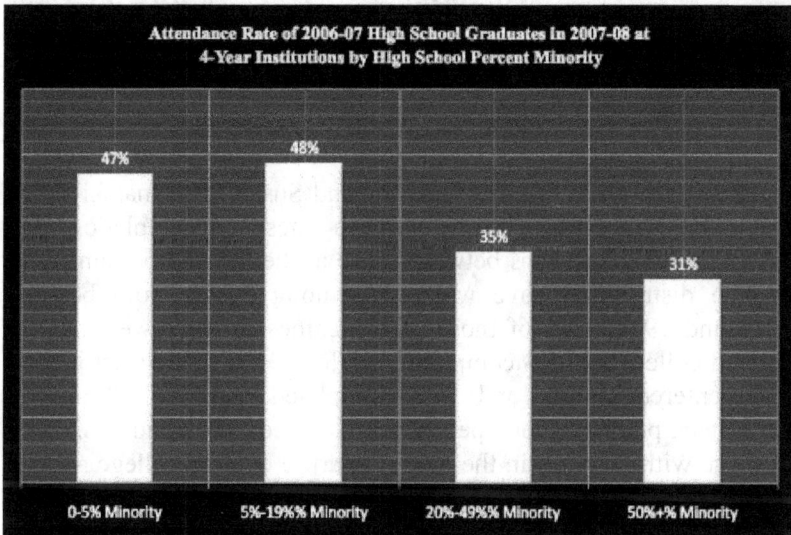

Attendance Rate of 2006-07 High School Graduates in 2007-08 at 4-Year Institutions by High School Percent Minority

Looking at the same data by the percentage of students approved for free or reduced-price lunch, the gradient is from 52% for students from schools where zero to 25% of the enrollment are from families poor enough to be eligible, to half that, 26%, for students from schools in which 76% to 100% are eligible for the National Lunch Program. Higher rates are found in private high schools with 19% or less minority enrollment, an average of 70% college attendance in the year following graduation, and even higher for those private high schools with less than 25% eligible for free and reduced-price lunch.

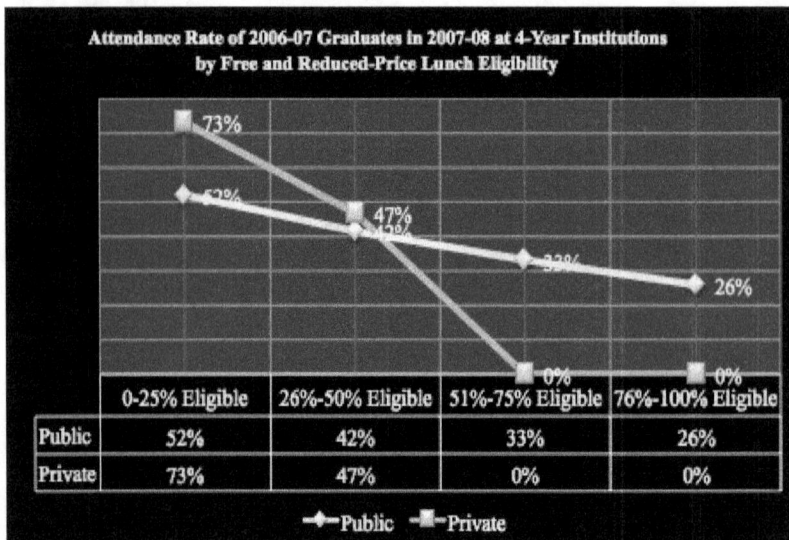

Attendance Rate of 2006-07 Graduates in 2007-08 at 4-Year Institutions by Free and Reduced-Price Lunch Eligibility

	0-25% Eligible	26%-50% Eligible	51%-75% Eligible	76%-100% Eligible
Public	52%	42%	33%	26%
Private	73%	47%	0%	0%

—◆—Public —■—Private

Recent work by Martha J. Bailey and Susan M. Dynarski shows that although general college entrance rates and completion rates have improved, the gaps between those at the top and bottom of the income distribution have widened. Among people born between 1961 and 1964, 19% of those with incomes in the lowest quartile entered college and 5% completed, while 58% at the highest income level entered college and 36% completed, gaps of 39 and 31 percentage points. Among people born between 1979 and 1982, 29% of those with incomes in the lowest quartile entered college and 9% completed, while 80% of those in the highest income quartile entered college and 54% completed: gaps of 51 and 45 percentage points.[97]

In a May 15, 2014 article in *The New York Times* Piketty, was quoted as saying that "it certainly does not follow that everyone has access to the same opportunities to acquire skills of every variety.

Indeed, inequalities of training have to a large extent simply been translated upward . . ."[98] Piketty noting that "social mobility has been and remains lower in the United States than in Europe," gives as "One possible explanation for this . . . the fact that access to the most elite US universities requires the payment of extremely high tuition fees . . .

> Research has shown that the proportion of college degrees earned by children whose parents belong to the bottom two quartiles of the income hierarchy stagnated at 10-20 percent in 1970-2010, while it rose from 40 to 80 percent for children with parents in the top quartile. In other words, parents' income has become an almost perfect predictor of university access . . . This inequality of access also seems to exist at the top of the economic hierarchy not only because of the high cost of attending the most prestigious private universities . . . but also because admissions decisions clearly depend in significant ways on the parents' financial capacity to make donations to the universities . . . the average income of the parents of Harvard students is currently around $450,000, which corresponds to the average income of the top 2 percent of the US income hierarchy. Such a finding does not seem entirely compatible with the idea of selection based solely on merit.[99]

There are few, very few, Black households with incomes at the Harvard average.

Black postsecondary enrollment in degree-granting institutions has tripled since 1976, from just over one million to just short of three million (14% of the total), of whom 1.1 million were male and 1.9 million female. Of those, the number of Black *undergraduates* was 2.6 million in 2012 (15% of the total), of whom 970,000 were male and 1.6 million female. The six-year undergraduate completion rates for African Americans of both genders were below those of all other groups, with the 35% six-year completion rate for male Black undergraduates thirteen points below that of male Hispanic undergraduates, twenty-five points below that of male White students and half that of male Asian students. The Black/Hispanic differential in completion rates appears to rule out simple economic explanations, but may be attributable to segregation effects, as the greater degree of Black residential segregation is accompanied by a greater degree of educational segregation, that is, the concentration of Black students from every family income level in schools where there are few opportunities for a k-12 college preparatory education.

College completion rates for Black students vary by gender more than those for other racial or ethnic groups, with an eight percentage point gap in favor of Black women, as compared to six points for Hispanic and Asian women and four for White women.[100]

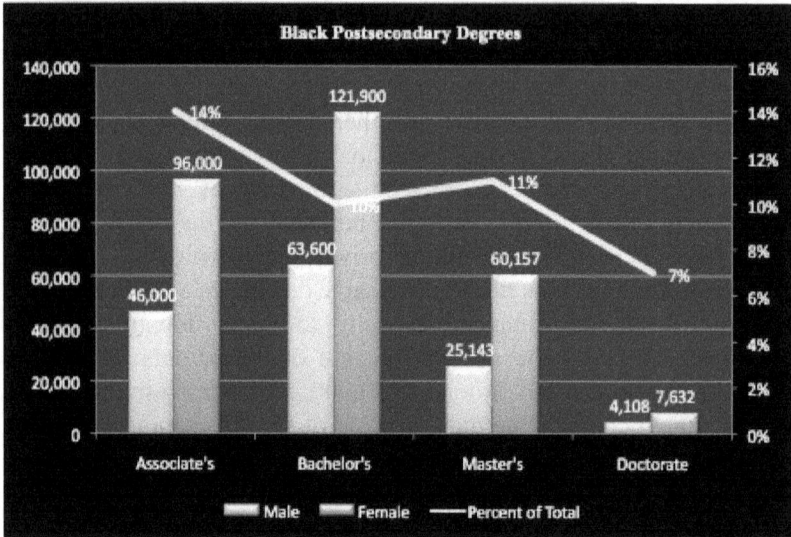

As we go up the educational ladder, the percentage of Black students declines (14% of Associate's, 7% of Doctorates) and the number of male Black students declines precipitously, so that for all postsecondary degrees earned by Black students, two are earned by Black women for each earned by a Black man. It should go without saying that this has serious economic as well as cultural and intellectual consequences.

The Hammer of Caste: The Criminal Justice System

The National Research Council of the National Academies, operating under grants from the MacArthur Foundation and the U.S. Department of Justice, issued a report in April, 2014, entitled "The Growth of Incarceration in the United States: Exploring Causes and Consequences." The issuing organization, the funders, and the panel that created the report could not be more respectable and mainstream. As they would say in Britain, the panel was a gathering of the great and the good.

The report's summary begins: "After decades of stability from the 1920s to the early 1970s, the rate of incarceration in the United States more than quadrupled in the past four decades."[101] The researchers found that this increase in incarcerations was not caused by an increase in crime rates. While rates for most types of crimes were falling, incarceration rates rose steadily and precipitously. Drug arrests, in particular, rose, and rose in a racially disparate fashion, so that by 1989 drug arrests for African Americans, which already had been taking place at double the rate for Whites, increased to four times the White rate, despite evidence that drug usage in the African American community has been consistently slightly lower than the rate for White, non-Hispanic, Americans.[102] The panel found that "The unprecedented rise in incarceration rates can be attributed to an increasingly punitive political climate . . . This provided the context for a series of policy choices . . . that significantly increased sentence lengths, required prison time for minor offenses, and intensified punishment for drug crimes." The authors of this quasi-governmental report attribute the origins of these policy choices to a specific group of individuals: the inner circle of the Nixon administration, with its "war on crime" consciously arising from its political Southern Strategy. "As top Nixon aide H.R. Haldeman explained, Nixon 'emphasized that you have to face the fact that the whole problem is really the blacks. The key is to devise a system that recognizes this while appearing not to . . .'"[103] In other words, in order to win elections in the South, the Nixon administration decided to criminalize African Americans, as had been done under Jim Crow.

The strategy has been followed by other politicians at the state and local as well as federal levels. The National Research Council report traces the causes of the resulting tragedy not to factors within the Black community, but to decisions repeatedly made in the White House, in many state houses, in police headquarters, in judges' chambers across the land. Again: "High rates of incarceration in the United States and the great numbers of people held in U.S. prisons and jails result substantially from decisions by policy makers to increase the use and severity of prison sentences . . .

The increase in U.S. incarceration rates over the past 40 years is preponderantly the result of increases both in the likelihood of imprisonment and in lengths of prison sentences—with the latter having been the primary cause since 1990. These increases, in turn, are a product of the proliferation in nearly every state and in the federal system of laws and guidelines providing for lengthy prison sentences for drug and violent crimes and repeat offenses, and the enactment in more than half the states and in the federal system of three strikes and truth-in-sentencing laws.[104]

In spite of these draconian measures, the researchers were unable to find definitive evidence of a reduction in crime. On the other hand, "The rise in incarceration rates marked a massive expansion of the role of the justice system. In the nation's poorest communities . . .

[t]he vast expansion of the criminal justice system has created a large population whose access to public benefits, occupations, vocational licenses, and the franchise is limited by a criminal conviction . . . Disfranchisement of former prisoners and the way prisoners are enumerated in the U.S. census combine to weaken the power of low-income and minority communities."[105]

That final remark is telling. Michael Katz has noted that Oscar Lewis, for example, "understood that poverty resulted in part from a lack of power."[106] The National Research Council report shows one way in which "the power of low-income and minority [that is, Black] communities" is weakened.[107]

The policy of incarcerating African Americans has focused specifically on African American men and in particular on poorly educated young adult African American men. "Among prime-age black men, around 16 percent of those with no college and fully a third of high school dropouts were incarcerated on an average day in 2010.

Thus at the height of the prison boom in 2010, the incarceration rate for all African Americans is estimated to be 1,300 per 100,000. For black men under age 40 who had dropped out of high school, the incarceration rate is estimated to be more than 25 times higher, at 35,000 per 100,000."[108]

The authors for the National Research Council report, working from earlier research by report co-authors Bruce Western and Betty Pettit, calculated lifetime risks of imprisonment for African American men: "Similar to the rise in incarceration rates, most of the growth in lifetime risk of imprisonment was concentrated among men who had not been to college. Imprisonment risk reached extraordinary levels among high school dropouts. Among recent cohorts of African American men, 70 percent of those who dropped out of school served time in state or federal prison." In Western and Pettit's famous phrase, "For these men with very little schooling, serving time in state or federal prison had become a normal life event."[109] This applies to approximately 2 million men between the ages of 18 and 54, with the highest concentration in urban areas.

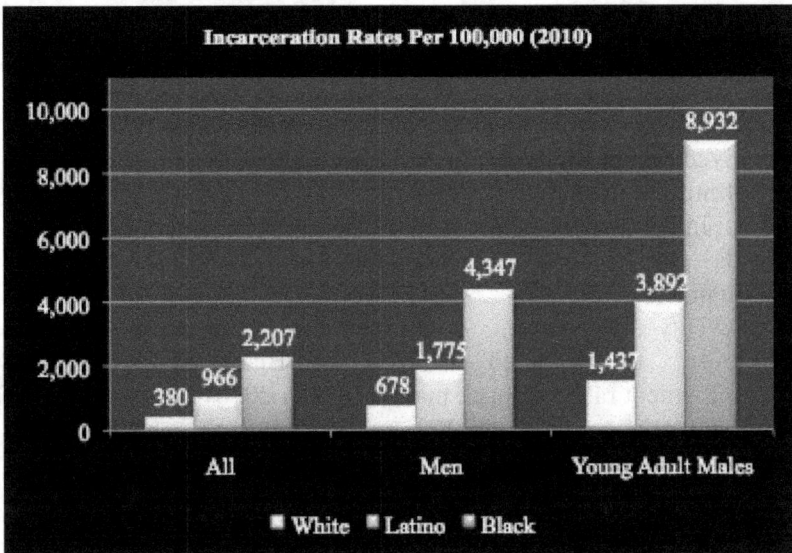

Incarceration Rates Per 100,000 (2010)

120,000 of the 1.3 million young adult African American males between 25 and 29, and 360,000 of the four million between 20 and 34 are incarcerated. But only a minority of those under the control of the criminal justice system are behind bars. Michael Katz found that "Every day one of three black men in their twenties 'is under some form of criminal justice supervision . . . either in prison or jail or on probation or parole.' By and large, they exit prison lacking job skills, unattractive to employers, and headed for poverty, the irregular labor market, and, too often, crime and repeat incarceration."[110] We can estimate that in many African American communities half or more of the men will have spent time in prison, unable to contribute to the support of their children while incarcerated, being able to do so only with difficulty if at all afterwards: under-educated, virtually unemployable, disfranchised. It should be noted that a large percentage of prisoners are incarcerated for parole violations, which can be something as trivial as going to a late movie (or as serious as voting with a felony conviction). In this way, repeated incarcerations, recidivism, is built into the system. What is the effect of this on the hypersegregated Black community? We will look at the effects on children in a moment, but first let us consider the purely economic effects.

The 2010 Census found that 72% of working age (20 to 64) African American males were then in the workforce, as compared to 85% of White males. In other words, 13% more African American men were *out* of the workforce than would be the case if their situation were similar to those for White males. They were neither employed nor in the unemployment accounting system. That would be 1.4 million men. Some of these are "discouraged workers," others are not in the general economy at all. They are incarcerated or living outside the system—"on the run"—as described by Alice Goffman.[111]

Seventy-eight percent of White males in the workforce were employed, as compared to 61% of Black males and the unemployment rate for Black males (10% in 2010) was twice that of White males. Combining the 13% excess "out of the workforce" and the 5% excess over the White unemployment percentage, we approach 20% of the working age male Black population not in a position to contribute to the income of the Black community, who would have been able to do so if they had the same employment profile as White men.

This calculation can be extended by noting that the median income of male full-time, year-round workers for African Americans is $37,271 and that for White Americans is 33% more: $49,616. Part of the reason for this difference is to be found in the incarceration rate and all that entails. Part is due to education attainment differentials. As Oliver and Shapiro have observed: "In taking young prime-age working and school-age males out of the possibility of securing schooling or gaining a foothold in the labor market,

> the racialization of U.S. imprisonment ensures that this population will not be able to begin the process of wealth accumulation at an early age, increasing the racial wealth gap between them and their white counterparts. Given that their

presence in prison creates a stigma that has a negative effect on labor market and economic outcomes during their post-prison reentry, this group will be further disadvantaged in attempting to build wealth over their life course.[112]

Wakefield and Wildeman found that "A criminal record imposes a drop in earnings of about 10 percent to 30 percent . . . some of which is attributable to the stigma employers attach to a criminal record . . ."[113] Western and Petit detail this: "Serving time reduces hourly wages for men by approximately 11 percent, annual employment by 9 weeks and annual earnings by 40 percent . . . By age 48, the typical former inmate will have earned [a total of] $179,000 less than if he had never been incarcerated . . . Incarceration depresses the total earnings of . . . black males by 9 percent."[114]

This, too, contributes to the lack of intergenerational transfer of capital otherwise prevalent in the United States, there being no capital to transfer. "Analyses of relative economic mobility . . . reveal much less mobility for [formerly] incarcerated men than for non-incarcerated men.

> For the formerly incarcerated who had earnings in the bottom fifth, or quintile, of the distribution in 1986, two-thirds (67 percent) remained at the bottom of the earnings ladder 20 years later in 2006 . . . By comparison, only one-third of men who were not incarcerated during that time frame remained stuck at the bottom. Moreover, the odds of moving from the bottom of the earnings distribution to the very top quintile were particularly low for offenders. They had only a 2 percent chance of making such a climb, compared with a 15 percent chance for those who had not served time behind bars. Analyzing relative family income mobility over those two decades yields similar results.[115]

The mass incarceration of young adult African American men affects equally remarkable numbers of the next generation in the Black community, contributing to the reproduction of caste status from generation to generation. The NRC report states that "According to the most recent estimates from the Bureau of Justice Statistics, 53 percent of those in prison in 2007 had minor children.

> In that year, an estimated 1.7 million children under age 18 had a parent in state or federal prison . . . In 2007, black . . . children in the United States were 7.5 . . . times more likely . . . than white

children to have a parent in prison."[116]
Sixty-two percent of black children in 2009 whose parents had not completed high school experienced parental imprisonment by age 17.[117] The "daily risk of parental incarceration for black children [was] 11.42 percent by 2008, a far cry . . . from the 1.75 percent of white children who can expect to have a parent incarcerated [on a given day] in 2008 . . ."[118] For White children born in 1990 the risk of paternal imprisonment was 7.8% for children of high school dropouts; 4.8% for children of high school graduates, 1.1% for children of college graduates. On the other hand, "Over half (50.5%) of black children born in 1990 to high school dropouts had their father imprisoned . . . About 13 [sic: 13.8%] percent of black children of college-educated parents had a parent sent to prison," as did 20% of high school graduates.[119] Therefore, in total, "one in four (25.1%) black children born in 1990 had their father imprisoned by age fourteen."[120] It is striking that the percentage of Black children of incarcerated college educated parents is nearly twice that of White children of incarcerated high school drop-outs. For the descendants of enslaved Africans, even a college education does not provide adequate protection against state policies of mass incarceration.

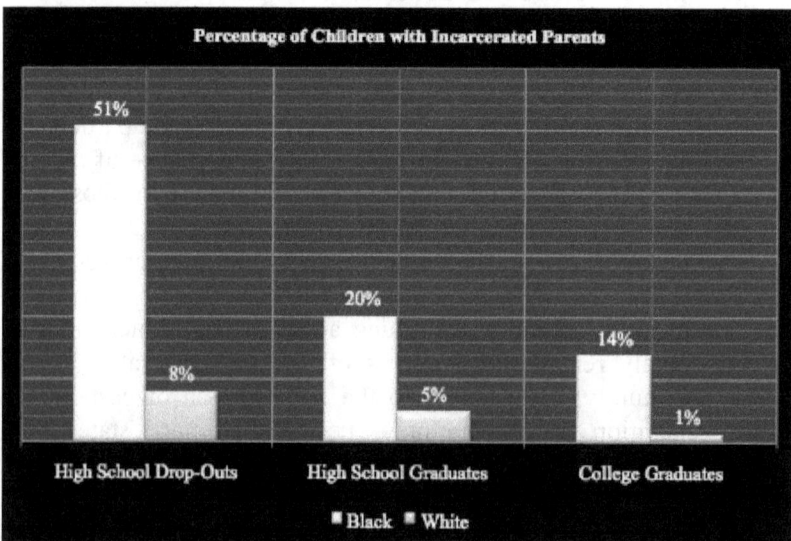

Percentage of Children with Incarcerated Parents

	High School Drop-Outs	High School Graduates	College Graduates
Black	51%	20%	14%
White	8%	5%	1%

Black   White

Mass incarceration has a direct, and very large, role in the intergenerational impoverishment of the Black community. Incarcerated men with children cannot contribute to the household incomes of the mothers (or grandmothers) of those children; formerly incarcerated men may not be welcomed into their children's households and whether or not they live with their children and their partners they are unlikely to make much of a contribution to family incomes. An estimate of a 60% national high school graduation rate for African American males implies that 28% of all African American males in a given cohort will spend time in prison. Adding in those with educational qualifications from high school diplomas to advanced degrees who also have been incarcerated, we find that there are an estimated one-third to 40% of African American males who at some point in their adult lives will have spent time in prison. Selecting the mid-point of Bruce Western's income penalty estimate, this points to a 30% reduction in potential lifetime earnings for the Black community from mass incarceration alone, a community which in any case has little prospect of incomes above the bottom quintiles. This is a powerful force for "sedimentation." Not only will these men live in, or close to, poverty, but their partners and children will do so as well.[121]

Chetty and his colleagues found that "The fraction of children living in single-parent households is the single strongest correlate of upward income mobility among all the variables we explored . . .

One natural explanation for this spatial correlation is an individual-level effect: children raised by a single parent may have worse outcomes than those raised by two parents . . . family structure correlates with upward mobility not just at the individual level but also at the community level, perhaps because the stability of the social environment affects children's outcomes more broadly.[122]

Or because, as we have seen, poverty itself limits upward mobility, for individuals and for their communities, an effect that is particularly powerful in African American communities. While 5.5% of White families consist of a female householder, no husband present, with related children under 18 years of age (in the awkward Bureau of the Census phrases), three times as many, 16.7% of Black families are in that category. For women over 15 years of age there is near perfect symmetry between the races in regard to marital status:

Half (49.8%) of White women are now married and a quarter (25.6%) have never been married; half (47.4%) of Black women have never been married and a quarter (25.5%) are now married. Thirty percent of White women, ages 15 to 50, who have given birth in the past 12 months were unmarried, as compared to two-thirds (67.3%) of Black women ages 15 to 50, who have given birth in the past 12 months.[123] In the Black community, children born to married couples are an exception. Michael Katz finds that these low "marriage rates among black women [can be traced] to the lack of marriageable men—a situation with roots in . . . joblessness and incarceration"[124] Although incarceration is more prevalent among men with lower levels of educational attainment, this lack of marriageable men is also vividly apparent for women who have attained postsecondary education. People tend to marry within their education level and, as we have seen, at higher education levels there are nearly twice as many Black women as Black men.

A principal effect of all these factors is the increased likelihood that the families of Black children will have incomes below the poverty level. In the White community that rate for single-parent families is 38%, in the Black community 48% (as compared to the married couple families, at poverty rates of 7.5% and 11%, respectively). And thus while 14% of White children live in poverty, 35% of Black children do so. We would expect, then, that upward mobility for Black children would be less than half as likely as for White children by virtue of family structure alone, a family structure in areas of concentrated poverty that is in large part a product of mass incarceration.

Black poverty is not a static condition, a pathology, but a manifestation of institutional racism. Institutional racism is an *action* continuously undertaken and accomplished by decisions taken about education and criminal justice system policies and practices by specific individuals, from chief state school officers to teachers in the classroom, from judges on the bench to cops on the beat.[125] The following chapters illustrate this by examining the condition of the descendants of enslaved Africans in a range of American cities.

Those chapters describe the chains of Black America that maintain the caste-status of the descendants of enslaved Africans in eight cities: Chicago, Cleveland, Memphis, Milwaukee, New

Orleans, New York City, Philadelphia and Rochester (NY). There is nothing special about these cities; many others have school systems that fail their African American students and racialized criminal justice systems that criminalize Black men. However, this set seems sufficient to make the point. There is also a chapter describing Prince George's County, Maryland, a suburb of Washington, D.C., where conditions and outcomes, although not ideal, are nonetheless sufficiently different as to demonstrate that comparatively low incomes and educational attainment, comparatively high incarceration rates, are not somehow in the nature of Black Americans but are products of institutional racism.

Each of these chapters is similarly structured to *Chapter One: The National Picture.* There are descriptions of demographics, income and wealth inequalities and the education and criminal justice systems. Each ends with an attempt to model a more equitable social structure for that city. A final chapter summarizes this material and suggests what steps can be taken, and by whom, to end the caste status of the American descendants of enslaved Africans.

Chapter One: Notes

[1] I have not included data about Hispanic/Latino Americans in this study as, in my opinion, they are following a trajectory similar to that of other immigrant groups, such as the Irish in the nineteenth century and the Italians in the early twentieth and are, in any case, highly heterogeneous. As observed by Massey and Denton: "Despite their immigrant origins, Spanish language and high poverty rates, Hispanics are considerably more integrated in U.S. society than blacks" Massey, Douglas S. and Denton, Nancy A. *American Apartheid: Segregation and the Making of the Underclass.* Cambridge, MA: Harvard University Press, 1993, p. 77).

[2] Demographic data from the Bureau of the Census, unless otherwise indicated.

[3] National Center for Health Statistics. Health, United States, 2012: With Special Feature on Emergency Care. Hyattsville, MD. 2013. http://www.cdc.gov/nchs/data/hus/hus12.pdf#018

[4] CIA World Fact Book, 2012.

[5] The rate for Western Europe is 4 and that for Eastern Europe is 10 deaths per thousand live births. National Center for Health Statistics. Health, United States, 2012: With Special Feature on Emergency Care. Hyattsville, MD. 2013.

[6] Wakefield, Sara and Wildeman, Christopher. Children of the Prison Boom: Mass Incarceration and the Future of American Inequality. Oxford: Oxford University Press, 2014, p. 99.

[7] Kaiser Family Foundation. Health Coverage by Race and Ethnicity: The Potential Impact of the Affordable Care Act, March 13, 2013. http://kff.org/disparities-policy/issue-brief/health. The Affordable Health Care Act has begun to alleviate this situation.

[8] http://www.hhs.gov/healthcare/facts/factsheets/2012/04/aca-and-african-americans04122012a.html

[9] There is a custom, particularly among business interests in the United States, of defining class by spending patterns—participation, or not, in "The American Way of Life": two cars in every garage, two mortgages on every house This is not particularly useful for analytical purposes.

[10] "The median income of black families in 1990 was virtually the same it had been in 1970." Oliver, Melvin L. and Thomas M.

Shapiro. Black Wealth/White Wealth: A New Perspective on Racial Inequality. Tenth-Anniversary Edition. New York: Routledge, 2006, p. 28.

[11] DeNavas-Walt, Carmen and Bernadette D. Proctor, U.S. Census Bureau, Current Population Reports, P60-249, Income and Poverty in the United States: 2013, U.S. Government Printing Office, Washington, DC, 2014.

[12] Coleman-Jensen, Alisha, Christian Gregory, and Anita Singh. Household Food Security in the United States in 2013: Statistical Supplement, AP-066, U.S. Department of Agriculture, Economic Research Service, September 2014, table S-1.

[13] Pew Charitable Trusts [Lopoo, Leonard and DeLeire, Thomas]. Pursuing the American Dream: Economic Mobility Across Generations., July 2012, p. 18.

[14] American Community Survey, 5-year survey.

[15] http://www.census.gov/hhes/www/income/data/historical/families/

[16] Bivens, Josh; Gould, Elise; Mishel, Lawrence and Shierholz, Heidi. Raising America's Pay: Why It's Our Central Economic Policy Challenge. Washington, D.C.: Economic Policy Institute, June 4, 2014. http://www.epi.org/publication/raising-americas-pay/

[17] Piketty, pp. 257-8.

[18] Bivens, Josh; Gould, Elise; Mishel, Lawrence and Shierholz, Heidi. /

[19] U. S. Census. Wealth and Asset Ownership. http://www.census.gov/people/wealth/

[20] Urahn, Susan K.; Currier, Erin; Elliott, Diana; Wechsler, Lauren, and Wilson, Denise. Pursuing the American Dream. Philadelphia: Pew Charitable Trusts, 2012, p. 18. http://www.pewstates.org/uploadedFiles/PCS_Assets/2012/Pursuing _American_Dream.pdf

[21] "Income is adjusted for family size. Wealth is adjusted for age and includes home equity. Numbers in each column may not sum to 100 percent due to rounding." Pew, p. 18.

[22] United States Census, Wealth and Asset Ownership of Households, Table 5. www.census.gov/people/wealth

[23] Unlike income, wealth is more unevenly distributed in the Black community than in White America. The top 10% of Black households holds 67% of the wealth of the Black community, as

compared to 51% for the White top 10%. On the other hand, the threshold for the wealthiest 10% of African American households is just $234,252, as compared to $702,950 for the wealthiest 10% of White households. See Kochhar, Rakesh; Fry, Richard and Paul Taylor. Wealth Gaps Rise to Record Highs between Whites, Blacks, Hispanics. Pew Research Social and Demographic Trends, Chapter 8. 2011/07/26. http://www.pewsocialtrends.org/2011/07/26/wealth-gaps-rise-to-record-highs-between-whites-blacks-hispanics/

[24] Tippett, Rebecca; Jones-DeWeever, Avis; Rockeymoore, Maya; Hamilton, Darrick and Darity, William, Jr. Beyond Broke: Why Closing the Racial Wealth Gap is a Priority for National Economic Security. Chapel Hill: Center for Global Policy Solutions, May 2014, p. 7.

[25] Katz, Michael B. The Undeserving Poor: America's Enduring Confrontation with Poverty. Oxford: Oxford University Press (2nd edition), 2013, p. 40.

[26] Rank, Mark Robert. One Nation, Underprivileged: Why American Poverty Affects Us All. Oxford University Press, 2005, p. 11.

[27] Rank, pp. 69-70.

[28] Rank, pp. 66-7.

[29] Rank, p. 50.

[30] Rank, pp. 3-4.

[31] Katz, Michael B. The Undeserving Poor: America's Enduring Confrontation with Poverty. Oxford: Oxford University Press (2nd edition), 2013, p. 75.

[32] Katz, p. 79.

[33] Katz, p. 114.

[34] Katz, p. 139.

[35] Katz, , p. 144.

[36] Rank, p. 29.

[37] Rank, p. 13.

[38] Rank, pp. 23-4.

[39] Rank, p. 24.

[40] HUD data.

[41] Rank, pp. 96-7. Chart adapted from Rank, Table 4.3, p. 96.

[42] Rank, p. 97.

[43] Coleman-Jensen, Alisha, Christian Gregory, and Anita Singh. Household Food Security in the United States in 2013, ERR-173,

U.S. Department of Agriculture, Economic Research Service, September 2014.

[44] Oliver, Melvin L. and Thomas M. Shapiro. Black Wealth/White Wealth: A New Perspective on Racial Inequality. Tenth-Anniversary Edition. New York: Routledge, 2006, p. 137.

[45] Alexander, Michelle. The New Jim Crow Mass Incarceration in the Age of Colorblindness. New York: The New Press, 2012.

[46] Blackmon, Douglas A. Slavery by Another Name: The Re-Enslavement of Black Americans from the Civil War to World War II. New York: Random House, 2009.

[47] Oliver and Shapiro, p. 4.

[48] ". . . first, whether it be a question of homesteading, suburbanization, or redlining, we have seen how governmental, institutional, and private-sector discrimination enhances the ability of different segments of the population to accumulate and build on their wealth assets and resources, thereby raising their standard of living and securing a better future for themselves and their children." Oliver and Shapiro, p. 22.

[49] Oliver and Shapiro, p. 41.

[50] Massey, Douglas S. and Denton, Nancy A. American Apartheid: Segregation and the Making of the Underclass. Cambridge, MA: Harvard University Press, 1993, p. 46. I understand that Richard Rothstein is working on a book on this matter in relation to the current situation in the St. Louis area.

[51] Massey and Denton, p. 9.

[52] Massey and Denton, p. 2.

[53] Massey and Denton, p. 3, quoting Clark, Kenneth B. Dark Ghetto: Dilemmas of Social Power. New York: Harper and Row, 1965, p. 11.

[54] Massey and Denton, pp. 2-3.

[55] Massey and Denton, p. 148.

[56] See, for example, "For black Americans, financial damage from subprime implosion is likely to last," Washington Post, 2012/07/08.

[57] Chetty, Raj, Hendren, Nathaniel, Kline, Patrick and Saez, Emmanuel. *Where is the Land of Opportunity? The Geography of Intergenerational Mobility in the United States.* NBER, May 2014, pp. 2-3. http://obs.rc.fas.harvard.edu/chetty/mobility_geo.pdf.

[58] Oliver and Shapiro, pp. 159-60.

[59] Oliver and Shapiro, p. 173.

[60] Pew, p. 19.

[61] Pew, p. 20.

[62] Isaacs, Julia B. "Economic Mobility of Black and White Families" in Isaacs, Julia B; Sawhill, Isabel V. and Ron Haskins. Getting Ahead or Losing Ground: Economic Mobility in America. The Brookings Institution, 2008. http://www.brookings.edu/~/media/research/files/reports/2008/2/economic%20mobility%20sawhill/02_economic_mobility_sawhill

[63] Mazumder, Bhashkar. "Black-white differences in intergenerational economic mobility in the United States." Economic Perspectives. Federal Reserve Bank of Chicago, 2014, pp. 8-9. https://www.chicagofed.org/digital_assets/publications/economic_perspectives/2014/1Q2014_part1_mazumder.pdf

[64] Sharkey, Patrick. Neighborhoods and the Black-White Mobility Gap. Philadelphia: The Pew Charitable Trusts, 2009, p. 9. http://www.pewstates.org/uploadedFiles/PCS_Assets/2009/PEW_NEIGHBORHOODS(1).pdf. Sharkey has now further reported on this research in his book Stuck in Place: Urban Neighborhoods and the End of Progress toward Racial Equity.

[65] Sharkey, p. 11. Chetty et al add: "we show that upward income mobility is significantly lower in areas with larger African-American populations. However, white individuals in areas with large African-American populations also have lower rates of upward mobility, implying that racial shares matter at the community level" p. 3.

[66] Rank, p. 74.

[67] Sharkey, p. 15.

[68] Massey and Denton, p. 144; 181.

[69] Wilkes, Rima, and John Iceland. "Hypersegregation." Encyclopedia of Social Problems. Ed. Thousand Oaks, CA: SAGE, 2008. 464-67. SAGE Reference Online. Web. 12 Apr. 2012.

[70] "The notion embodied in the 'sedimentation of racial inequality' is that in central ways the cumulative effects of the past have seemingly cemented blacks to the bottom of society's economic hierarchy. A history of low wages, poor schooling, and segregation affected not one or two generations of blacks but practically all African Americans well into the middle of the twentieth century." Oliver and Shapiro, p. 5.

[71] Wilkes and Iceland.

[72] Massey and Denton, p. 57.

[73] Sharkey, p. 5.

[74] Piketty, Thomas. Capital in the Twenty-First Century. Trans. Arthur Goldhammer. Cambridge, MA.: Harvard University Press, 2014, p 313.

[75] Bivens, Josh; Gould, Elise; Mishel, Lawrence and Shierholz, Heidi. Raising America's Pay: Why It's Our Central Economic Policy Challenge. Washington, D.C.: Economic Policy Institute, June 4, 2014. http://www.epi.org/publication/raising-americas-pay/

[76] Chetty, Raj, Hendren, Nathaniel, Kline, Patrick and Saez, Emmanuel. *Where is the Land of Opportunity? The Geography of Intergenerational Mobility in the United States.* NBER, May 2014, p. 4; p. 20. http://obs.rc.fas.harvard.edu/chetty/mobility_geo.pdf

[77] Kornrich, Sabino and Furstenberg, Frank. Investing in Children: Changes in Parental Spending on Children, 1972-2007. Demography (2013) 50:1-23.

[78] A caution: the numbers of adults in these categories, as reported by their children, are not necessarily the same as those self-reported to the Census or those that might be obtained from school and college records.

[79] Enrollment data in this section is from: U.S. Department of Education, National Center for Education Statistic, The Condition of Education, Status of Rural Education, May, 2013, nces.ed.gov/programs/coe/indicator_tla.asp.

[80] Massey and Denton caution that "Relatively high levels of black suburbanization in some metropolitan areas can be deceiving, however, because many black 'suburbs' are simply poor, declining cities that happen to be located outside the city limits. Camden, New Jersey, for example, accounts for a sizable portion of Philadelphia's suburban black population, and East St. Louis, Illinois, likewise represents a large share of St. Louis's suburban blacks; but neither 'suburb' fits the idea of suburban life" (p.69.).

[81] Rank, p. 73.

[82] In Rank, p. 73.

[83] Kornrich, Sabino and Furstenberg, Frank. Investing in Children: Changes in Parental Spending on Children, 1972-2007. Demography (2013) 50:1-23.

[84] U.S. Department of Education Office for Civil Rights. Civil Rights Data Collection. Data Snapshot: School Discipline. Issue Brief No. 1 (March 2014).

[85] U.S. Department of Education Office for Civil Rights. Civil Rights Data Collection. Data Snapshot: School Discipline. Issue Brief No. 1 (March 2014).

[86] Massey and Denton, p. 141.

[87] Massey and Denton, p. 153.

[88] Massey and Denton, pp. 141-2,.

[89] Rank, pp. 207-8.

[90] Rank, p. 210.

[91] Rueben, Kim and Murray, Sheila. Racial Disparities in Education Finance: Going Beyond Equal Revenues. Urban Institute Discussion Paper N. 29, November 2008. http://www.urban.org/UploadedPDF/411785_equal_revenues.pdf

[92] Rueben and Murray, page 8.

[93] Heuer, Ruth and Stephanie Stullich. Comparability of State and Local Expenditures Among Schools Within Districts: A Report from the Study of School-Level Expenditures. U.S. Department of Education, Office of Planning, Evaluation and Policy Development, Policy and Program Studies Service, 2011, p. 29.

[94] Spatig-Amerikaner, Ary. Unequal Education: Federal Loophole Enables Lower Spending on Students of Color. Center for American Progress, August 2012.

[95] Spatig-Amerikaner, p. 14.

[96] Baker, Bruce, David Sciarra and Danielle Farrie. Is School Funding Fair? A National Report Card. Education Law Center, New Jersey. Second edition: June 2012, pp. 5-6.

[97] Cited in the New York Times, June 18, 2014, page B6.

[98] Piketty, p. 420.

[99] Piketty, pp. 484-5.

[100] U.S. Department of Education, National Center for Education Statistics, Digest of Education Statistics, 2012, Table 376.

[101] National Research Council of the National Academies. "The Growth of Incarceration in the United States: Exploring Causes and Consequences." Jeremy Travis and Bruce Western, Editors; Washington, D.C., April, 2014, p. 1.

[102] National Research Council, p. 50.

[103] National Research Council, p. 116.
[104] National Research Council, p. 70.
[105] National Research Council, p. 7.
[106] Katz, p. 14.
[107] The National Research Council and similar reports appear to use the phrase "low-income and minority communities" and like phrases as a euphemism for communities of the descendants of enslaved Africans.
[108] National Research Council, p. 66.
[109] National Research Council, p. 68.
[110] Katz, pp. 227-8.
[111] Goffman, Alice. On the Run: Fugitive Life in an American City. Chicago: University of Chicago Press, 2014.
[112] Olive and Shapiro, pp. 225-6.
[113] Wakefield, Sara and Wildeman, Christopher. Children of the Prison Boom: Mass Incarceration and the Future of American Inequality. Oxford: Oxford University Press, 2014, p. 17.
[114] The Pew Charitable Trusts, 2010. Collateral Costs: Incarceration's Effect on Economic Mobility. Washington, DC: The Pew Charitable Trusts.
[115] The Pew Charitable Trusts, 2010. Collateral Costs.
[116] National Research Council, p. 260.
[117] National Research Council, p. 262.
[118] Wakefield and Wildeman, p. 32.
[119] Wakefield and Wildeman, pp. 36-8.
[120] Wakefield and Wildeman, p. 33.
[121] Carson, E. Ann, "Prisoners in 2013, U. S. Department of Justice, Office of Justice Programs, Bureau of Justice Statistics, September 2014, NCJ 247282. http://www.bjs.gov/content/pub/pdf/p13.pdf
[122] Chetty, p. 40.
[123] It is little noted that out-of-wedlock births in the White community have now surpassed the level of "pathology" identified in the Moynihan report on the Negro family.
[124] Katz, p. 225.
[125] For an example at the local level, in New York City, "the Vera Institute of Justice, found that race was a significant factor at nearly every stage of criminal prosecutions in Manhattan, from setting bail to negotiating a plea deal to sentencing." New York Times, July 8,

2014, citing Kutateladze, Besiki Luka and Nancy R. Andiloro. "Prosecution and Racial Justice in New York County" – Technical Report, Vera Institute Of Justice, January 31, 2014. There is also pervasive individual racism in America. See, for example, "Racial Bias, Even When We Have Good Intentions," by Sendhil Mullainathan, New York Times, January 3, 2015. http://www.nytimes.com/2015/01/04/upshot/the-measuring-sticks-of-racial-bias-.html?abt=0002&abg=1

Chapter Two: Chicago

Let the Midnight Special shine her light on me,
You take the Illinois, and come to Kankakee.[1]

Chicago was one of the main destinations of the Great Migration; the source of that beacon of hope shining south along the tracks of the Illinois Central Railroad.[*] That light, that beacon, that hope, has been nearly extinguished.

*　　　　*　　　　*

The 860,000 African Americans now living in Chicago are much less than half as likely to have a college education than White residents of the city, more than twice as likely to be unemployed, almost twice as likely not to be in the labor force at all, much less likely to be in management or professional occupations, much more likely to be in service occupations. Chicago's Black household incomes are half those of White households, the poverty rate of individual Black residents of Chicago is more than twice that of individual White residents and the poverty rate of Black families nearly three times as high as that of White families. At the other end of the scale, 20% of White families have incomes over $150,000 per year, as compared to just 4% of Black families. Over 90% of Chicago's Black households have no net assets apart from small amounts of equity in their own homes: they could not pay an unexpected medical bill of a few hundred dollars without borrowing. By some of these measures life for the descendants of enslaved Africans is better today in Chicago than in Mississippi; in some ways not as good; in general, a wash.

Few Black children in Chicago grow up to have incomes equal to that of their parents, as low as those may be, and most will have lower incomes yet as a result of the concentration of inferior schools,

---

[*] Kankakee is a city and county a little south of Chicago. It fits the song's rhyme scheme.

heightened police activity and unemployment in Chicago's extraordinarily segregated Black neighborhoods. Chicago was a pioneer in real-estate-agent-driven "block busting" and similar tactics playing on racism to increase profits. The White/Black "Index of Dissimilarity" for the city, a measure of segregation on which values of 60 or higher are considered very high, was 82.5 in 2010.[2] The result has been that in some cases adjacent census tracts have mirror-image homogenous populations, one 90% or more Black, the next, across the street, 90% or more White.

Demographics

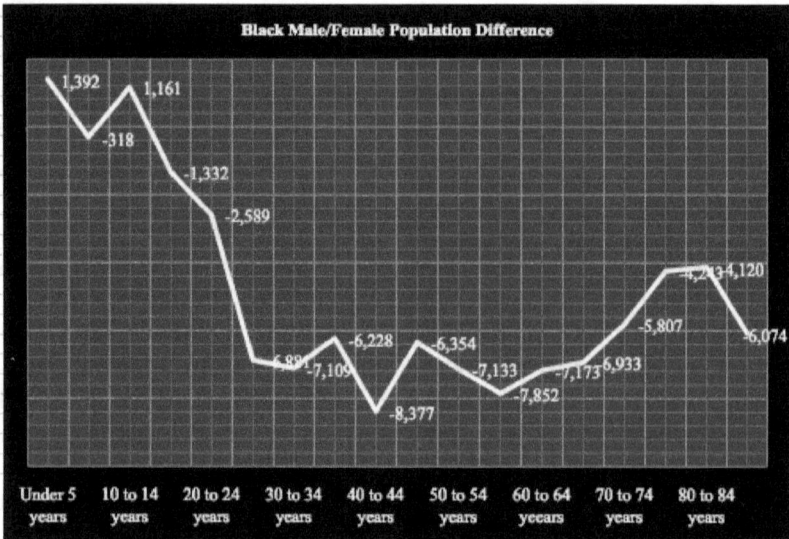

Black Male/Female Population Difference

The age distributions of the Black and White populations, unlike those in many other cities, are quite similar, but the gender distributions within the races vary considerably. There are exactly equal percentages of White, non-Hispanic, males and females, but females constitute 55% of the Black population, males just 45%. Every Chicago Black-age-cohort from 25 to 69 years of age shows a deficit of approximately 6,000 males as compared to females in that cohort. Why is that? One reason might be that Chicago is notorious for the homicides of young Black men. Total homicides in the city vary from 350 to 400 annually: 80%

of the victims are Black. However, even 300 murders across all age groups account for only a small percentage of the missing working-age Black males among Chicago residents. More die from preventable disease. Many of the rest are in jail.

The health of African Americans in Illinois is not as good as that of White, non-Hispanic, residents of the state. This disparity begins at birth, when, for the usual reasons of poor nutrition and healthcare, 17% of non-Hispanic Black births are pre-term, as compared to 11% of non-Hispanic White births. Fourteen percent of Black births are of low birth-weight infants, twice the percentage of non-Hispanic White births. More Black men than White men and twice the percentage of Black women as White women report fair or poor health status. One study found that "Black Cook County residents suffered 266.4 more premature deaths than did White residents in 2007, a ratio of 2.5 premature Black deaths for every premature White death."[3]

Category	Cook County	U.S.A.
Overall Premature mortality	239.6[†]	231.1
White	179.5	216.7
Black	445.9	373.7
Overall All-cause mortality	759.2	760.2
White	687.1	749.4
Black	1,042.9	958.0
Overall Heart disease mortality	202.0	190.9
White	194.7	191.4
Black	261.8	251.9
Overall Infant mortality rate (%)	7.5	6.7
White	4.3	5.6
Black	13.8	12.9
Overall Low birth weight rate (%)	8.9	8.2
White (%)	6.9	7.1
Black (%)	13.9	13.4

[†] Per 100,000

Income

The 2010 Census found that the African American unemployment rate in Chicago was twice that of White, non-Hispanic, residents of the city, 11% as compared to 5%, continuing a long-term trend. The percentage of those in the labor force who were unemployed was even more disparate: 19% to 7%. The reason for this is that while 30% of the White population is not in the labor force, the percentage of the Black population not in the labor force—neither employed nor counted as actively looking for employment—is a much higher 43%.

Looking more closely at Chicago's workforce, nearly half (46%) of the city's White workforce is in management and only 15% in service occupations, while 25% of the city's Black workforce is in service occupations and just 28% in management. There are enormous disparities in income distribution in Chicago. White median household income, $61,000, is twice that of Black median household income: $31,000. Just 13% of White families have incomes under $25,000 per year, while 36% of Black families have incomes below that poverty threshold. Nearly half, 45%, of Black residents of the city have incomes below the poverty level; just 13% of the White residents live in poverty.[4] Two-thirds of Black families in Chicago have incomes so low that their children qualify for the National Lunch Program.

The percentage of very poor Black families is nearly a quarter of the total Black population, while that of White families is just 6%. The lowest quintile (20%) of Black families, by income, comes in at just over $15,000, while the lowest White quintile has incomes over $35,000 per year. Or to put that another way, half of Chicago's Black families have incomes that would put them in the lowest 20% of White families. On the other end of the scale, the upper 20%, the highest quintile, of White families have incomes over $150,000 per year, as compared to just 4% of Black families. The highest quintile of Black families has incomes starting at about $70,000 per year. In total, aggregate White income in Chicago is $46 billion per year, Black aggregate income a third of that, $16 billion, a far greater difference than can be attributed to the difference in population.

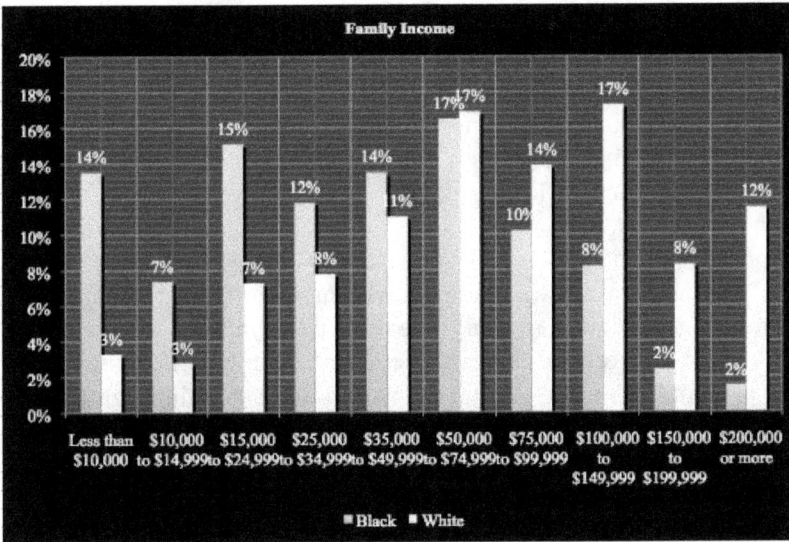

Family Income

Black *White*

Wealth

Wealth, unlike income, can be passed from one generation to another. It is crucial for family and neighborhood stability. It is the basis of capitalism itself. Money can be invested so that it earns income (such as rental property, stocks and bonds) or it can be put into non-income producing assets, such as one's own home. We know from the Census that 30% of Chicago's White households have incomes from interest, dividends or net rental income, compared with 7% of the city's Black households. This indicates that 93% of Chicago's Black households have no net wealth, apart from equity in their own homes.

Researchers at the Bureau of the Census have found that national Black household mean net worth, excluding equity in their own home, is $50,000, that of White households is $300,000. Under these assumptions the net worth of all of Chicago's Black households comes to $1 billion, not including home equity, and those of the city's White households totals $49 billion. Including home equity, the wealth of Chicago's White households is approximately $80 billion, that of the city's Black households $5 billion. These calculations obviously understate the wealth of both groups, as they are based on national averages and Chicago has an unusual number of members of the top one-tenth of one percent of both races. But billionaires aside, the total wealth of White Chicago's households is probably forty times that of the Black households of the city. Not only are most Black Chicagoans individually poor, the wealth of Black Chicago, as a community, is insignificant compared to the wealth of the metropolis as a whole. This has obvious implications related to political influence.

Mobility

Research has shown that even without regard to parental income, "spending childhood in a high-poverty neighborhood versus a low-poverty neighborhood raises the chances of downward mobility by 52 percent."[5] Chicago is a highly segregated city, with high poverty rates in its Black neighborhoods. Some census tracts in Black neighborhoods have poverty rates reaching 60%, while some nearby White neighborhoods have poverty rates under 10%. Few Black children in Chicago grow up to have incomes equal to that of their parents, as low as those may be, and most will have lower incomes yet as a result of the concentration of inferior schools, heightened police activity and unemployment in Chicago's Black neighborhoods.

Intergenerational *wealth* mobility is even less likely for Chicago's African Americans than intergenerational income mobility. Nationally, twice as many White as Black Americans raised in the middle quintile accumulate more wealth than had their parents. Only African Americans raised in the poorest households exceed their parents' "wealth," which in any case is likely to be barely existent or negative.[6] Less than a quarter of African Americans raised in the middle quintile of national wealth distribution achieve greater wealth than their parents. On the other hand, 68% of African Americans raised in that middle quintile of wealth end up in the bottom two quintiles as adults.[7] It is therefore unlikely that there is much intergenerational family income or wealth upward mobility in Chicago's Black community.

This calls the question: what are the causes of the vast racial inequities in the city? Two are easily identified: the operations of the schools and those of the police.

The Anvil of Education

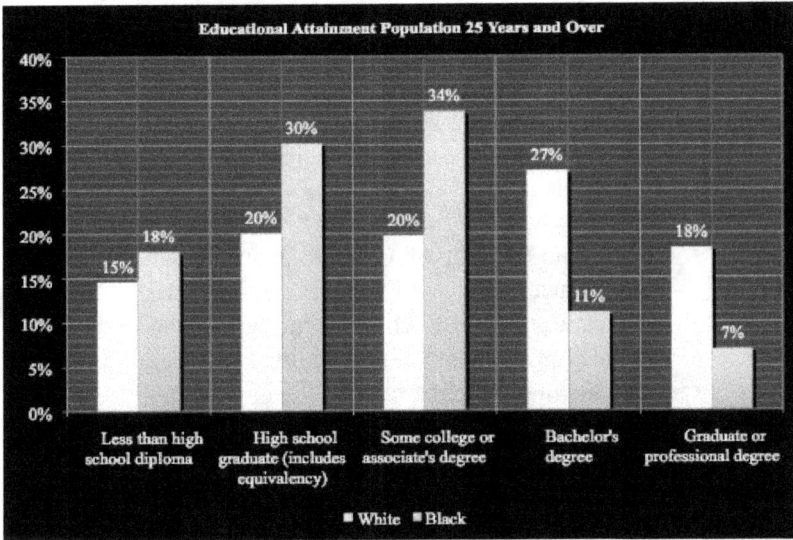

Educational Attainment Population 25 Years and Over

	White	Black
Less than high school diploma	15%	18%
High school graduate (includes equivalency)	20%	30%
Some college or associate's degree	20%	34%
Bachelor's degree	27%	11%
Graduate or professional degree	18%	7%

Elementary and Secondary Education

> Our vision is that every student in every neighborhood will be engaged in a rigorous, well-rounded instructional program and will graduate prepared for success in college, career and life. *Chicago Public Schools.*[8]

Half of the adults in Black Chicago have only a high school diploma or less and some of those counted as high school graduates have equivalents, such as GEDs, which is not the same thing (and many of which are obtained in prison, which functions as a de facto supplementary education system for Chicago's Black residents). Just 18% have a Bachelor's degree or more. This is crucial: income is directly related to education and, for Black men, incarceration for those without a high school diploma is more likely than not. The comparatively low educational attainment of Chicago's Black adults is a consequence of the failure of the Chicago school district to provide adequate educational opportunities in the schools in the city's hypersegregated Black neighborhoods.

The Chicago public schools continue to produce young Black people with the same unsatisfactory education levels as their parents.

Only slightly more than half of Chicago's Black students in grade 9 in 2009 graduated with a high school diploma in 2013, as compared to 69% of the district's White, non-Hispanic, students. The attitude of the district to its Black students is illustrated by the fact that when the district decided to close nearly fifty schools, 87% of the students affected were Black. And the recent proliferation of charter schools has simply made matters worse: increasing segregation and decreasing achievement.[9]

Some numbers:

- Forty-one percent of Chicago's public school students are Black, 9% are White, non-Hispanic, 45% are Hispanic. 87% are eligible for either the free or the reduced price meals of the National Lunch Program.
- The average teacher salary (2011) is $70,000. Nearly a quarter of those teachers are absent more than 10 days of the school year.
- Sixty-nine percent of out-of-school suspensions and 71% of expulsions are inflicted on the 41% of the district's students who are the descendants of enslaved Africans.

The National Assessment of Educational Progress (NAEP) reports concerning the crucial grade 8 level of basic skills achievement show that while the district's schools have brought half (51%) of its White, non-Hispanic, students to grade-level Proficiency in reading, they have only done so with 11% of their Black students. Just 9% of the district's Black students eligible for the National Lunch Program are Proficient or above in reading, but 20% of the district's relatively few Black students from more prosperous families, ineligible for free or reduced price meals, are Proficient. *None* of the district's Black students from the city's 18% of Black families with parents who did not complete high school achieved proficiency in reading by grade 8; just 6% of those with a parent who graduated from high school achieved proficiency; 12% who had a parent with some college education and 15% with college graduate parents achieved proficiency in grade 8 reading.[‡]

---

‡ In comparison, 63% of the district's White, non-Hispanic, students from more prosperous families, ineligible for free or reduced price meals, are Proficient in grade 8 reading. There were insufficient numbers of White, non-Hispanic students whose parents had not completed college to report.

In brief, the district teaches nearly two-thirds of its White, non-Hispanic, students to read at grade level by grade 8. It fails to teach nearly 90% of its Black students to read at or above grade level by grade 8.

Given this failure to teach basic skills and the routine displacement of African American students from the classroom, it is surprising that even slightly more than half of Chicago's Black students in grade 9 in 2009 graduated with a high school diploma in 2013. Which brings us to ask: What is the value of a Chicago school district diploma? What does it really mean? How well-prepared are its graduates for college and career?

Postsecondary Education

We can consider high school graduation as an indicator of career preparation by examining the district's success in preparing its Black students for Associate's degrees. The pipeline to an Associate's degree for Chicago's African American students begins with 18,000 Black students in grade 9, of whom approximately 9,400 are given diplomas four years later. The seven-campus City Colleges of Chicago system admitted 8,361 students in the fall of 2008, 3,436 of whom were Black (1,399 of those were men), all of whom, for the sake of argument, we will assume to be Chicago school district graduates (to balance the number who seek Associate's degrees in other institutions). In the summer of 2012 the City Colleges of Chicago graduated 561 students in 150% of normal time, 208 of whom were Black (84 of those were men), giving an overall graduation rate of 7% and a graduation rate for Black students of 6%.

In other words, by this measure, the Chicago public school district failed to prepare 93% of its graduates for successful pursuit of an Associate's degree, that now-basic certification required for skilled employment.

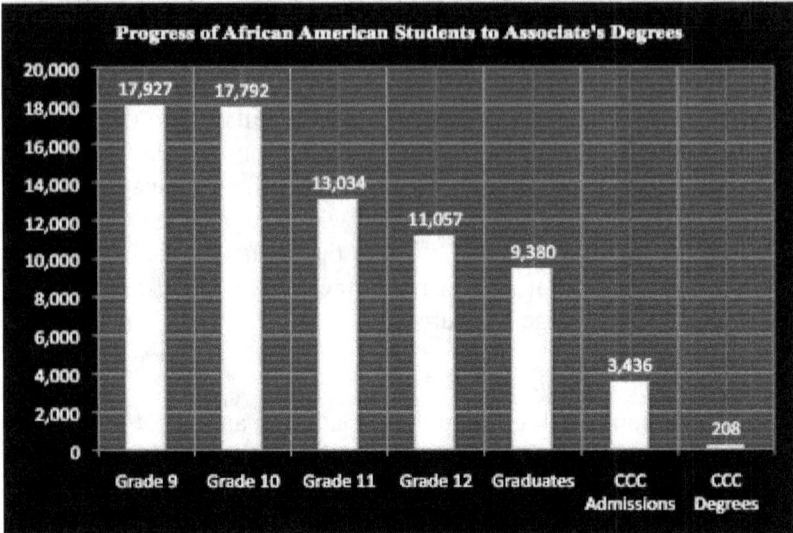

Progress of African American Students to Associate's Degrees

Grade 9	Grade 10	Grade 11	Grade 12	Graduates	CCC Admissions	CCC Degrees
17,927	17,792	13,034	11,057	9,380	3,436	208

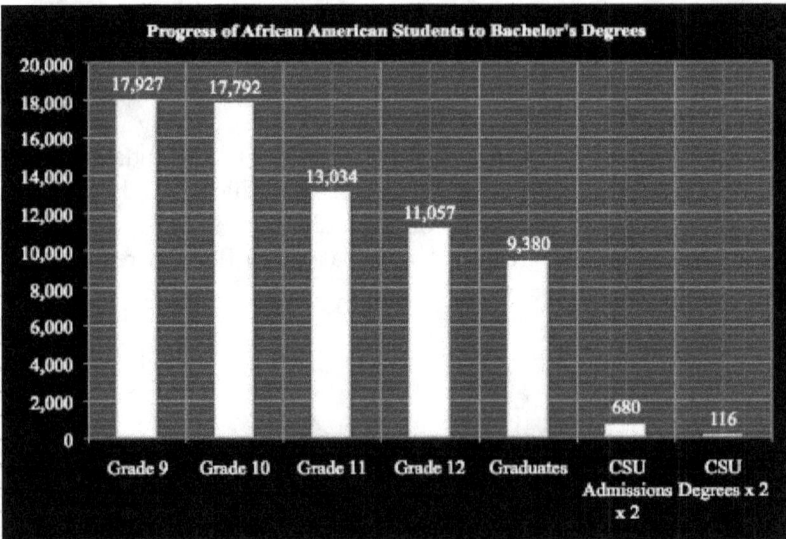

Progress of African American Students to Bachelor's Degrees

Grade 9	Grade 10	Grade 11	Grade 12	Graduates	CSU Admissions x 2	CSU Degrees x 2
17,927	17,792	13,034	11,057	9,380	680	116

78

Chicago has many four-year colleges and universities, including some that draw students from the entire world. Chicago State University is one with a more local catchment area. It admitted 423 first-time degree-seeking undergraduates in fall 2006, 340 of whom were Black (93 of those were men). In 2012 it graduated 75 students with Bachelor's degrees in 150% of normal time, 58 of whom were Black (14 of those were men), giving an overall graduation rate of 18% and a graduation rate for Black students of 17% (15% for African American men).[§] Again for the sake of argument, we will double the numbers of Chicago State University to represent district graduates who enroll in 4-year colleges. (See graph above.) This gives us about 680 admissions and 116 graduates with Bachelor's degrees in 150% of normal time.

In round numbers, of 18,000 African Americans entering grade 9 of the Chicago schools, 200 (1%) would be expected to attain Associate's degrees and half that number (and percentage) Bachelor's degrees. If we multiply these numbers by, say, 5, we are still well below 10% of district African American students whom the schools have prepared for college. In other words, from the point of view of the descendants of enslaved Africans, the Chicago school district fails in a key part of its mission 90% of the time.

The Hammer of Caste: The Criminal Justice System

And then there are the police. The laws against possession and use of marijuana, cocaine and the rest are arguably in place in order to have the effect that they do in fact have: to criminalize Black men. The mere documentation of the operation of these laws is a demonstration of their true purpose.

Illinois imprisons 258 White, non-Hispanics, per 100,000 population and nearly ten times that proportion of the state's Black residents: 2,128 per 100,000.[10] The resulting prison population of the state was approximately 48,000 on June 30, 2012, the latest date for which information is available.[11] Almost exactly half of those prisoners came from Cook County, and nearly a third of those were

---

[§] Another large Chicago postsecondary institution, the University of Illinois at Chicago, admitted just 116 Black students from Chicago in Fall 2013, 50 of whom were men. (UIC Student Data Book.) The University of Chicago Black admissions and graduates are approximately 5% of its total (a few dozen), not all of whom are from Chicago.

incarcerated for drug offenses, most frequently, possession of a controlled substance.[12] The most frequent "controlled substance" in question was marijuana. According to the *Chicago Reader* newspaper, "Chicago police made tens of thousands of arrests in 2009 and 2010 for marijuana possession, including 47,400 in which that misdemeanor was the most serious charge . . .

- Of those arrested, 78 percent were black, 17 percent were Hispanic, and 5 percent were white.
- In those years 4,255 people pleaded or were found guilty of low-level marijuana possession after being arrested in Chicago: 89 percent were black, 9 percent were Hispanic, and 2 percent were white.[13]

It appears that the Chicago police were arresting 24,000 residents per year for marijuana possession, of whom 18,700 were African American, approximately 8% of the city's adult Black males each year. What are the chances that a young Black man in Chicago would *not* be arrested by, say, age 30? How does this compare to arrests for marijuana possession of young White men, who are as likely, if not more likely, to use marijuana than are young Black men?

A May, 2014, study by the Illinois Consortium on Drug Policy of The Institute for Metropolitan Affairs at Roosevelt University found that "Illinois ranked third in the nation for the black to white racial disparity of marijuana possession offenders, despite the fact that marijuana use is the same in both groups . . . In Illinois, African Americans were about 7.6 times more likely to be arrested than whites . . . Illinois's rate of black to white disparity was more than 200% higher than the national average (7.56 v. 3.73)."[14] In Cook County African Americans comprise nearly 73% of arrestees.[15] Although under a recently enacted local law possession of small amounts of marijuana can be dealt with by a ticket, rather than arrest, "Only 7% of cases involving misdemeanor marijuana possession resulted in a ticket in Chicago, with the remaining 93% resulting in arrest."[16] The Chicago neighborhoods with high marijuana arrest rates are nearly all high majority Black neighborhoods.[17] Those Chicago neighborhoods with African American populations over 90% may experience marijuana arrest rates over 3,000 per 100,000 inhabitants.

Marijuana is in wide use in the United States, legal in an increasing number of states. It is used by approximately equal proportions of Americans of each race and ethnic group. In Chicago the police have discretion over whether to give a ticket to a person they find in possession of marijuana or arrest them. If that person is Black, 93% of the time the police choose arrest. It is difficult to view this practice by the Chicago police department as anything other than a way in which large numbers of African American men can be criminalized. An arrest record, even one for such a trivial cause, is enormously damaging to the victim. "All individuals, including those with marijuana misdemeanor offenses, may be subject to extensive background checks or a criminal record check.

> Licensed professionals with a misdemeanor criminal conviction on record could face having their license revoked or suspended (e.g., those licensed in the areas of law, education, and healthcare). Additionally, if someone with a conviction on record is seeking a license in any of these fields, their conviction may make them ineligible.[18]

This has direct economic effect on Black Chicago, as education and healthcare are among the chief employers of Chicago's African American workforce.

The drug laws have deleterious consequences beyond arrest for possession. People generally buy drugs from others of their own race or ethnic group, retailers who find this employment available when others may be closed to them. These dealers are liable to more severe jail sentences. And as disputes in an illegal trade cannot be settled in the courts, they are settled by recourse to the ubiquitous supply of guns. And so forth.

There are 14,000 persons on parole in Cook County and 25,000 on probation. If we estimate the number incarcerated at approximately that of those on parole, and take it that three-quarters of the total are African American men, we can estimate that there are at any one time between 30 and 40,000 adult African American male residents of Chicago under the control of the criminal justice system: 15%.[19] That is an average, of course; in some Chicago neighborhoods a third or more of the male adults might be under the control of the criminal justice system—unable to work for many large employers, liable to be picked up by the police (if not already incarcerated) at any moment for trivial violations of parole, unlikely to make enough money to lift their households out of poverty, or to pay the rent for an apartment in a neighborhood with good schools— if they could rent an apartment in a Chicago neighborhood with good schools.

Modeling a More Equitable Chicago

Inequity in Chicago—the caste-like subordination of much of the Black population—is enforced on the one hand by the education system, which prepares fewer than 10% of its Black students for success in college or well-paying careers. It is also enforced by the criminal justice system, with which five times as many Black as White men, proportionately, are entangled. A first, simple step toward progress would be to end the unequal enforcement of drug laws. As it is unlikely that this would be accomplished by bringing the arrest rates of White Chicago residents up to those of Black Chicago residents, it most likely would result in thousands of the latter walking free, able to contribute to economies of their families, neighborhoods and the city. (It would also save tens of millions of dollars in costs to the police department.)

Ending the unequal enforcement of drug and other laws can be done any day the Mayor wishes to do so.

Increasing the high school graduation rate of Black students in the Chicago public schools to that of White students, or higher, would reduce the pool of undereducated African American men that the state's prisons draw from by half or more, significantly lowering their incarceration rate—if policing practices are reformed—and increasing labor force participation. An increase in educational attainment will also have strong positive effects on incomes. We can model these effects by setting educational attainment of adults 25 years of age and older at the current level of White residents of Chicago. Then, at current average national Black incomes at each level of educational attainment, increasing Chicago's Black educational attainment levels to the current levels for White residents of Chicago would increase the community's annual income by $5.2 billion.

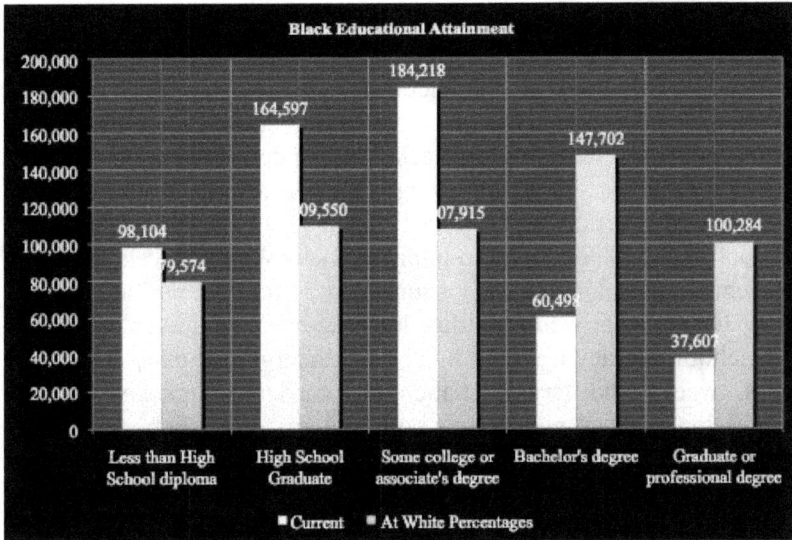

In a virtuous circle, other things being equal, this increase in college-educated adults, with its concomitant increase in family incomes, would then further increase Black student achievement levels.

Model Black Community Income Calculations					
Educational Attainment	Black Wages	Current Numbers	Model Numbers	Current Income (billions)	Model Income (billions)
Less than a high school diploma	24,544	98,104	79,574	$2.408	$1.953
High school diploma	33,852	164,597	109,550	$5.572	$3.708
Some college, no degree	37,804	184,218	107,915	$6.964	$4.080
Bachelor's degree	57,616	60,498	147,702	$3.486	$8.510
Graduate or professional	86,077	37,607	100,284	$3.237	$8.632
Totals	239,893	545,024	545,024	$21.667	$26.883

The changes posited by this modeling exercise are not extraordinary. The first is simply an internal policy change by the Police Department, which is under the control of the city's powerful mayor. It could happen tomorrow, as in New York City the notorious "stop-and-frisk" targeting of Black youth ended over-night without a noticeable increase in crime. Improving the schools would be more difficult, in practice, as more complicated, but quite possible given the political will. The road to improved achievement levels for Black students in Chicago is clearly signposted by the "Abbott" decision in New Jersey: improved facilities; learning-oriented universal full-day pre-school; literacy teaching in all-day kindergarten; extended school days, weeks and terms; challenging curricula; intensive teacher professional development in both subject area knowledge and appropriate pedagogy. These measures, standard practice in other developed countries, have resulted in near-doubling of achievement levels in some high-poverty New Jersey districts and similar efforts in districts near Washington, D.C. have led to similar outcomes.

These changes could be begun by the mayor, chief of police, district attorney and the chief executive officer of the Chicago schools any time they decide to do so. The question, therefore, is not *how* to bring about the better lives sought by the generation of the Great Migration. It is *why* are those with the power to improve the lives of Black residents of Chicago not doing it?

Notes: Chapter Two

[1] Cohen, Norm. *Long Steel Rail: The Railroad in American Folk Song*. University of Illinois Press (2nd ed.), 2000, p. 479.

[2] http://www.s4.brown.edu/us2010/segregation2010/city.aspx?cityid=1714000

[3] Evans, Benjamin F., Zimmerman, Emily, Woolf, Steven H., Haley, Amber D. Food Access and Health in Cook County, Illinois. Technical Report. Center on Human Needs, Virginia Commonwealth University, Richmond, Virginia, 2012.

[4] Bureau of the Census, Selected Economic Characteristics, 2006-2010 American Community Survey, DPO3.

[5] Sharkey, Patrick. Neighborhoods and the Black-White Mobility Gap. Philadelphia: The Pew Charitable Trusts, 2009, p. 9. http://www.pewstates.org/uploadedFiles/PCS_Assets/2009/PEW_NEIGHBORHOODS(1).pdf.

[6] Pew, p. 19.

[7] Pew, p. 20.

[8] About CPS. cps.edu/Pages/home.aspx

[9] See, Fitzpatrick, Lauren. Study: Charter schools have worsened school segregation. Chicago Sun-Times, October 13, 2014, citing a recent University of Minnesota Law School Institute on Metropolitan Opportunity study.

[10] http://www.prisonpolicy.org/profiles/IL.html

[11] Illinois Department of Corrections, FY12 Annual Report, http://www2.illinois.gov/idoc/reportsandstatistics/Pages/AnnualReports.aspx

[12] 2004 Statistical Presentation—Illinois Department of Corrections.

[13] http://www.chicagoreader.com/chicago/chicago-marijuana-arrest-statistics/Content?oid=4198958

[14] Kane-Willis, Kathleen; Aviles, Giovanni; Bazan, Marcia; Fraguada Narloch, Vilmarie. Patchwork Policy: An Evaluation of Arrests and Tickets for Marijuana Misdemeanors in Illinois. Illinois Consortium on Drug Policy. The Institute for Metropolitan Affairs. Roosevelt University. May 2014, p. iv.

[15] Kane-Willis, Aviles, Bazan, Fraguada Narloch, p. 5. Chart:

[16] Kane-Willis, Aviles, Bazan, Fraguada Narloch, p. 10.

[17] Kane-Willis, Aviles, Bazan, Fraguada Narloch, p.19.

---

[18] Kane-Willis, Aviles, Bazan, Fraguada Narloch, p. 4.

[19] In 2010, there were 7,631 African American men in Cook County correctional facilities for adults and 738 Black women. (This compares with 2,748 White men and 295 White women.[19]) There were 14,000 prisoners on parole in Cook County, which is nearly twice the expected proportion. "The [Cook County] Adult Probation Department receives nearly 14,000 new probation supervision cases annually and has an active caseload of approximately 25,000 probationers, 86% of whom have been sentenced for felony offenses."
http://www.cookcountycourt.org/ABOUTTHECOURT/OfficeoftheChiefJudge/ProbationDepartments/ProbationforAdults/AdultProbationDepartment/Profile.aspx

Chapter Three: Cleveland

Our next example is Cleveland, a city of 400,000 people, the center of a metropolitan area with a population of two million. Cleveland has a world-class orchestra and an equally fine and renowned art museum. Case Western Reserve University is one of the highest-ranking research universities in the United States. The medical research and treatment facilities in Cleveland bring the international wealthy and famous there for treatment. None of this alleviates the situation of the more than half the residents of the city who are the descendants of enslaved Africans.

State-of-the-art, high end, medical facilities do little for Black residents of Cleveland, men and women, who have poorer health than White residents and die earlier. Cleveland's Black men are even less healthy than the city's Black women. Relatively few male Black residents of the city live beyond retirement age. Nor do the city's postsecondary educational institutions significantly improve the lives of its Black residents. Cuyahoga Community College is the area's postsecondary institution of first resort, as it were. In a recent year it admitted 2,100 first time students. 780 of those admitted were Black, 316 of whom were men. Ninety of those 2,100 first-time students received Associate's degrees in the standard 150% of normal time. Eleven of those were Black students, four of whom were men.[1] Those 11 of 780 Black students were not necessarily all from Cleveland, nor were all four of the Black males who benefitted in this way.

Some other students attend Cleveland State University, hoping to obtain a Bachelor's degree, which is increasingly vital for employment, middle class incomes and, for Black men, avoidance of incarceration. Cleveland State University's first-time degree-seeking undergraduates in fall 2006 totaled nearly a thousand, 241 of whom were Black: 73 of those were men. Three hundred eighteen of that cohort, 39 of whom were Black, seven of whom were Black males, received Bachelor's degrees in the usual time. Not all those 32 Black women and seven Black men who grasped the brass ring of a four-year degree from Cleveland State University were necessarily from Cleveland. Some of those successful Black undergraduates may have come from elsewhere in Cuyahoga County, elsewhere in Ohio, or further afield.

Finally, to round out the sample, Case Western Reserve, a national research university, admitted 1,015 first time undergraduate students in fall 2006, 66 of whom were Black and 22 of whom were Black males. Nearly 800 of that group received Bachelor's degrees in the normal six years or less. Fewer than 50 of those were Black, just 14 were Black males. Not all of these, as well, would necessarily have been graduates of the Cleveland public schools. It is possible that very few were.

In that recent year, then, seven Black women and four Black men received Associate's degrees from Cuyahoga Community College, 64 Black women and 25 Black men received Bachelor's degrees from Cleveland State University and Case Western Reserve University combined. The Cleveland school district enrolled 42,500 students in 2011, 68% of whom were African American. As we shall see, each year it graduates perhaps 1,600 Black students out of a cohort of 3,000, half of the grade 9 cohort being male, according to the district, as are half of the graduates. Given the nature of these results, exact percentages hardly matter. We have something like 3,000 Black students going into the district's high schools, 1,600 graduating, 11 receiving Associate's degrees and 89 Bachelor's degrees by when they would be expected to attain them. It is clear that the district fails to prepare its Black students, and, in particular, its male Black students, for college or careers likely to produce an income sufficient to support a family, or provide them with the type of background necessary to fully appreciate the remarkable holdings of the Cleveland Museum of Art or the offerings available during the season in Severance Hall. It does, however, "prepare" many of its male Black students for incarceration.

Let us look at the condition of the Black residents of Cleveland in more detail.

Cleveland is a highly segregated city with a Black/White "Index of Dissimilarity" of 69 (meaning 69% of Black residents of Cleveland would have to move from one neighborhood to another in order for Black and White residents to be equally distributed). A Index of Dissimilarity of 60 is considered very high. The Cleveland metropolitan area has the extraordinary Index of Dissimilarity of 73: most African Americans in the area are confined within the

Cleveland city limits, most White, non-Hispanics, live in the suburbs.[2]

Just over one-third of the city's residents are White, non-Hispanic (148,000), over 53% (212,000) are Black. The two groups have quite different age distributions. There are much higher percentages of Black residents than White for each age cohort to age 19; higher percentages of White residents than Black from age 20 to 85 years and over. Among Black residents of Cleveland, the population percentages by gender are nearly identical until age 19, after which the percentages of women in each cohort are greater than the percentage of men in that cohort, until those cohorts 80 years and over include twice the percentage of women as men. Black men in Ohio are nearly twice as likely to report that they are in fair or poor health and to suffer from diabetes than are White men. A quarter of all Black women in the state reported that they are in only fair or poor health, as compared to 9% of White women. Ten percent of Black women in Ohio suffer from diabetes as compared to 4% of White women.[3] As so many Black men in Cleveland die young, the median age for Black men (32) is markedly lower than the median age for Black women (36). For White residents of the city the gender medians are higher and much more alike: 40 for men and 41 for women.[4]

Death rates for children and infants are a crucial indicator of community health. Those for Cleveland are particularly disturbing.[5]

	Child Deaths aged 1-14 years old (per 100,000 children)		Infant Deaths (per 1,000 live births)		Neonatal Deaths (per 1,000 live births)		Post-Neonatal Deaths (per 1,000 live births)	
	Cuyahoga	Cleveland	Cuyahoga	Cleveland	Cuyahoga	Cleveland	Cuyahoga	Cleveland
White, non-Hispanic	8.2	13.0*	5.0	4.8	3.8	3.6	1.2	1.2*
Black, non-Hispanic	15.3	20.3	15.6	18.1	10.5	11.7	5.1	6.4
Hispanic	5.8*	9.0*	6.4	7.7	2.1*	1.5*	4.3*	6.2*
Other	0.0	0.0	1.7*	8.3*	1.7*	8.3*	0.0	0.0

Black children in Cleveland are more than twice as likely to die before age 14 than White children in Cuyahoga County as a whole. Black infant death rates in the city are more than three times those in the County.

Black residents of Cleveland have poorer health than White residents and die earlier. Black men are even less healthy than Black women and die even earlier. Relatively few Black men in Cleveland live beyond retirement age.

Income

As with many formerly industrial cities, the largest percentages of Cleveland's workforce are employed in health and educational services: 19% of the White employed and 32% of Black workers. The White staff of hospitals, schools and colleges are likely to be doctors, teachers and administrators; the Black employees cafeteria workers and cleaners. Overall, one-third of Black workers, but only one quarter of White workers, are in service occupations. Further exacerbating these disparities, the Black unemployment rate in Cleveland is twice that of the White unemployment rate. The combination of lower status jobs and higher unemployment results in a median income for Black families in Cleveland of $27,451, while for White families it is $44,015. Black income per capita is $13,137 and White income per capita is $21,085: 39% of Black residents of the city have incomes below the poverty level, as compared to just over half that, 21%, of the White residents. Eighteen percent of Black households in the city consist of Black women raising children alone on incomes below the poverty line, as compared to 7% of White households. A quite remarkable quarter (24%) of Black households in Cleveland have annual incomes of less than $10,000, twice the proportion of the relatively poor White households in the city. While 9% of White households have incomes over $100,000, only 2% of Black households in Cleveland have incomes at that level and the percentage of Black households with incomes over $150,000 rounds to zero.

These differences are actually minimized by the considerable movement over the past decades of the more prosperous among the White population to the surrounding suburbs. Therefore it is useful to look at incomes in Cleveland's Cuyahoga County as a whole. Statistics for the county's Black residents are dominated by those for Cleveland; statistics for the county's White residents reflect the conditions in the White suburbs. The median income of Black families in the county (including Cleveland) is $35,656, for White families it is nearly twice that—$69,146. Thirty percent of Black residents of the county have incomes below the poverty level, three times the percentage for the county's White residents.

Discussions of inequality commonly begin by dividing the population into groups of twenty percent of the total, "quintiles." The mean income of the highest income fifth of Cleveland's Black population is just above that of the fourth quintile of the White US population.[6] The incomes of Black families in Cleveland are not only lower than the White national averages, they are lower, and increasingly lower for higher incomes, than the national averages for Black families alone. In other words, the poorest Black families are relatively twice as poor as the poorest White families and the poorest Black families in Cleveland are even worse off than the poorest Black families in the country as a whole.

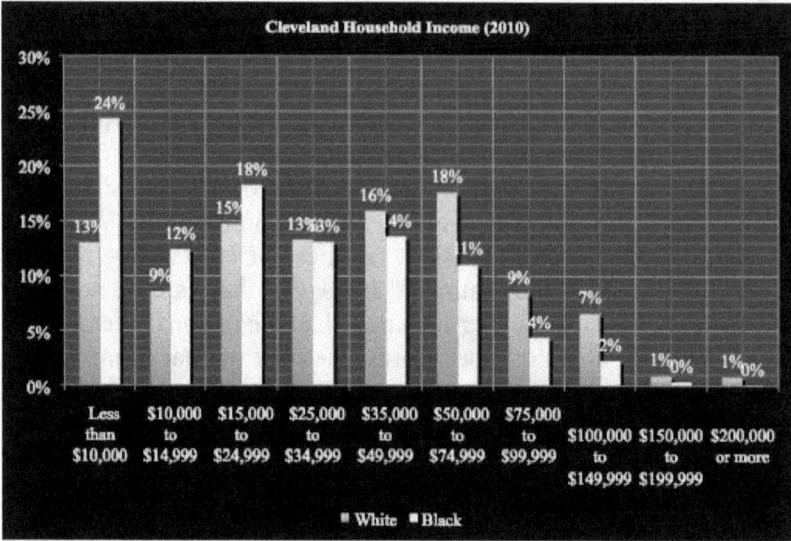

Cleveland Household Income (2010)

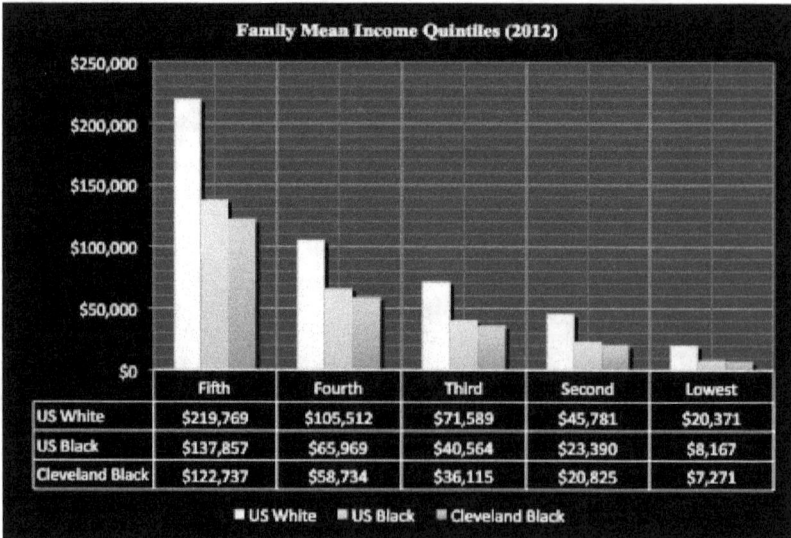

Family Mean Income Quintiles (2012)

	Fifth	Fourth	Third	Second	Lowest
US White	$219,769	$105,512	$71,589	$45,781	$20,371
US Black	$137,857	$65,969	$40,564	$23,390	$8,167
Cleveland Black	$122,737	$58,734	$36,115	$20,825	$7,271

■ US White   ■ US Black   ■ Cleveland Black

Wealth

Wealth is property, either "real" property, houses for instance, or investments. Just 4,000 (4%) of Cleveland's nearly 90,000 Black households had income from interest, dividends or net rental income in 2010. Thirteen thousand (18%) of Cleveland's not particularly prosperous 74,000 White households had such income. One hundred fifteen thousand (32%) of Cuyahoga's 360,000 White households had this non-wage income, compared to 9,000 (6%) of the county's 154,000 Black households. Thus, five times the percentage of the county's White families as the county's Black families have at least some "liquid" assets: buffers against emergencies or health catastrophes. Nationally, Black household mean net worth, excluding equity in their own home is $50,000, that of White households is over $300,000. Under these assumptions the net worth of all of Cuyahoga's Black households taken together totals $442 million, not including home equity, and those of the county's White households totals $38 billion. These calculations obviously understate White wealth in the county, as various billionaires, such as the Lerners and Gunds, have connections with the city. But billionaires aside, the wealth of White Cuyahoga County is at least 80 times that of the Black households of the county, and if home equity is included, probably much more than that.

Mobility

Intergenerational mobility is a key measure of economic equity. "The American Creed," as Gunnar Myrdal named it in *An American Dilemma,* holds that mobility is one-directional: up. But there are dreams and there is reality. Research has shown that even without regard to parental income, "spending childhood in a high-poverty neighborhood versus a low- poverty neighborhood raises the chances of downward mobility by 52 percent."[7] Few Black children in Cleveland grow up to have incomes equal to that of the family into which they were born and most will have lower incomes as a result of segregation's concentration of inferior schools, heightened police activity and unemployment in Black neighborhoods.

Intergenerational *wealth* mobility, or the lack thereof, is even more of a problem for African Americans than intergenerational income mobility. Twice as many White as Black Americans raised in

93

the middle quintile accumulate more wealth than had their parents. Only African Americans raised in the poorest households exceed their parents' "wealth," which in any case is likely to be barely existent or even negative.[8] Less than a quarter of African Americans raised in the middle quintile of national wealth distribution achieve greater wealth than their parents. On the other hand, 68% of African Americans raised in that middle quintile of wealth end up in the bottom two quintiles as adults.[9] It is therefore unlikely that there is much intergenerational family income or wealth upward mobility in Cleveland's Black community. The situation is different in areas of Cuyahoga County outside of the city, where the schools are better, the adults better educated with higher incomes and some wealth, chiefly as home equity. However, relatively few descendants of enslaved Africans live there.

The Anvil of Caste: Education
The Cleveland Metropolitan School District enrolled 42,500 students in 2011, 68% of whom were African American, 15% White, non-Hispanic, and 14% Hispanic. The average salary of teachers was $69,000. The student to teacher ratio was a quite high 17:1. All those comparatively well-paid teachers met state licensing and certification requirements and hardly any were in their first or second year of teaching. On the other hand, a remarkable three-quarters of the district's teachers were absent more than 10 days of the school year. These data in regard to the teaching staff are most unusual, the salaries higher, the proportion of new teachers lower, the student to teacher ratio and teacher absenteeism unusually high.[10]

Cleveland is one of the urban districts analyzed by the National Assessment of Educational Progress (NAEP). Grade 8 reading achievement, a key factor, has varied since 2003 for White students in the district from 14% scoring at or above grade level (Proficient and above) in 2003 to 26% in 2007, and then back down to 19% in 2013. Results for the district's Black students have been less variable, 8% at grade level in 2003 and 9% in 2013: 12% for Black girls and just 6% for Black boys. Or, to put this another way, the district fails to teach 94% of male Black students to read at grade level by grade 8. For Ohio as a whole, 16% of Black students read at grade level in grade 8, as do 43% of White students. In Ohio's suburban districts, 19% of Black students read at grade level, as do 47% of White students.

Educational attainment levels for suburban Cuyahoga County are quite different from those for Cleveland, especially for White residents. Of the 100,000 Black residents of the county's suburbs, 30,000 (30%) have Bachelor's degrees or above as compared to the 488,000 White suburban residents of the county, 179,000 (37%) of whom have Bachelor's degrees or above. Both Black and White residents of Cleveland's suburbs are comparatively highly educated, while neither Black or White students within the city itself are brought by the school district to an adequate educational attainment.

In Cleveland, as elsewhere, Black students can double their opportunity of learning basic skills by moving to the suburbs.

We can calculate the *numbers* of students reading at grade level (Proficient and above) with parents at various educational attainment levels by aligning NAEP and Census data. Twenty-three percent of White and 25% of Black adult Cleveland residents over 25 years of age reported to the Census that they had less than a high school diploma, equivalent to NAEP's "Did not finish high school."[11] Thirty-five percent of Whites and 36% of African Americans said that they were high school graduates with a diploma or GED, equivalent to NAEP's "Graduated high school." Twenty-four percent of Whites and 31% of African Americans reported some college or associate's degree, equivalent to "Some education after high school" and 17% of Whites and 8% of African Americans reported attaining a Bachelor's degree or higher: "Graduated College."[*]

---

[*] Two things are notable about these distributions: the low level of educational attainment of White Cleveland residents, relative to the White population of the county, where, for example, 33% of adults have a Bachelor's degree or above, and the sharp drop in Black educational attainment at the college level.

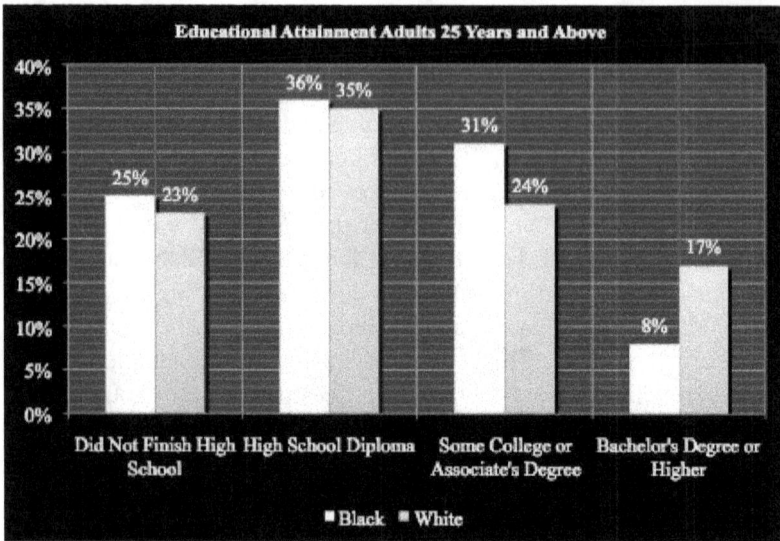

None of the 2,100 grade 8 Black students in Cleveland schools who reported that neither of their parents had a high school diploma read at grade level or above. Just 30 Black students reported that at least one of their parents completed high school while they themselves read at grade level. One hundred thirty-one Black students read at grade level in grade 8 and had at least one parent who had some college. And fifteen of Black students at grade 8 read at grade level and reported that at least one of their parents had a college degree. (The number of Black students in grade 8 reading at grade level who are the children of college graduates is lower than that of those whose parents have "some college" because there are fewer adult Black college graduates.)

Whichever way we calculate it, fewer than 10% of grade 8 Black students in Cleveland have been taught to read at or above grade level.

The Cleveland school district's Plan for Transforming Schools has as its goal "to ensure that every child in Cleveland attends a high-quality school and that every neighborhood has a multitude of great schools from which families can choose.

To reach this goal, Cleveland must transition from a traditional, single-source school district to a new system of district and charter schools that are held to the highest standards and work in partnership to create dramatic student achievement gains for every child.[12]

Charter schools in Ohio, according to NAEP, bring 17% of students at or above Proficient in reading at grade 8. Non-charter schools bring 40% at or above proficient. For Black students, state-wide, those in charter schools scored at or above proficient in 2013 10% of the time; those not in charter schools reached grade level 19% of the time. If results for charter schools in Cleveland are similar to those for the state as a whole, creating a "system of district and charter schools" will dilute the efficacy, such as it is, of the district schools.

High school graduation rates for Cleveland students in 2011-2012 were 42% for both Black and White students, that is, nearly 60% of those students enrolled in grade 9 in 2008-09 did not graduate at the end of the 2011-12 school year. Given that 90% of Black students in grade 8 cannot read at grade level, it is remarkable that the district manages to graduate as many students as it does.

How well prepared are those students to whom the district gives diplomas? Not very, given that, as we have seen, we have something like 3,000 Black students at grade 9 in the district's high schools, 1,600 graduating, eleven of those going on to college receiving Associate's degrees and 89 Bachelor's degrees within 150% of normal time.

The Hammer of Caste: The Criminal Justice System

The incarceration rate for Black residents of Ohio, 2,336 per 100,000, is more than five times that for White, non-Hispanic, residents of the state (422 per 100,000). While African Americans comprise 12% of the state's population, they account for 43% of those in the state's prisons and jails.[13] Commitments to state prisons for drug offenses is the largest category for which Ohioans are incarcerated (5,278 of 20,120).[14] According to the Ohio ACLU "In 2010 in Cuyahoga County, Caucasians accounted for 63.6% of the population and African Americans were 29.7%. However, African Americans accounted for 70.3% of those sent to prison."[15] In 2010 there were 1,811 Black residents in correctional facilities for adults and 389 in college/university housing in Cleveland. By way of comparison, there were 782 White residents of Cleveland in correctional facilities for adults and 2,411 in college/university student housing. There were an additional 139 White, non-Hispanic, incarcerated adults in the county outside the city (and 3,938 more White residents of college dormitories) and an additional 282 incarcerated Black adults and 411 African Americans in dormitories. The assertion that there are more African Americans in prison than in college is simply a statement of fact in Cleveland.

Assuming the usual gender and age proportions of people who are imprisoned, we can count 1,500 Black male residents of Cleveland between the ages of 20 and 40 as incarcerated and three times that number as imprisoned, on parole or on probation. It would appear, then that six percent of the men in those cohorts are in prison and, therefore, 18% are under the control of the criminal justice system. This would account for 4,500 of the 5,500 "missing" working age Black men in the city, that is, the excess of the Black male over Black female numbers in those age groups.

An indicator of drug use perhaps more accurate than arrests is the rate of drug-induced deaths. This rate in 2010 was slightly over 11 per 100,000 for Black residents of Cleveland and Cuyahoga County as a whole. For White, non-Hispanics, it was 16.2 in Cuyahoga County and 32.4 in the city of Cleveland: three times the Black rate.[16] Professor Mona Lynch concluded one of her studies of racial bias in the enforcement of drug laws by stating that Cuyahoga County was "overzealous in pursuing low level cases as felonies, that this overzealousness seems to be happening primarily or exclusively in cases that originate within the city of Cleveland, and that there are racially based inequities that exist within the county's criminal justice system."[17] She attributed these "racially based inequities" to a policy decision by the Cleveland Police Department "to concentrate a significant share of its law enforcement resources within certain sections of the city.

> So not only are city residents as a whole more likely to be subject to felony charges on low level drug instrument cases than their suburban counterparts, but within the city, those areas that have the highest percentages of African-Americans are especially likely to be subject to police surveillance and arrests.[18]

While in Milwaukee, for example, and Ferguson, Missouri, the criminalization of African American men is largely achieved by means of traffic law enforcement, and in New York it was achieved in large part by "stop-and-frisk," in Cleveland, possession of drug paraphernalia was for many years the strategy of choice: the police searching the homes of Black residents of Cleveland for such evidence, while refraining to do so in the White suburbs; charging Black residents of Cleveland with a felony for this offense, while residents of the White suburbs, if by chance found with drug paraphernalia, were charged only with a misdemeanor.[19] Eventually, in November, 2008, as in New York more recently when a new mayor ended stop-and-frisk, Cleveland mayor Frank Jackson (the son of a mixed race couple) directed the police to bring its drug offense policy in the city into line with that of the suburban authorities.[20]

The results of this policy change have been impressive. In the January, 2010, census of prisoners in Ohio there were 9,391 prisoners from Cuyahoga County (19% of the total for the state), 6,876 of whom were Black and 2,076 of whom were White. Drug offenses were 16% of the total. In the January, 2014, census of prisoners in Ohio there were 8,190 prisoners from Cuyahoga County, 5,942 of whom were Black, and 1,819 of whom were White. Drug offenses were down to 14% of the state total.[21] The change in the classification of drug offensives is clearly a large part of the reason for this 10% decline in incarcerations of Black residents of Cuyahoga County. Other reasons are the aging of the population and an increase in the number of alternative to incarceration options.[22]

On the other hand, recently, "The Department of Justice has completed its civil pattern or practice investigation of the Cleveland Division of Police ("CDP" or "the Division").

> We have concluded that we have reasonable cause to believe that CDP engages in a pattern or practice of the use of excessive force in violation of the Fourth Amendment of the United States Constitution. We have determined that structural and systemic deficiencies and practices—including insufficient accountability, inadequate training, ineffective policies, and inadequate engagement with the community—contribute to the use of unreasonable force.[23]

These practices and deficiencies of the police disproportionately affect Black Cleveland.[†]

[†] The killing of 12-year-old Tamir Rice by a police officer on November 22, 2014 was a recent example.

99

Modeling a More Equitable Cleveland

It is not very complicated to model a more equitable city of Cleveland. All that need be done is to apply the data for Black residents of Cuyahoga County beyond the city limits to the city itself and then, if we wish to be more ambitious, the data for White residents of the Cuyahoga County suburbs to both the Black and White residents of the city.

First, then, applying the data for Black residents of Cuyahoga County beyond the city limits to the city itself would significantly change the distribution of household incomes. The percentage of households living in dire poverty, with incomes under $10,000 per year, would be cut in half, from 24% to 12%. Incomes below the poverty level, approximately $25,000 per year, would fall from 54% to 32%. Incomes over $75,000 per year would rise from 6% to 19%. There would be 10,600 fewer households in dire poverty, 20,000 fewer below the poverty line, 10,000 more with incomes over $75,000 per year. Median household income would rise from $28,000 per year to about $38,000.

How would this be accomplished? One strategy would be to improve educational attainment. Bringing the city's adult educational attainment for Black residents into line with that of suburban Black residents would reduce the percentage of those without high school diplomas from 25% to 13% and increase the percentage of those with a Bachelor's degree or above from 8% to 20%.

Income is directly related to educational attainment. Nationally, median earnings for Black workers, aged 25 and over, vary from $16,000 for those without a high school diploma to nearly $55,000 for those with an advanced degree.[24] A change in the distribution of educational attainment from that current for African Americans in the city of Cleveland to that for Cuyahoga County suburban African Americans alone would increase the collective income of Cleveland's African Americans from $3.3 billion to $3.9 billion.[25] Education is also a factor in employment (or unemployment) rates. Increases in educational attainment result in decreases in unemployment rates. The 2006-10 average unemployment rate for African American residents of Cleveland was 23%, that for suburban Cuyahoga County African Americans ages 16 and over was 15%. Aligning educational attainment in Cleveland with that of the

100

suburbs would increase employment by 8%, bringing total income for the Black community to $4.2 billion.

Modeling on White Cuyahoga County suburban educational attainment has even more marked results. The percentage of the adult population without a high school diploma would be 8%, rather than 25%, the percentage with a Bachelor's degree or higher would be 36%, rather than 8%. At present employment rates, total income would be $4.4 billion, at suburban employment rate for African Americans total income would be $4.8 billion, as compared to today's total income for Cleveland's Black residents of $3.3 billion: a 45% increase.

Another, complementary, strategy would be to bring arrest and incarceration rates for Black residents of Cleveland in line with those for White residents of Cuyahoga County. Ending the disparate classification of crimes for possession of crack cocaine apparatus was a good first step and, as we have seen, other factors have lowered the overall number of commitments to prison of Cuyahoga County (chiefly Cleveland city) residents. Given typical felony sentences of seven years, it would be expected that most of the disparately sentenced Black residents of Cleveland would be released by 2020. Nonetheless, the effects of the history of felony sentences for African Americans for the same offenses resulting in misdemeanor sentences for White, non-Hispanics, will continue to disrupt Cleveland's Black community for many years to come. A June, 2011, report from the Ohio ACLU found that for every 100 ex-felons in the state there are approximately 12 fewer employed people and that "previously incarcerated males receive nine fewer weeks of annual employment and a 40% decrease in yearly earnings compared to males who had not been incarcerated."[26] Fewer felony commitments, more effective re-entry programs, particularly basic education and work skills, and strong enforcement of guidelines prohibiting hiring discrimination against ex-felons will be needed for fundamental improvement in economic conditions in Cleveland's Black community and with those improvements, improvements also in social and cultural conditions.

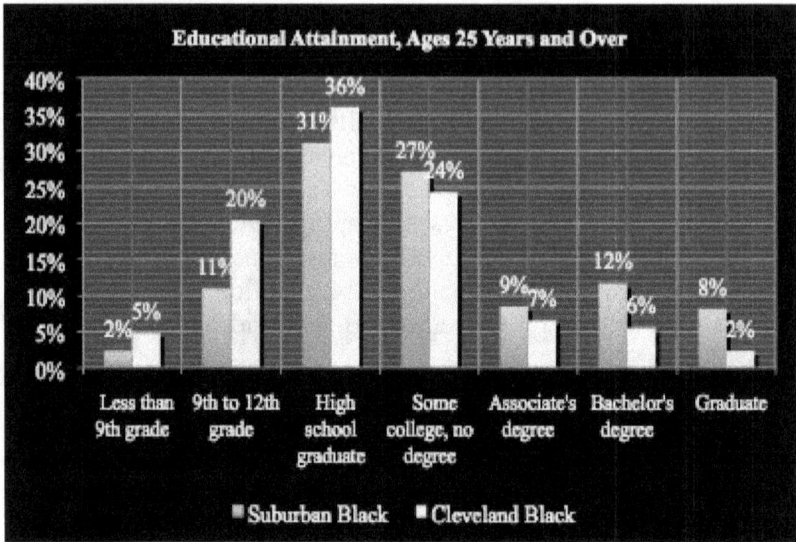

Educational Attainment, Ages 25 Years and Over

	Less than 9th grade	9th to 12th grade	High school graduate	Some college, no degree	Associate's degree	Bachelor's degree	Graduate
Suburban Black	2%	11%	31%	27%	9%	12%	8%
Cleveland Black	5%	20%	36%	24%	7%	6%	2%

■ Suburban Black   ■ Cleveland Black

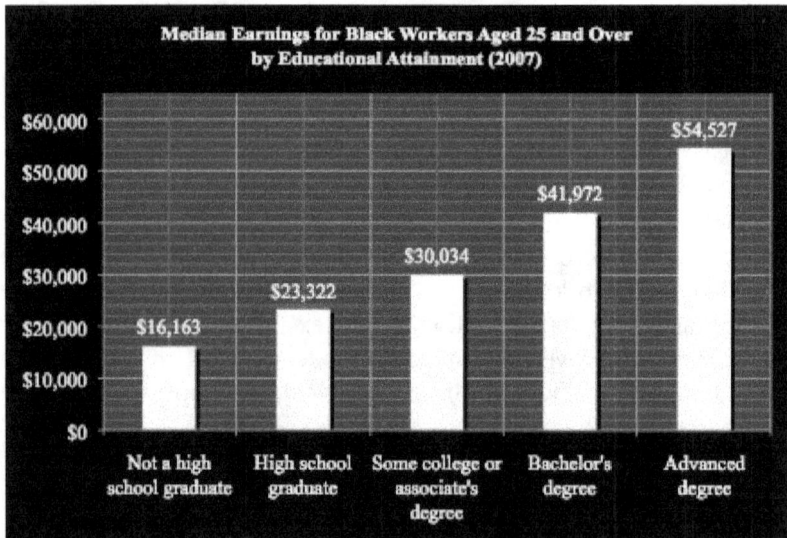

Median Earnings for Black Workers Aged 25 and Over by Educational Attainment (2007)

Not a high school graduate	High school graduate	Some college or associate's degree	Bachelor's degree	Advanced degree
$16,163	$23,322	$30,034	$41,972	$54,527

What are the necessary pre-conditions for these actions? Given the record of the Cleveland police department it is helpful that the Department of Justice is taking it under federal supervision. Egregious policies, such as those in place until recently in regard to cocaine paraphernalia, do not exist in a vacuum. They are part of a culture of racially-based attitudes and actions, including, but not limited to, the policy of more heavily policing Black than White neighborhoods. A properly supervised department would be one in which the deployment of personnel, the numbers and types of interactions with the public, arrests and prosecutions were held to strictly equitable norms. In other words, it is necessary for the Cleveland police department (and, no doubt, the rest of its criminal justice system) to function in the city's Black neighborhoods as its peers function in the White suburbs.

The Cleveland public school system *can* be improved. It can be improved by hiring more teachers, teachers more willing and able to teach the city's children. It can be improved by providing intensive early childhood education, beginning at age two, if not before. It can be improved with longer school days, longer school years, curricula designed to higher standards, intensive teacher professional development. A better educated Black community, one supported by rather than subjected to the criminal justice system, would, in time, break free of the chains of caste and become, as they say, more like America.

The mayor, chief of police, district attorney and superintendent of schools could begin to make these changes any time they decide to do so.

Notes: Chapter Three

[1] U. S. Department of Education, National Center for Education Statistics, IPEDS Data Center.
http://nces.ed.gov/ipeds/datacenter/Data.aspx
[2] Logan, John. US 2010: Discover America in a New Century, Brown University, http://www.s4.brown.edu/us2010/index.htm. Map from NEO CANDO, http://neocando.case.edu/neocando/map.jsp
[3] Kaiser Family Foundation, State Facts.
[4] Bureau of the Census, 2010 Census Summary File 2, Table DP-1.
[5] Table from Cuyahoga Health Improvement Partnership. Community Health Status Assessment for Cuyahoga County, Ohio. March 21, 2013.
http://www.naccho.org/topics/infrastructure/accreditation/upload/full-chachipcombined-3-20-13.pdf
[6] US data from U.S. Census historical income data, http://www.census.gov/hhes/www/income/data/historical/families/. Cleveland data estimated from national distributions among quintiles.
[7] Sharkey, Patrick. Neighborhoods and the Black-White Mobility Gap. Philadelphia: The Pew Charitable Trusts, 2009, p. 9.
http://www.pewstates.org/uploadedFiles/PCS_Assets/2009/PEW_NEIGHBORHOODS(1).pdf.
[8] Pew, p. 19.
[9] Pew, p. 20.
[10] United States Department of Education, Office for Civil Rights.
[11] A caution: the numbers of adults in these categories, as reported by their children, are not necessarily the same as those self-reported to the Census or those that might be obtained from school and college records.
[12] Cleveland's Plan for Transforming Schools.
http://www.clevelandmetroschools.org/cms/lib05/OH01915844/Centricity/Domain/4/ClevelandPlanExecutiveSummary.pdf
[13] http://www.prisonpolicy.org/profiles/OH.html
[14] Ohio Department of Rehabilitation and Correction, 2014 Annual Report.
http://www.drc.ohio.gov/web/Reports/Annual/Annual%20Report%202014.pdf

[15] Ohio ACLU, "Overcharging, Overspending, Overlooking: Cuyahoga County's Costly War on Drugs." Executive Summary. June 16, 2011. http://www.acluohio.org/assets/issues/DrugPolicy/DrugPolicyAllian ceReport2011_0616.pdf

[16] Cuyahoga Health Improvement Partnership. Community Health Status Assessment for Cuyahoga County, Ohio. March 21, 2013, p. 148.

[17] Lynch, Mona. "Selective Enforcement of Drug Laws in Cuyahoga County, Ohio: A Report on the Racial Effects of Geographic Disparities in Arrest Patterns," ACLU Ohio, p. 7.

[18] Lynch, Mona. "Selective Enforcement of Drug Laws in Cuyahoga County, Ohio: A Report on the Racial Effects of Geographic Disparities in Arrest Patterns," p. 12.

[19] Lynch, Mona. "Crack Pipes and Policing: A Case Study of Institutional Racism and Remedial Action in Cleveland," Law & Policy, Vol. 33, No. 2, April 2011, p. 192.

[20] Lynch, Mona. "Crack Pipes and Policing: A Case Study of Institutional Racism and Remedial Action in Cleveland," p. 203.

[21] Ohio Department of Rehabilitation and Correction DRC DataSource Reports - Institution Census Reports. Mr. Steve Van Dine kindly guided me to this resource.

[22] Caniglia, John. "Cuyahoga County judges sending far fewer felons to prison, marking major shift in Ohio's corrections system." The Plain Dealer, October 25, 2013. http://www.cleveland.com/metro/index.ssf/2013/10/cuyahoga_count y_judges_sending.html

[23] U.S. Department of Justice, Civil Rights Division. United States Attorney's Office, Northern District of Ohio, December 4, 2014.

[24] U. S. Census. Educational Attainment in the United States: 2007. Population Characteristics, January 2009. http://www.census.gov/prod/2009pubs/p20-560.pdf

[25] A caution: These calculations assume that all persons over 25 years of age are workers. This is obviously not the case, but the results are indicative of the change to be expected at this stage of the modeling process.

[26] Ohio ACLU, "Overcharging, Overspending, Overlooking: Cuyahoga County's Costly War on Drugs." Executive Summary.

June 16, 2011.
http://www.acluohio.org/assets/issues/DrugPolicy/DrugPolicyAllian
ceReport2011_0616.pdf

Chapter Four: Memphis

"And then I got to Memphis."
Martin Luther King, Jr.

Martin Luther King delivered his last sermon—"I've been to the mountaintop"—in Memphis on April 3, 1968. He was assassinated the next day. Although, or perhaps because, Memphis is the metropolis of the Mississippi Delta, the agricultural region extending south from the city to Vicksburg, the city's history is one of racial violence. The native inhabitants of the region were driven out in the early nineteenth century to be replaced by the descendants of enslaved Africans force-marched from the exhausted cotton fields of the older southern states. Reconstruction was violently resisted by much of the White population, many of whom were recent Irish immigrants. Much of the twentieth century history of Memphis was characterized by Jim Crow laws and customs and later the struggle against them.

Since 1879 Hohenberg Brothers Cotton Company (now Cargill Cotton) has traded with the plantations down the river between Memphis and Vicksburg. Now FEDEX, with its headquarters in Memphis, trades around the world. Nevertheless, the Memphis area is one of the poorest, if not the poorest, metropolitan area in the United States.

African Americans form the majority of the city's population, 411,000 to the White population of 195,000, although there are nearly another 200,000 White (and 75,000 Black) residents in the surrounding Shelby County. The median age of Memphis's White population is 41, that of the Black population 31, the difference primarily attributable to the considerably smaller percentage of school-age White children in the city and the shorter lives of the area's Black residents. Twenty-nine percent of the city's Black population is under 17 years of age, compared to just 17% of the White population. An additional 17% of the White population of the city is over 65 years of age, compared to just 8% of the Black population.[1] Shelby County has the lowest life expectancy at birth for Black residents of any Tennessee metropolitan region and the greatest difference between Black and White life expectancies: 7.3 years.[2] There are more Black males than Black females in the age groups under 18 years, then more Black women than men in each older age group. As a consequence there are 22,000 more Black working age women than Black working age men in Memphis, a topic to which we will return below.

Memphis, like Cleveland and Chicago, is a highly segregated city. Some areas of Memphis are 97% Black.[3] Therefore the White/Black Index of Dissimilarity for Memphis is very high: two-thirds of Black residents would have to move from one neighborhood to another if the city were to be integrated.[4] Suburban Shelby County is nearly as segregated, with some areas almost exclusively White. Residential segregation in the county, especially between Memphis and the suburbs, is linked to the extreme segregation of the schools.

Income Disparities

> It's all right to talk about streets flowing with milk and honey, but God has commanded us to be concerned about the slums down here and His children who can't eat three square meals a day. MLK, April 3, 1968.

While the percentage of Black adults in the labor force (62%) is only slightly under that for White adults (65%), the unemployment rate for Black residents of Memphis is twice as high (11% compared to 5%). The White per capita income in Memphis is more than twice the Black per capita income of $14,807. The poverty rate of Black families is three times that of White families; half of the Black families in which a woman is raising her children without a husband live in poverty. Twenty-one percent of Black families have incomes under $15,000, but only seven percent of White families are that poor. Thirty-one percent of White families have incomes over $100,000 per year, but only 8% of Black families in Memphis are that prosperous. As a matter of fact, there is a higher percentage of White families in Memphis with incomes over $200,000 than of Black families with incomes over $100,000.

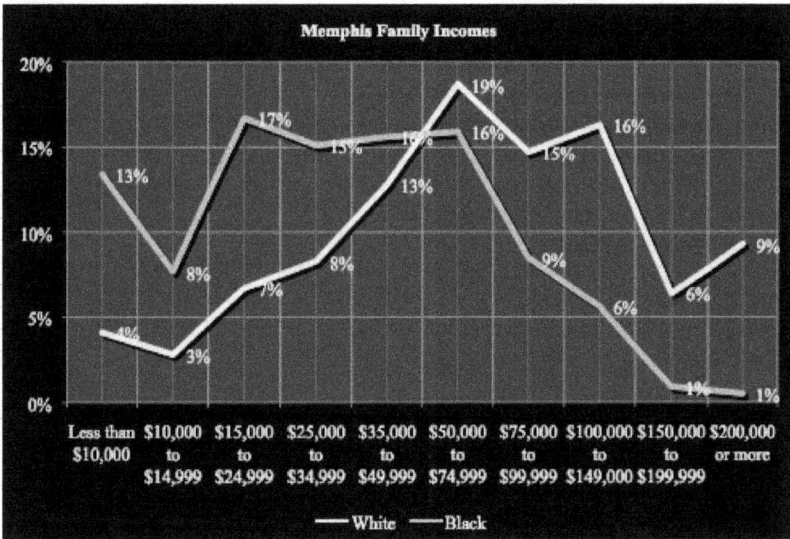

Memphis Family Incomes

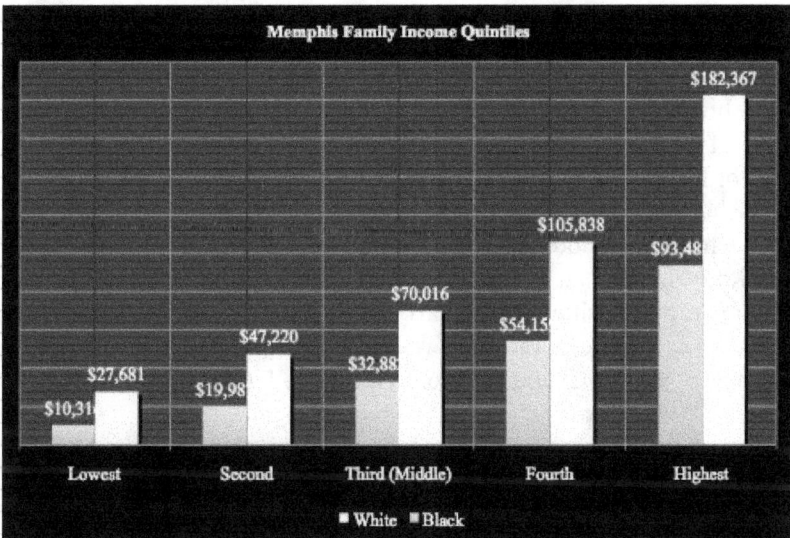

Memphis Family Income Quintiles

We can examine income distributions by charting the population
quintiles for Black and White Memphis families, using the

percentages for each group for the nation as a whole and extrapolating from family medians. The income of the average family in the highest quintile for Black residents of Memphis ($93,488) is just over half that of White residents in the highest quintile and lower than that for White residents in the fourth White quintile. The average income of the White family in the lowest quintile is nearly three times that of the average income of a Black family in the lowest Black quintile. Eight percent of White families in Memphis have incomes under the poverty level, as do 27% of Black families. Black families in Memphis have considerably lower incomes than White families and the distribution of Black incomes is compressed: 80% have incomes lower than that of the average White family.

Disparities of Wealth

Just 4% of Black Memphis households receive interest, dividends or net rental income, while nearly 30% of White households had income from those sources. This implies that 96% of Black households in Memphis have no financial resources other than equity in their homes, if that, which means that they have no resources in case of an unexpected medical bill, a bail demand or other emergency. Total home equity for Memphis's White community is on the order of $6.6 billion; for the Black community, $3.6 billion. Using national averages, the investment wealth of the 30% of White households with liquid assets we can estimate to be on the order of $8.7 billion, that of the 4% of the city's Black households with liquid assets $286 million, giving total Black wealth in Memphis, including home equity, of about $4 billion, White wealth of more than $15 billion. When we look at this together with the income disparities, particularly at the extremes, it is apparent that from an economic point of view Black Memphis is as much a caste apart as when W. C. Handy wrote *The Beale Street Blues*.

Mobility

As is generally the case in the U.S., and particularly in Memphis, relatively higher income Black families are likely to live where their (Black) neighbors have lower incomes, the schools and other social services (under-) resourced accordingly. Few Black children in Memphis will grow up to have incomes equal to that of the family into which they were born and most will have lower incomes simply because of the effects of this residential and educational segregation. Research has shown that there is little chance of upward income mobility for children raised in impoverished neighborhoods like those of Black Memphis and a very good chance of downward mobility—that their adult incomes will be lower than those of their parents.[5]

The Anvil of Caste: Education

The history of public education in Memphis has been the story of efforts to provide good educations for all the children in conflict with an insistence by some on privileging the education of children from higher income, especially White, families. The segregated system constructed and maintained during the Jim Crow reaction to Reconstruction illustrated this in bricks and mortar, or their absence, with solidly built, adequately staffed and well-equipped schools for White children and over-crowded, inadequately staffed, flimsily constructed schools for Black children.[6] Court-ordered desegregation after the *Brown v. Board of Education* decision eventually led to an overwhelmingly Black Memphis City School District and a predominately White Shelby County District. In the last few years, the Memphis City district dissolved itself, merging with the County district in order to bring integration, at least at the district level, then the cities and towns in the former County district formed their own districts, which brings things today to something like the status quo pro ante. At the end of 2014 there was a "Shelby County" district including only Memphis and the unincorporated areas of the county, and half a dozen small, predominately White, suburban districts.

In 2013, the then-Memphis-City School District had 215 schools serving just over 100,000 students, 82% of whom were African American and 7% of whom were White. Eighty-nine percent were eligible for free or reduced price lunches. In spite of the fact that per student expenditure was $11,500, the average teacher salary in Memphis in 2010 was just $46,800. Only 6% of the district's teachers were in their first or second year of teaching, but 22% had not met all state licensing and certification requirements. On the other hand, in the then-Shelby-County district, outside of Memphis, with its White majority, the average teacher salary was $52,500 and

99% of that district's teachers had met all state licensing and certification requirements.[7]

For the state of Tennessee as a whole, the 2013 NAEP grade 8 reading assessment showed improvement over that for 2009. Just 6% Black students in Tennessee's city schools who were eligible for the National Lunch Program (most of whom are in Memphis) scored at or above Proficient, that is, grade level, in the 2009 assessment, while twice that percentage, 12%, did so on the 2013 assessment. (There are not enough Black students in Tennessee's suburban and rural schools for NAEP to report achievement levels.) By way of comparison, in 2013 26% of White students in city schools eligible for the National Lunch Program scored at or above grade level, as did 45% of White students in city schools who were not eligible; 31% of eligible White students in suburban schools and 53% of ineligible suburban White students were at or above Proficient. These 2013 levels and improvements since 2009 generally track national trends for each category, 11% of eligible Black students in city schools, nationally, scoring at or above grade level and 28% of eligible White students, nationally, scoring at or above grade level in grade 8 reading.

Memphis is not one of the districts assessed by the National Assessment of Educational Progress (NAEP). The state of Tennessee itself measures student skills and academic progress with a Tennessee Comprehensive Assessment Program: TCAP. Scores in reading are reported as averages for grades 3 through 8, combined, and for grade 7. In 2013 the average for all Memphis students in grades 3 through 8 was 29% at Proficient or above (6% Advanced), while that for all students in grade 7 was 25% (5% Advanced). These are similar to the NAEP assessments for the state at grade 8 (30% Proficient, 3% Advanced) and can be used as proxies for those. Black students in grades 3 through 8 scored at Proficient or above 25% of the time (4% of those scored Advanced) and in grade 7 22% (4% Advanced). In other words, three-quarters of Memphis Black students are not reading at grade level by grade 9.[8]

All students were twice as likely to reach grade level by the state's standards in the suburban schools near Memphis than in the city's schools and three times as likely to reach the Advanced level. Black students were also much more likely to reach grade level in the suburban schools and approximately twice as likely to reach the Advanced level in the suburban schools as in the city schools.

TCAP	Memphis City	Shelby County
	% at or Above Proficient (Advanced)	
Grades 3 to 8 All Students	29% (6%)	62% (18%)
Grades 3 to 8 Black Students	25% (4%)	44% (8%)
Grade 7 All Students	25% (5%)	56% (17%)
Grade 7 Black Students	22% (4%)	37% (7%)

The state lists the graduation rate for Memphis in 2012 as 70.3% for all students, 70.5% for African American students and 73.1% for White students. The state lists the graduation rate for Shelby County in 2012 as 90.5% for all students, 88.8% for African American students and 93.1% for White students. The Memphis graduation rates are quite extraordinary, given the state's own test data. One explanation might be found in the ACT scores for the districts. (The ACT is a standard test used for college admission.) The 2013 mean composite ACT score for the Memphis City School District was 16.2.[9] Half of students, nationally, taking the ACT, scored between 20 and 21. Just 23% scored at or below 16.[10] This implies that although seventy percent of Memphis students graduate from high school, few of them are career or college ready.

Census data on educational attainment of the adult population of Memphis seems to bear out this interpretation. While 81% of Black respondents reported that they were high school graduates or higher (as did 90% of White respondents), just 13% of Black respondents as compared to 41% of White respondents said that they had a Bachelor's degree or higher.

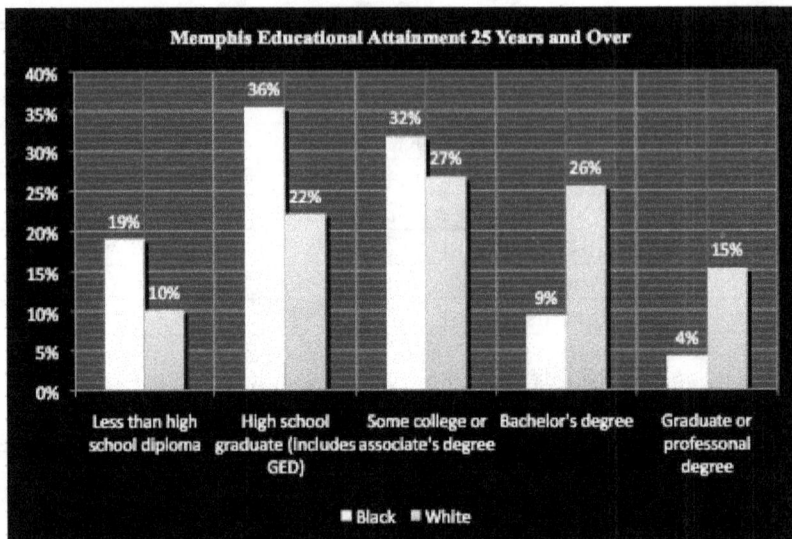

We can take another approach to this. There are two large postsecondary institutions in the Memphis area: Southwest Tennessee Community College and the University of Memphis. The U.S. Department of Education's Integrated Postsecondary Education System (IPEDS) provides enrollment and graduation data for these institutions. According to IPEDS Southwest Tennessee Community College admitted 2,882 first time undergraduate students in Fall, 2009; 1,988 of those were Black, 672 were Black males. By August, 2012, there were 93 completers (Associate's degree recipients) within the standard measure of 150% of normal time: 45 were Black, 16 were Black males. The University of Memphis admitted 2,163 first-time undergraduates in the Fall of 2006; 835 were Black, 265 were Black males. In 2012, there were 823 graduates receiving Bachelor's degrees within 150% of normal time; 210 were Black, 70 were Black men.

Let us assume that all the Black students at Southwest Tennessee Community College and the University of Memphis were graduates of the Memphis city schools. (Of course some were from other districts and some students from the Memphis city schools went elsewhere, but for the sake of the argument, we will assume that these at least approximately balance.) There were 8,000 Black students in grade 9 of the Memphis school district, including 4,617

Black males in the 2008/9 school year. Four years later 6,919 Black students graduated, including 3,360 Black males. Of these Memphis graduates, 1,988 went to Southwest Tennessee Community College and 835 went to the University of Memphis, 672 and 265 of whom, respectively, were Black males. Forty-five Black students graduated with Associate's degrees from Southwest Tennessee Community College within 150% of normal time, 16 of whom were Black males. Two hundred and ten Black students graduated from the University of Memphis with Bachelor's degrees within 150% of normal time, 70 of whom were Black men.[*]

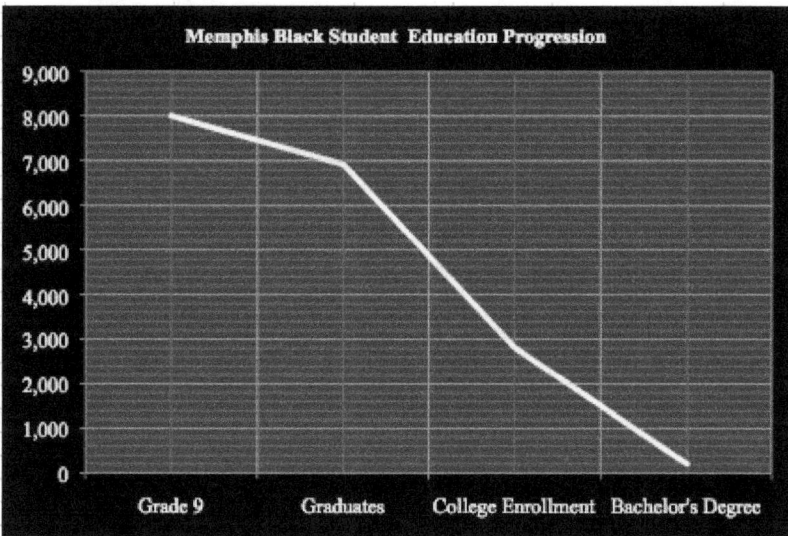

Memphis Black Student Education Progression

If the progression from the first year of high school in Memphis for Black students through graduation, college matriculation and degrees is anything like that indicated by these approximations, it cannot be said that the district is preparing its students well for college and careers. This matters enormously because higher education is an entry point to civilization itself. Once through that

---

[*] Memphis's elite liberal arts Rhodes College admitted 452 students in fall 2006, 34 of whom were Black, 8 of whom were Black men. Six years later, there were 366 graduates within 150% of normal time, 26 of whom were Black, 7 of whom were Black men.

door a person can travel through science, the arts, the humanities, coming into contact with entire worlds far from her or his family's neighborhood and quite possibly bringing what they learn there back to that family and neighborhood to further enhance their human development.

There are also the issues of employment, income and wealth. In the United States today, except for the inheritors of great fortunes, these are interconnected. Adults without a high school degree can look forward to an unemployment rate of more than twice the average of all workers and an income of less than half the average.[11] Each additional educational level decreases the unemployment rate and increases income. As we have seen, the Black/White education differentials in Memphis are considerable. If Black educational attainment were at White levels, there would be 17% more Black adults with Bachelor's degrees and 11% more with further degrees, significantly lowering the unemployment rate of the Black community and raising its income level.

It would also, other things being equal, lower the incarceration rate.

The Hammer of Caste: The Criminal Justice System

Racially unequal operations of the Memphis-area criminal justice system begins in the schools. In the 2011 school year, the U.S. Department of Education's Office for Civil Rights counted 26,000 out-of-school and 11,500 in-school suspensions and 4,400 expulsions in the 100,000 student Memphis public schools, over 90% of which were of Black students. There were also 100 each of referrals to law enforcement and school-related arrests. These school discipline actions in Memphis were nearly evenly divided between male and female students, 57% to 43%, affecting about one-third of each. The then-Shelby County district, not including Memphis, gave 4,600 in-school and 3,500 out-of-school suspensions and expelled 423 students, out of a total enrollment of approximately 47,000 students. Black students accounted for two-thirds of these school discipline cases, nearly twice their percentage in the total enrollment. Four hundred-thirty-seven students were referred to law enforcement by the Shelby system and 310 students had school-related arrests. Again, two-thirds of these were Black students. In other words, school discipline actions in the suburban schools affected about one-quarter of Black students, most of whom were male. The chances of a male Black student being suspended, expelled or arrested in suburban Shelby County approached 50%. In that single year, nearly 1,000 Black students in the Memphis area became known to the police, while at least 40,000 others had school discipline records. These are most unusual numbers. New York City, with ten times as many students, had fewer than 14,000 out-of-school suspensions and exactly 332 expulsions.

Given that 8,600 of the state's incarcerated population are enrolled full-time in Adult Basic Education/GED classes and an additional 420 are enrolled part-time, it appears that nearly a third of those incarcerated in the state's prisons have not completed high school.[12] One way of putting this would be to say that many Black children in Shelby County, and especially in Memphis City, spend their school years being readied for incarceration rather than being educated.

Tennessee's incarceration rate for African Americans, 1,962 per 100,000, is four times that for the state's White, non-Hispanic, population (503 per 100,000).[13] A consequence of the so-called war on drugs was that the number of people incarcerated in the state of Tennessee increased from under 7,500 in 1978 to nearly 30,000 in 2011. Today, approximately 20% of those incarcerated in the state's prisons are there for drug offenses. These offenses are divided between "cocaine" (2,818) and "other" (3,351). The average sentence for cocaine is 17 years, for "other," 8 years.

It is well-established that drug use among Black and White Americans is roughly equivalent. It is therefore notable that the Black/White arrest ratio for drug offenses in Memphis is 3 to 1.[14] In fiscal year 2012-2013, 17% of the 15,000 annual inmate admissions in the state's prisons were from Memphis's Shelby County. There are usually about 3,000 adults in the Shelby County Jail (as distinct from the state prisons). Yearly bookings in the jail average 56,000.[15] Almost all of these would be Black males, of whom there are 120,000 between the ages of 18 and 64. Thus, on average, bookings in the Shelby County Jail are equivalent to half the working age population of Black men in the county. Of course this is deceptive. Some of the bookings, a few hundred, are of women; some are of White residents, male and female. Some people are booked more than once in a year. It is not as if half the working age Black men in the county were actually booked each year. Perhaps only a third of the working age Black men in the county are booked each year.

According to the 2010 Census, when there were about twice as many Black as White residents in the county, there were about the same number of White men in Shelby County college dormitories as in the county's jails and prisons and nearly four times as many White women in the dormitories as in cells. The situation is quite different for the county's Black residents. There are ten times as many Black men incarcerated in the county as in dormitories and less than twice as many Black women in the dormitories as in cells.[†] It would seem from these figures that if the laws were equitably enforced in Shelby County there would be 10,000 more White men in jail, or at least 4,500 fewer Black Shelby County men incarcerated, depending on which way the criminal justice system decided to equitably enforce the law.

As about a quarter of the 22,000 missing Black working age men in Memphis are in the county jail, the others probably in other Tennessee prisons, the criminal justice system of Shelby County, and, more generally, the state, has an enormous impact on African American life in southwestern Tennessee. It polices, as it were, the caste boundaries of the descendants of enslaved Africans as effectively as it once policed Jim Crow.

Modeling a More Equitable Memphis
The task of modeling a Memphis where the schools graduate students well-prepared for college and careers and where there are no longer enormous racial disparities in the numbers of residents arrested and incarcerated requires fundamental reformation of the criminal justice system's policies and practices and improvements in the public school system.

Memphis's incarceration rate disparities are driven by the irrationality of drug laws and their inequitable application. The sale and use of marijuana is now legal in some states and many localities.

[†] 1,152 White males and 380 White females in Shelby County correctional institutions for adults and 1,046 White males and 1,267 White females in college/university student housing; 5,188 Black males and 570 Black females in Shelby County correctional institutions for adults and 488 Black males and 949 Black females in college/university student housing.

Penalties in regard to the use of the powder and crystal forms of cocaine are being equalized. If the will for wholesale reform in Memphis is absent, these and similar matters could be attended to step-by-step. One approach (out of many possible) would be for the county sheriff to announce that the drug laws would be enforced evenly across the county. If it appeared likely that 10,000 young adult White males were liable for arrest and incarceration for drug offenses, it is possible that possession of marijuana would be de facto legalized. If it appeared likely that hundreds of upper middle class White residents of Shelby County were to be at risk of prison sentences averaging 17 years for their cocaine use, both the legal status of that habit and the consequences might quickly change. If recreational use and sale of drugs were legalized, a large part of the city's underground drug economy would disappear along with its associated violence.

Turning then to education, we have seen that Shelby County suburban schools have better outcomes and narrower gaps for Black students than the Memphis schools. For example, Houston High School, in the Shelby County suburb of Germantown had a 2012 graduation rate of 89% for Black students, just 7 points under the graduation rate for White students in the school. Houston Middle School brought 83% of its students to grade level in Reading/English Language Arts, including 62% of African Americans. Collierville High School in that suburban community, had a combined ACT score of 24 and a graduation rate of 93% for its African American students, just 4 points below that of its White students. Collierville Middle School brought 79% of its students at grade level in Reading/English Language Arts, including 57% of African Americans.[16] These can be benchmarks for modeling the potential effects of improvements in the Memphis schools.

Producing those improvements has been a long-term goal of the Memphis community, district personnel and national reformers. Much good work has been done with the professional development of teachers and administrators. The essential ingredient if educational outcomes within Memphis are to reach (or surpass) those of suburban schools like those in Germantown and Collierville is investment. Educational funding is usually measured by governmental support for schools. This is important, but in many places it is not the full story. Investments in children's education begins at birth, if not before, and usually those investments are much greater for children from prosperous families than for those from impoverished families. Studies going back half a century or more have found that middle class toddlers know more words than those from impoverished families, of any race, in part because their parents know and use wider vocabularies, in part because of differing "ways with words," in Shirley Brice Heath's phrase: the customs and practices of communication with children. By the time those middle class toddlers are two or three years old they have begun an endless round of lessons of one type or another, lessons, perhaps most importantly, in experiencing lessons themselves. This represents an investment of parental time, usually that of a spouse not otherwise or not fully employed, and often cash as well. These investments continue throughout the k-12 years, with afterschool and summer school classes and the usual weekend excursions to science museums and summer excursions to, say, Spain.

Now, it is possible, and a very good thing, to help parents who are not already doing so to use middle class ways with words, but many simply do not have the time or backgrounds for this and some see these as culturally inappropriate practices. As for pre-pre-school, after school and summer lessons, not to mention trips to Spain, people living in poverty, by definition, do not have the discretionary incomes to spend on these, no matter how much they would like to. Judge John Dietz in the recent Texas school finance case, pointed to the importance of determining "the cost of providing all students with a meaningful opportunity to acquire the essential knowledge and skills reflected in the state curriculum and to graduate at a college- and career-ready level."[17] That cost includes the extra-curricular investments just outlined as well as those more generally involved with the support of traditional school systems. The proverbial even playing field for Memphis would be defined by challenging curricula, highly qualified teachers, well-equipped schools as well as universal pre-kindergarten; literacy-oriented early childhood education; extended school days and school years to support children from impoverished households at least as well as the educational development of children from the prosperous households of Germantown and Collierville are supported by their families.

Let us assume that these reforms resulted in the educational attainment of Black adults in Memphis equaling that of White residents of the city. That would mean that instead of only 13% of Black adults reaching the crucial level of Bachelor's degrees or above, 41% would do so. That would increase the number of those higher-earning Black residents by over 66,000, bringing with it the concomitant advantages of income, wealth and socio-economic mobility. Given current earning and unemployment rates by educational attainment, this would result in an increase in total Memphis Black community income from $8 billion to perhaps $16 billion per year.[18] It is clear that the bulk of this increase would come from the increased income (and decreased unemployment) flowing from the achievement of a college degree. We can then make the same experiment with community wealth. If we set Memphis's Black mean net worth at the White figures, we could anticipate a very large increase in the total wealth of the Black community (and of the city as a whole).

None of this will happen immediately, but all of it is possible if the educational system of Memphis meets its potential and the criminal justice system begins to operate on behalf of all the area's residents.

These changes could be begun by the mayor, chief of police, sheriff, district attorney and the various superintendents of schools any time they decide to do so.

Notes: Chapter Four

[1] U.S. Census. Selected Population Profile 2010-2, American Community Survey, S0201.

[2] Office of Policy, Planning and Assessment (2010). Life Expectancy in Tennessee, 2004-2006. Tennessee Department of Health, Nashville, TN.

[3] Social Explorer (old version). http://www.socialexplorer.com/89AACD3A4F1E4E1/explore

[4] http://www.s4.brown.edu/us2010/segregation2010/city.aspx?cityid=4748000

[5] Sharkey, Patrick. Neighborhoods and the Black-White Mobility Gap. Philadelphia: The Pew Charitable Trusts, 2009, p. 9. http://www.pewstates.org/uploadedFiles/PCS_Assets/2009/PEW_NEIGHBORHOODS(1).pdf.

[6] An account of this history for Memphis can be found in Pohlmann, Marcus D. Opportunity Lost: Race and Poverty in the Memphis City Schools. Knoxville: The University of Tennessee Press, 2008.

[7] U.S. Department of Education, Office for Civil Rights, Civil Rights Data Collection.

[8] Tennessee Department of Education, Data. http://www.tn.gov/education/data/download_data.shtml

[9] The state average was 19.3 and that for Shelby County was 20.9. Tennessee Department of Education, Data.

[10] The ACT. http://www.actstudent.org/scores/norms1.html

[11] Chart from New York State Education Department. http://www.p12.nysed.gov/irs/ela-math/2014/2014Grades3-8ELAMath-final8-13-14.pdf.

[12] Tennessee Department of Correction, Decision Support: Research & Planning Division, FY 2013 Statistical Abstract, October 2013.

[13] Prison Policy Initiative.

[14] Beckett, Kathrine. Race and Drug Law Enforcement in Seattle. Report Prepared for the ACLU Drug Law Reform Project and the Defender Association, September 2008, p. 9. https://www.aclu.org/files/assets/race20and20drug20law20enforcement20in20seattle_20081.pdf

[15] Shelby County Sheriff's Office. http://www.shelby-sheriff.org/jl/

[16] Tennessee Department of Education, State Report Cards. http://edu.reportcard.state.tn.us/pls/apex/f?p=200:20:3966078826724 869::NO

[17] *Texas Taxpayer & Student Fairness Coalition (TTSFC) v. State*, August 28, 2014.

[18] Earnings and unemployment rates by educational attainment, 2013. Bureau of Labor Statistics. http://www.bls.gov/emp/ep_chart_001.htm.

Chapter Five: Milwaukee

When China was still Communist and exotic I arranged an international exchange program for teachers from the United States who would go there to teach English and teachers from China who would come to this country to teach Chinese language and culture. Milwaukee was one of the American host cities. One day the person I was working with at the University said that there was a problem we had not discussed: where the Chinese exchange teacher would live. "You see," she said, "We have a White section of the city and a Black section, but we don't have a Chinese neighborhood." I thought that was funny. I don't think so any more.

Milwaukee, Wisconsin, is a mid-sized, Midwestern city, just far enough from Chicago to escape most of its economic gravitational pull. Milwaukee, among the most segregated of American cities, is "hypersegregated." The Black-White Index of Dissimilarity is 70 (60 is considered very high).[1] The metropolitan area has a population over two million; Milwaukee County has a population just under one million, the city about 600,000.[2] The Black population of Milwaukee County, 250,000, is about twice the national average percentage; the Hispanic population, 130,000, just under the average national percentage for that group. As the Chinese population is only 1,300, the city is probably still without a Chinese neighborhood.

Ancestry and religion are perhaps more important in Milwaukee than in many other parts of the United States. A quarter of the population of Milwaukee County reports German ancestry. The next two largest groups with European ancestry are of Polish and Irish descent. Between them they account for about half of the county's residents and because of their even greater share of the population in the past they dominate its image and cultural heritage today. The "we" of those traditionally dominating the city and its institutions, are of German, Polish or Irish descent. "They" are the descendants of enslaved Africans.

The economy of Milwaukee County, historically based on the brewing of beer, manufacturing and the marketing of products from the local agricultural interior, in a familiar pattern is now predominately supported by education, social services and health care, which between them employ a quarter of the workforce. However, manufacturing still provides just under 15% of the county's employment, followed by retail trade and professional and managerial services. Although total workforce and educational attainment statistics are close to national averages,[*] household income in Milwaukee is lower. Median household income in Milwaukee County is $42,000 per year, compared to the national average of $51,400. A larger proportion in Milwaukee County than the national average live on incomes below $25,000 per year, a lower proportion have incomes over $200,000 per year, and there are higher poverty rates than the national averages. Twenty-seven percent of families with related children under 18 years of age have incomes below the poverty line, as do 48% of those of women raising their children without a man in the house.

If, however, we look at the data for Milwaukee County's White, non-Hispanic, residents alone, the picture is quite different. The White median household income in Milwaukee County is $51,000 per year, ranking with the highest in the developed world; just 22% have incomes under $25,000 per year and 3% have incomes over $200,000. Only eleven percent of White families with related children under 18 years of age have incomes under the poverty line, as do 30% of White women raising children on their own. Eighty-nine percent of the White adult population have high school diplomas or the equivalent; 32% have Bachelor's degrees or higher qualifications. Only eleven percent did not graduate from high school. White Milwaukee County differs economically from the nation as a whole only slightly and that at the extremes, with both fewer poor families and fewer high income families.

It is apparent from the disparities between the general statistics for the county and those for the White population that the Black population probably is not doing as well as the county's White population and that is indeed the case. There are higher percentages of Black than White households at each of the lower income levels from less than $10,000 per year to $35-49,000, after which the percentage of Black households at each income level drops

---

[*] Eighty-six percent of the adult population have high school diplomas or the equivalent; 28% have Bachelor's degrees or higher qualifications. Fourteen percent have not graduated from high school.

precipitously until that above $150,000 rounds to zero. Black median household income is $27,000 per year: half that of the county's White residents, just three-quarters of the national average for Black households and far below the average for the world's most developed countries. Half of the county's Black residents have incomes in the bottom quartile of all Milwaukee area incomes, that is, 80% of Milwaukee residents have incomes higher than the average Black resident of the county.[3] In Black Milwaukee County, sixty percent of households live on incomes below $35,000, qualifying their children for the National Lunch Program. The income of a Black household with two school teachers would be among the highest 5% of all Black households in the county.

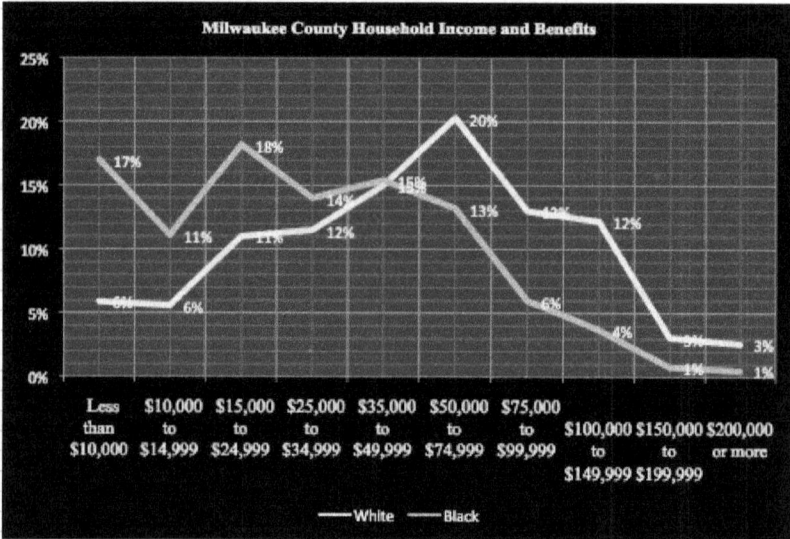

Milwaukee County Household Income and Benefits

There are other indicators of racial inequalities in Milwaukee. We will turn to those involving education below. For the moment we might add to those for income some of those involving health. Life expectancy at birth for White male residents of Wisconsin is 78 years; for White women it is 83 years. Life expectancy at birth for Black male residents of Wisconsin is 71, for Black women 77 years.[4] According to the Kaiser Family Foundation, 14% of Black men in Wisconsin report having "fair" or "poor" health, twice the percentage of White men. For women the situation is more extreme:

24% of Black women, as compared to 8% of non-Hispanic White women report their health as "poor" or only "fair." Nine percent of Black men and women have been diagnosed with diabetes, as compared to just 2% of White men and 3% of White women. The White rates of ill-health are lower than national averages for the White, non-Hispanic, population of the state and Wisconsin's Black rates are higher than national averages for America's Black population.

African American residents of Milwaukee County (and Wisconsin in general) have half the median household income of the area's Whites, four times the percentage of families with children living in poverty, two to three times the percentage with poor or fair health, three to four times the rate of diabetes and six to seven years less life expectancy than White residents. In effect they live in another country from the area's White residents, a country even poorer than that inhabited by the average African American family.

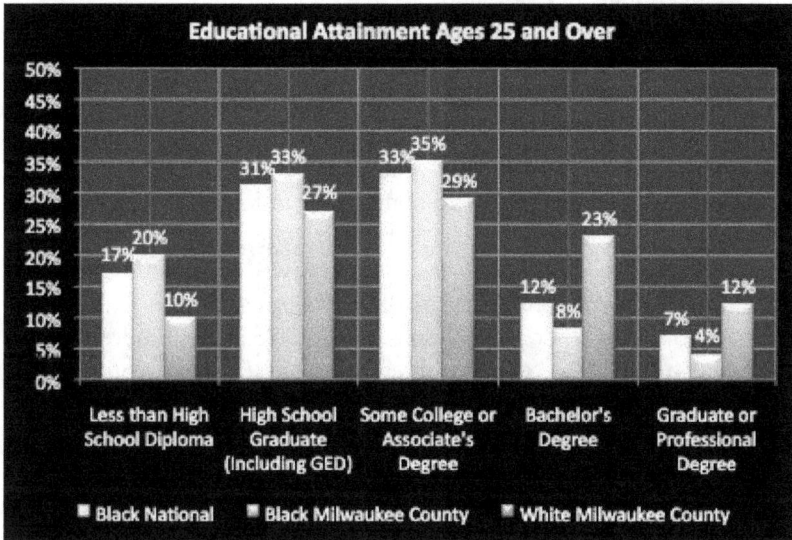

It is generally accepted that the chief determinate of income for Americans in the twenty-first century, except for those inheriting great wealth, is the quality and extent of their education. Nationally, 19% of African Americans over 25 years of age have graduated from college, as compared to the 30% of White Americans who have a

Bachelor's degree or higher. In Milwaukee County, just 12% of African Americans have graduated from college, as compared to 35% of White residents of the county.

White Milwaukee residents are more highly educated than White, non-Hispanic, Americans in the rest of the country, while Black residents of the county have not been as well-educated as White residents of Milwaukee County or as African Americans generally. This has a direct effect on incomes. The national median full-time annual wage for adults without a high school diploma in 2014 was $24,960; with a high school diploma it was $34,320.[5] Workers with some college averaged incomes of $36,717 per year and for those with a Bachelor's degree it was $57,460. Five additional years of education approximately doubles incomes. Although Black incomes are 80% of those figures at each educational level (perhaps a racial penalty), the relationship holds: $19,968 without a high school diploma, $27,466 with one; $29,374 with some college and $45,968 a year with a Bachelor's degree.

If we assume that wages in Milwaukee County are in step with national averages, we would expect that the 20% of Black adults in the county without high school diplomas, if they were in full-time employment, would earn about $20,000 per year; the 33% with high school diplomas and no further education would earn, on average, $27,000 per year, the 35% with some college $23,499, and the 12% with Bachelor's degrees would earn $46,000 per year. With those assumptions we can make a comparative community income calculation: 100 White adult, full-time wage earners in Milwaukee County would together bring home $4,039,186. One hundred Black adult, full-time wage earners in Milwaukee County would bring home $2,665,465: just two-thirds of that of the White group. The difference of educational attainment, and the lower wages paid to Black workers at every educational level, produces a 34% "race-based" reduction in the community's income as compared to the White community.[6] The superior earning power of college graduates is particularly crucial for community incomes.

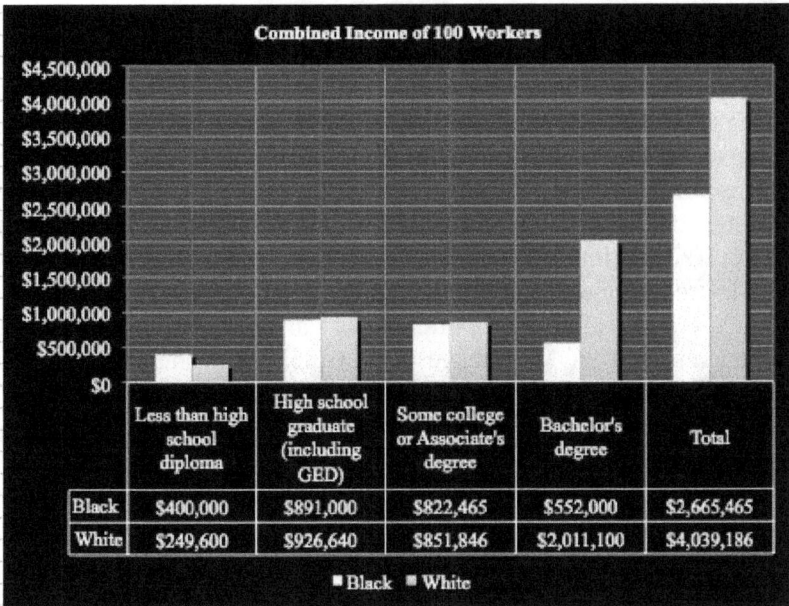

	Less than high school diploma	High school graduate (including GED)	Some college or Associate's degree	Bachelor's degree	Total
Black	$400,000	$891,000	$822,465	$552,000	$2,665,465
White	$249,600	$926,640	$851,846	$2,011,100	$4,039,186

■ Black ■ White

There are other factors that lead to further deficiencies in the income of Milwaukee's Black community as compared to that of the county's White population. The unemployment rate and the percentage of adults not in the labor force at all are much higher for Black adults than for Whites. Milwaukee County's Black adult unemployment rate was 12% of those in the labor force in 2012, while 40% of African Americans over 16 years of age were not in the labor force (that is, neither employed nor actively looking for "on the books" work). This would imply that more than half of Milwaukee County's African-American adults have no full-time regular incomes. The comparable figures for the county's White, non-Hispanic, adults are 5% unemployed and 31% not in the labor force: 36% as compared to 52%—sixteen percentage points.[†] In other words, there are nearly one-third fewer adult full-time wage earners in the Black community as compared to the White community in Milwaukee County, and, as we have seen, those who

---

[†] For both groups, those not in the labor force as defined by the Census include homemakers, the disabled and those living on investment incomes, among others. Other things being equal, one would expect members of poorer communities to have higher workforce participation, if lower wages.

are full-time wage earners make, collectively, one-third less than their White counterparts. We find, then, that Black aggregate income is 20% of that of White Milwaukee County's aggregate income, even though the Black population is 40% of the White population. Given these conditions, it is no surprise that in 2012 four times the proportion of Black families as White families in Milwaukee had incomes below the poverty line: 36% of Black families as compared to just 9% of White families.

These income disparities naturally result in great differences in what members of each community can afford. Just under 60% of White residents of Milwaukee live in their own homes, twice the proportion of Black residents. Less than a quarter, 23%, of Whites paid 30% or more of gross income in rent as compared to 36% of Blacks. Just under 30% of Black residents of Milwaukee County were without a car, as compared to only 10% of Whites. Four percent of Whites commuted to work by public transportation; 14% of Black Milwaukee workers used public transportation.

Category	White	Black
Home owners	60%	30%
Paid 30% or more income in rent	23%	36%
Car owners	90%	70%
Commute to work by car	89%	80%
by public transportation	4%	14%

Black residents of Milwaukee, as a group, have lower incomes than White residents of the county. They are less likely to be in the labor force and if they are in the labor force they are more likely to be unemployed. Black residents of the county are half as likely to own their own homes, half again as likely to pay more than 30% of their gross income in rent, less likely to own cars and three times as likely to be dependent on public transportation to get to work.

The housing issue is particularly egregious in Milwaukee. Not only is the city hypersegregated, the local banks have a history of actively discouraging home ownership among the city's African Americans. Barbara Miner cites a study that "found that loan denials in Milwaukee affected middle-class blacks the most, with lending disparity between whites and nonwhites growing in higher-income brackets.

> As a *Milwaukee Journal* article noted, the study "is troubling, because it raises the possibility that many blacks do not encounter less racism as they move up the economic ladder; they encounter more."[7]

In this way, even relatively prosperous descendants of enslaved Africans in Milwaukee are confined to the city's Black ghettos.

Being "allowed" to buy a house is not enough. Loans offered, when they are offered, are often unconventional and the terms onerous. Consequently, the foreclosure crisis was particularly severe in Black areas of Milwaukee. Indeed, the map of foreclosed houses for sale in Milwaukee County is virtually a map of the city's segregated Black neighborhoods. Oliver and Shapiro have argued that *wealth* differentials between Black and White communities are crucial to understanding the socio-economic situation of African Americans. "The notion embodied in the 'sedimentation of racial inequality' [i.e., caste] is that in central ways the cumulative effects of the past have seemingly cemented blacks to the bottom of society's economic hierarchy . . .

> Wealth is one indicator of the material disparity that captures the historical legacy of low wages, personal and organizational discrimination, and institutionalized racism.[8]

As stated earlier, wealth is conventionally divided between home equity and investments.

White residents of Milwaukee County are six times as likely as Black residents of the county to have investment income: 30% of Milwaukee County Whites in 2012 had interest, dividends or net rental income as compared to 5% of Black county residents. Milwaukee County's White community, which is less than three times the size of the Black community, has a net investment wealth more than 100 times that of the county's Black community: $26 billion, as compared to $226 million.[9] Adding home equity to the value of other investments, the wealth of the White community is "only" 34 times that of the county's Black community: over $40 billion as compared to $1.2 billion. In a country where wealth is (increasingly) power, Milwaukee's Black community is relatively powerless in the face of the wealth of the area's White community.

Mobility

Median family (as opposed to household) income in Milwaukee County in 2012 was $69,283 for White families and $28,388 for Black families (the latter considerably lower than the national median Black family income in 1990, adjusted for inflation[10]). The chances of a child brought up in a family with an income of $70,000 reaching the top quintile is 19%; the chances of that child falling to the bottom quintile is nearly the same. The chances of a child brought up in a family with an income of $30,000 reaching the top quintile is 11%, the chance of falling to the bottom quintile is more than twice as much.[11] Or to put that another way, the odds are two-to-one against a Black child in Milwaukee of doing much better in life than that child's parents, who, in general, are not doing very well at all.

Milwaukee's Black community is a caste, for all practical purposes restricted to its ghetto, where 40% of the children are born into the nation's lowest quintiles in income, averaging $13,000 across those two quintiles. The Black distribution of family incomes is off-set downward from the White by between one and two quintiles in Milwaukee. That is, the mean Black family income of the richest 20% is approximately that of the mean White family income of the second highest White 20%, while the mean Black family income of the middle 20% is similar to that of the mean White income of the lowest-income 20% of White families. It is therefore unlikely that there is any meaningful intergenerational family income upward mobility in Milwaukee's Black community. Unless there is fundamental change, many will remain, generation after generation, at the poverty level in income with little wealth and little hope of improving their situation.

How does this happen? Patrick Sharkey's analysis is particularly pertinent in hypersegregated Milwaukee. His national data showed that most Black children grow up in neighborhoods with high poverty rates; most White children grow up in very low poverty rate neighborhoods.[12] He found, further, that there are "extremely high rates of downward mobility among blacks raised in neighborhoods" with high rates of family poverty.[13] What causes these enormous disparities? In addition to the operations of the real estate and banking businesses, the education system is a way that state institutions themselves limit opportunities for African Americans. As we have seen, other things being equal, the main source of differences in income of those living on wages is the level of education, which is to a large extent dependent on opportunities for acquiring the requisite skills and knowledge during primary and secondary school.

Mark Robert Rank noted that "patterns of racial residential segregation ensure that more black children find themselves in schools that are severely segregated and that lack resources than do white children from similar social class backgrounds."[14] The underfunding of schools in Black neighborhoods affects less impoverished Black families as well as the poor. Sharkey, Massey and Denton agreed that in hypersegregated areas like Milwaukee many middle class African American families are unable to find housing in areas with good schools, with dire consequences: "one consequence of this pattern is that middle-class status is particularly precarious for blacks, and downward mobility is more common as a result."[15] Or as Massey and Denton put it: "Segregation . . . is directly responsible for the creation of a harsh and uniquely disadvantaged black residential environment, making it quite likely that individual blacks themselves will fail, no matter what their socioeconomic characteristics or family background. Racial segregation is the institutional nexus that enables the transmission of poverty from person to person and generation to generation . . ."[16]

There is another factor, especially significant in Milwaukee: extraordinary rates of incarceration of African American residents. We will turn to that after considering the effects of the city's education system in creating and maintaining Milwaukee's caste boundaries.

The Anvil of Caste: Education

The common association of the poverty of Black families with the comparative lack of educational achievement and educational attainment of many African American children is valid, but all too often the chain of causality is run the wrong way. It is not that poverty is the incurable cause of a lack of educational achievement, it is that the lack of educational opportunities is a significant cause of poverty. The reason that Milwaukee's Black children are not as well educated as they should be is that the schools they attend are not as good as they should be. And the reasons for that include school district and state financial and other institutional policies and individual actions. As we have seen, many American school districts continue to provide more support to schools in middle class (read: White) neighborhoods while reducing support to schools in poor (read: Black) neighborhoods. School district boundaries themselves are another way in which resources are apportioned so that those schools serving children with higher income parents receive more resources than those serving children from lower income families. For example, the teacher salary differentials between schools in Milwaukee and the nearby, largely White, Waukesha school district are very large: average salaries are $58,000 in Milwaukee; $81,000 in Waukesha. Is it a coincidence that the Waukesha schools have much better learning outcomes than those in Milwaukee—even for children who are Black or whose families have low incomes?

An analysis of the quality of education available to Milwaukee's Black children can begin with data about basic skills. Here, again, the U. S. Department of Education's National Assessment of Educational Progress (NAEP) is a good general indicator of the education provided to students by their schools in the district. Reading is the essential skill and by grade 8 the Milwaukee schools have had nearly a decade to teach it to their students.

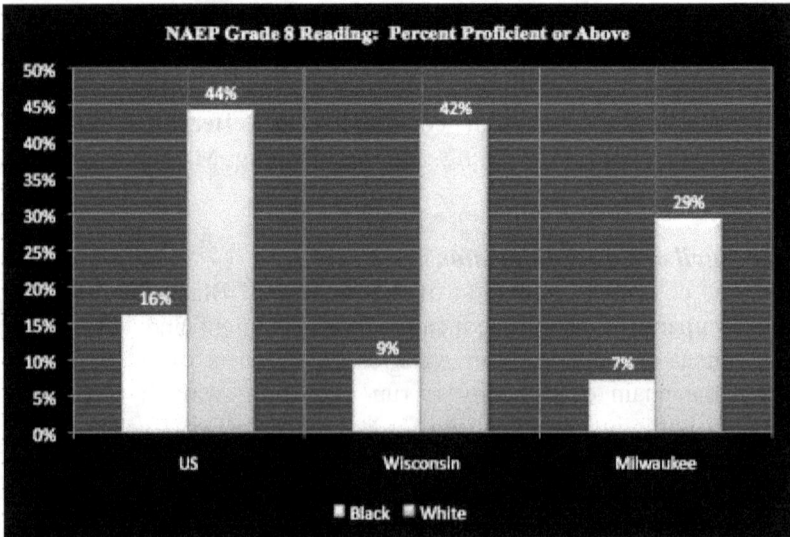

NAEP Grade 8 Reading: Percent Proficient or Above

White students, nationally, are about two-and-a-half times as likely to read at or above grade level at grade 8 as Black students. But in 2013, while Wisconsin's schools brought 42% of their White students they only brought 9% of their Black students to grade level or above (NAEP Proficient or Advanced) in grade 8 reading. Schools in Wisconsin, then, do just over half as well, comparatively, as the national average in teaching Black students to read, while they teach White students to read at close to the national average. In Milwaukee the disparity is slightly lower due to lower scores for White students. Milwaukee's public schools brought just 29% of their White students and 7% of their Black students to grade level in grade 8 reading.

White students do not learn to read as well in Milwaukee as in the state or in the nation as a whole. That difference might be attributed either to some characteristic of Milwaukee's White students, as compared to those in the rest of the state, or to some characteristic of the Milwaukee public schools. If so, it is not family income. Although White families in Milwaukee are poorer than the state average, they are not dramatically poorer: median household income is $54,000 for White households in the state as a whole, $45,000 for White households in the Milwaukee school district. White families in Milwaukee have incomes well above the poverty line. The difference in family income is not sufficient to account for the difference in education outcomes. An analysis of a program allowing some Milwaukee public school students to transfer to schools in the suburbs found that those succeeding in transferring to those better-funded suburban schools, achieved higher scores than those who applied but failed to win a place.[17] It is therefore arguably more likely that the difference in grade 8 reading ability among White students in Milwaukee as compared to White students in the state as a whole has to do more with characteristics of the schools than with the economic status of student families. This would then apply to Black students as well. Confirmation of this school system effect might be found from observing that, nationally, as we have seen, NAEP results indicate that 16% of Black students score at grade level or above in grade 8 reading: more than twice the percentage in Milwaukee.[‡]

If Milwaukee's schools do not teach either their Black or White students to read as well as do other schools in the country, it is unlikely that they do better with any other subject. In brief, schools in Milwaukee do not fulfill their function of teaching their students the skills and knowledge they need for successful lives. They do not do this for most White students and they do this for hardly any Black students.

When we analyze grade 8 reading outcomes for Milwaukee by race and eligibility for the National Lunch Program, a measure of income, we find that just 5% of Black students in the district whose families are eligible for that program, that is, relatively poor, score at or above Proficient (grade level), while 20% of those from less impoverished families do so. For White students, 19% who are eligible for the National Lunch Program and 44% of those ineligible score at Proficient or above. (Just over a quarter of Milwaukee's White families but about 60% of the city's Black families have incomes in the range eligible for the National Lunch program.) Lower income White students and higher income Black students are both four times as likely to read at grade level than lower income Black students. Higher income White students are twice as likely as lower income White students and nearly nine times as likely as lower income Black students to read at or above grade level.

Turning to the influence of parental education levels, reading achievement for Milwaukee's Black students shows steady increases as reported parental educational attainment increases, doubling from 5% to 10% between students who reported that their parents were high school graduates and those who reported that at least one of their parents had graduated from college. *No* Black students in Milwaukee whose parents had not graduated from high school achieved proficiency. (No White students reported parental education attainment below college graduation.)

[‡] The overwhelming predominance of Milwaukee's Back population, compared to that of the state as a whole, complicates these calculations.

NAEP Milwaukee Grade 8 Reading: At or Above Proficient

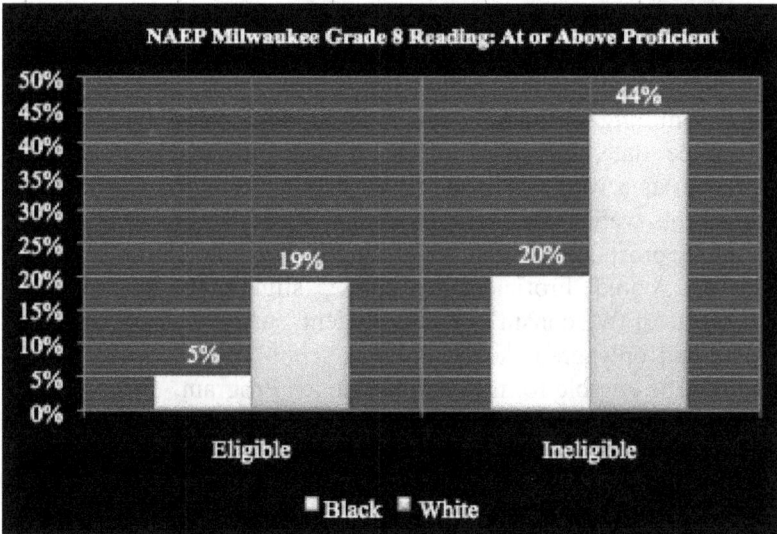

NAEP Milwaukee Grade 8 Reading: At or Above Proficient

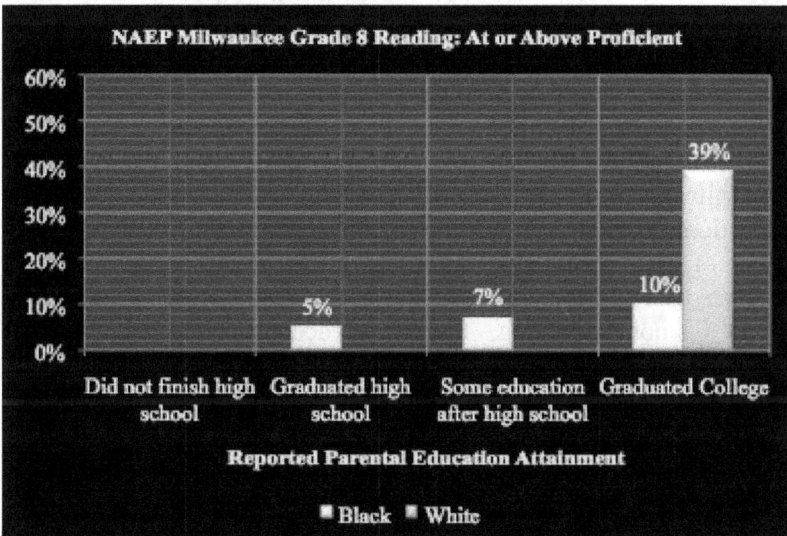

Of the approximately 3,000 Black students in grade 8 in the Milwaukee school district, just under 13% have a parent who was a college graduate. There are, then, fewer than 40 Black students with college-educated parents reading at or above grade level at grade 8. NAEP sampling limitations preclude further cross-tabulations for Milwaukee data, but if we look at data for Black students in Wisconsin as a whole, we find that 27% of those who reported that their parents were college graduates <u>and</u> whose families were among the more prosperous, that is, ineligible for the National Lunch Program, scored Proficient or above, slightly higher than the percentage of Wisconsin's White students who reported that their parents had only graduated from high school, and yet were not so poor as to be eligible for the National Lunch Program.

This analysis of Milwaukee and Wisconsin NAEP data can be summarized as follows: Higher family income doubles the level of reading proficiency for Black students, perhaps, in part, because of the additional investments those families make in the education of their children. Black students whose parents did not finish high school have no chance at all of achieving proficiency. Black students whose parents graduated from college have double the chance of Black students whose parents only graduated from high school of achieving proficiency in reading at grade 8, but there are very few of these. These factors are not independent. Virtually only those Milwaukee students with college-educated parents have family incomes making them ineligible for the National Lunch Program. And just ten percent of African American men and 14% of African American women in Milwaukee County report having a Bachelor's degree or higher. We can conclude that the education provided by the Milwaukee public schools provides little "value-added" to educational achievement for the students entrusted to them, Black or White. This is particularly disastrous for the vast majority of Black students who can count on few educational resources at home.

It is not surprising, then, that according to the National Assessment of Educational Progress, in 2013, out of 21 urban school districts, Milwaukee ranked above—and only slightly above—only Detroit and Cleveland in grade 8 reading for all students. For White students it ranked above only Philadelphia and Cleveland. For Black students it ranked last, below southern cities such as Atlanta;

Jefferson County, Kentucky; and Charlotte, below Chicago, Los Angeles and New York City.

Milwaukee's schools limit educational opportunities for Black students in many ways. Twenty-three percent of Black students in Wisconsin attend schools where more than 20% of teachers are not certified, compared to less than 1% of White students in the state.[18] Wisconsin is one of the eleven states reporting higher than national average gaps between the suspension rates of Black and White, non-Hispanic, students. The national average for out-school-suspensions in 2011-12 for African-Americans students was 20% and 6% for White students. In Wisconsin nearly one-third of Black students were pushed out of school by their educators with out-of-school suspensions, as compared to just 4% of White students.[19] The state is implicitly claiming by this that Black students are eight times as likely to misbehave as their White peers and more than half again as likely to misbehave as their peers in the national Black community. We can believe that, or believe that there is a highly abnormal propensity among the state's educators to exclude Black students from their classrooms.

A Milwaukee school board member stated as far back as 1979: "a high school cannot function when 70 percent of the kids can't even read at an eighth grade level."[20] Her analysis was unfortunately accurate: in 2012 just over one-third of the district's Black students and just over half of the district's White students received diplomas four years after grade 9. We can follow out the educational consequences of the failure of Milwaukee schools to teach Black students to read at grade level in middle school by concentrating on the education of male Black students, widely considered the most vulnerable group. In 2012, an estimated 860, 30%, of the 2,886 male Black students who were in grade 9 in the Milwaukee public schools four years earlier, graduated with a regular high school diploma, as compared to 52% of White students.[§] Given the school-administration-induced attrition by the infliction of out-of-school suspensions and given grade 8 reading levels, it is surprising that

---

[§] Grade 9 enrollment is greater than either grade 8 or grade 10 enrollment, indicating that it includes students who have been held back at that "gateway" grade and then dropped out the following year. Some graduation rate calculations are based on first time grade 9 students. This tends to obscure the issue of the quality of the education offered by the schools.

even 30% of Milwaukee's Black students graduated four years after grade 9. As for the rest, given national patterns, it is likely that 800 of those male Black students without diplomas will spend time in prison. That is, 800 of *each year's* high school cohort.[21]

This brings us to the question of the quality of those few diplomas awarded. How can we gauge the quality of the education of those receiving high school diplomas in Milwaukee? One indication of the quality of teaching and the amount of learning in Milwaukee schools is that the average Milwaukee school district ACT college entrance test composite test score, 15.9,[22] was at the 20th percentile, the equivalent of 400 on each of the two parts of the SAT, half the total points possible, slightly below that of Memphis.[23] As that is an average score, it follows that half of the district's students scored even farther below the ACT composite score average of 23 for White Wisconsin students. The Milwaukee school district ACT average is below that of the level of the bottom quartile of students admitted to Wisconsin universities. It is therefore likely that many of the African American students who do manage to graduate from the Milwaukee school district do not graduate prepared for college. They are just being passed along.

We can look at this in more detail. Milwaukee has two large universities: Marquette and the University of Wisconsin-Milwaukee. Undergraduate tuition at the University of Wisconsin-Milwaukee is nearly $10,000 per year. Undergraduate tuition at Marquette is over $35,000 per year. These figures amount to nearly fifty percent and over 150%, respectively, of median household incomes for Black families in Milwaukee. Of course, scholarships are available, but how many Milwaukee students with ACT scores of 16 or below would be eligible? Apparently very few. In the fall of 2006 Marquette enrolled 1,854 undergraduate, first-time, degree-seeking students; 95 of those were Black or African American, 35 were Black males. In 2012 Marquette graduated 1,476 students with Bachelor's degrees within 6 years, 55 of whom were Black and 20 of whom were Black men. The University of Wisconsin-Milwaukee enrolled 4,090 undergraduate, first-time, degree-seeking students in the Fall of 2006, 273 of whom were Black or African-American); 87 of those were men. In 2012 the University graduated 1,691 students with Bachelor's degrees within 6 years, 45 of whom were Black and 15 of whom were Black men.[24]

Some graduates of the Milwaukee schools may have enrolled in other universities, the University of Wisconsin-Madison, for example, or gone out of state. (Of course not all Black students at Marquette and University of Wisconsin-Milwaukee went through the Milwaukee public schools.) Let us make a generous allowance for these by doubling the totals for Marquette and University of Wisconsin-Milwaukee. That would give 400 university admissions of Black students, 244 being male African-Americans and 200 African American graduates, 70 of whom were Black males, out of a ninth grade class of more than 5,400 Black students, 2,800 of whom were Black males: a success rate of 3-4%.

There are a number of two-year degree granting institutions in Milwaukee County, by far the largest being Milwaukee Area Technical College. In 2009 it admitted 2,232 first-time undergraduates, of whom 546 were Black and 262 were African-American men. In 2012 it graduated 196 students within 150% of normal time for an Associate's degree, of whom 25 were Black and 20 African-American men.[25] This does little to change the picture. Milwaukee's Black students are not prepared for college or careers in significant numbers.

Milwaukee, and Wisconsin, are known for their ever-expanding voucher programs. Vouchers—the transfer of public funds from public school districts to charter, private and religious schools—were not a spontaneous growth in Milwaukee. According to Barbara Miner, the idea was promoted by "Milwaukee's Lynde and Harry Bradley Foundation . . . [which] has used its local and national clout and its bankroll to nurture, protect, and expand Milwaukee's voucher program. From 1986 to 2003, it made an estimated $41 million in grants for school voucher initiatives."[26] As a result, "By 2010, voucher schools in Milwaukee enrolled more than twenty thousand students . . ."[27] Interestingly, in "1989, the year before the voucher program began, there were 29,988 students in private schools in Milwaukee. In 2010, the number was almost exactly the same—29,528. The difference was that [in 2010] most of the students (20,996) received publicly funded vouchers to pay the tuition. Roughly 85 percent of those voucher students attended a religious school, in particular a Catholic or Lutheran school."[28] In other words, the result, if not the expressed intention, of the voucher campaign has been to use public funds to support religious schools. Whether or not this has been a good thing, or even constitutional, it has not significantly changed the distribution between public and private schools nor improved educational opportunities for Milwaukee's Black students.[**]

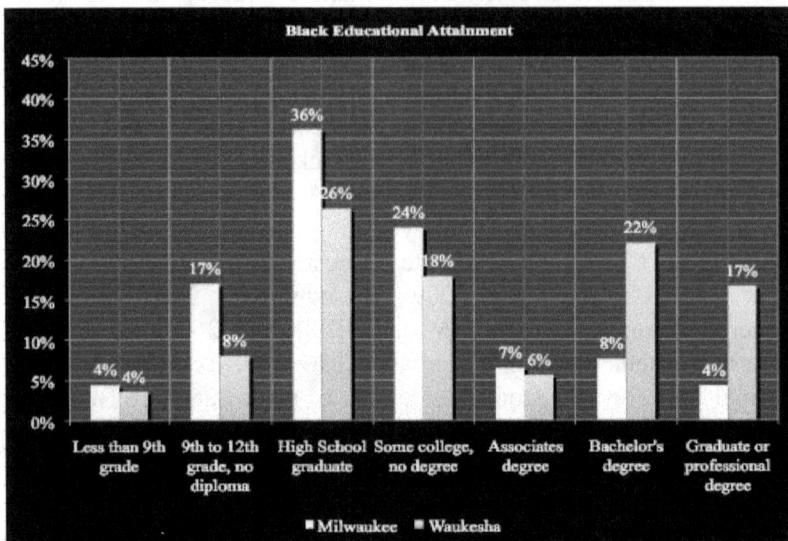

Education is the gateway to economic mobility. In Milwaukee that gateway is very narrow for Black families, whose children attend schools that by and large do not teach Black children to read. Most Black boys in Milwaukee do not graduate from high school and of those Black children who do so, few go on to college and fewer yet graduate.[29] School reform is a lengthy and complicated process, but it should not require extraordinary levels of effort and good will, as a first step, to bring educational outcomes for Black students in Milwaukee to the national average for Black students: to go from 7% at or above Proficient in reading at grade 8 to 16%. That would imply a doubling of the high school graduation rate as well, to something at or reasonably above 60%. It should be possible to go much further than that. Milwaukee is typical of "donut" school districts: crossing the district boundary to the nearest suburban

---

[**] According to NAEP Wisconsin's charter and non-charter schools provide nearly identical grade 8 reading outcomes.

districts vastly improves educational opportunities. Based on educational attainment figures there and national results for Black children whose parents have graduated from college, we can estimate that students in the neighboring Waukesha County schools achieve Proficient or above scores on grade 8 NAEP reading 30% of the time, four times the rate in Milwaukee's schools and twice the national average. Literacy rates at this level in Milwaukee's middle school would make the failure to graduate from high school uncommon, college attendance and graduation common. Just like in America.

The next logical question is why is it that the Milwaukee schools offer fewer educational opportunities to their Black students than other urban districts and than those of schools in the surrounding suburban schools districts? Miner, citing research by Michael Barndt and Joel McNally, has found that "'As the percentage of students of color has risen in the Milwaukee Public Schools, funding per pupil has plummeted compared to funding in overwhelmingly white suburban districts' . . .

In 1981, when the white and African American populations in Milwaukee were roughly equal, Milwaukee's 'shared costs per pupil' were only $127 below the suburban average. As the percentage of white students dropped in the Milwaukee Public Schools, the spending gap widened. By the 1998-99 school year, when whites were only 20 percent of the district's enrollment, the Milwaukee Public Schools had $1,254 per student less than the suburban average, based on "shared costs."[30]

Unlike the Milwaukee schools, the suburban Waukesha district, for example, has virtually no attrition of either Black or White students between grades 9 and 12. It may well be that higher teacher salaries lead to better educational outcomes. Otherwise, why are residents of Waukesha willing to fund teacher salaries at that level? The usual argument against this is that money does not matter. The refutation of this argument can be found any day in the business media reports of corporate executive salaries.

The Milwaukee education system is one institution that limits economic opportunities for African Americans. The criminal justice system is another.

The Hammer of Caste: The Criminal Justice System

Wisconsin's incarceration rate for its Black residents, 4,000 per 100,000, is the highest in the nation, perhaps in the world. There are currently 22,500 adults in Wisconsin's state prisons, 9,500 of whom are Black.[31] Given that the Black population of the state is just 7% of the White population, the state incarcerates Black residents at more than six times the rate at which it incarcerates White residents. As all but 6% of the state's prisoners are male, we can then calculate that about 9% of the state's male Black population between the ages of 18 and 64 is incarcerated in state prisons. It is not unlikely that twice that percentage will be incarcerated at some point during their adult lives and that on any given day nearly one-third of the adult male Black population of Milwaukee will be incarcerated, on parole or on probation. This has severely negative implications for their incomes and those of their families, as well as for the educations and life courses of their children.

How has this come about?

University of Wisconsin-Milwaukee researchers John Pawasarat and Lois M. Quinn have found that in 2013 "The prison population in Wisconsin has more than tripled since 1990,

> fueled by increased government funding for drug enforcement (rather than treatment) and prison construction, three-strike rules, mandatory minimum sentence laws, truth-in-sentencing replacing judicial discretion in setting punishments, concentrated policing in minority communities, and state incarceration for minor probation and supervision violations. Particularly impacted were African American males . . .[32]

Counting those in local jails, in addition to those in state prisons, thirteen percent of working age Wisconsin African American men were incarcerated, ten times the state and national rates for Whites. Pawasarat and Quinn further found that "From 1990 to 2011 Wisconsin incarcerated 26,222 African American men from Milwaukee County in state correctional facilities. As of January 2012, 20,591 men had been released back into the community and 5,631 were still imprisoned." Forty percent of those incarcerations were for drug offenses.[33] As a result, in Milwaukee County, "Over half of African American men in their 30s and half of men in their early 40s have been incarcerated in state correctional facilities."[34] Forty-one percent of African American men in the county between the ages of 20 and 54 are now or have been incarcerated in state correctional facilities.[35] Others are in or have passed through federal prisons and local jails.

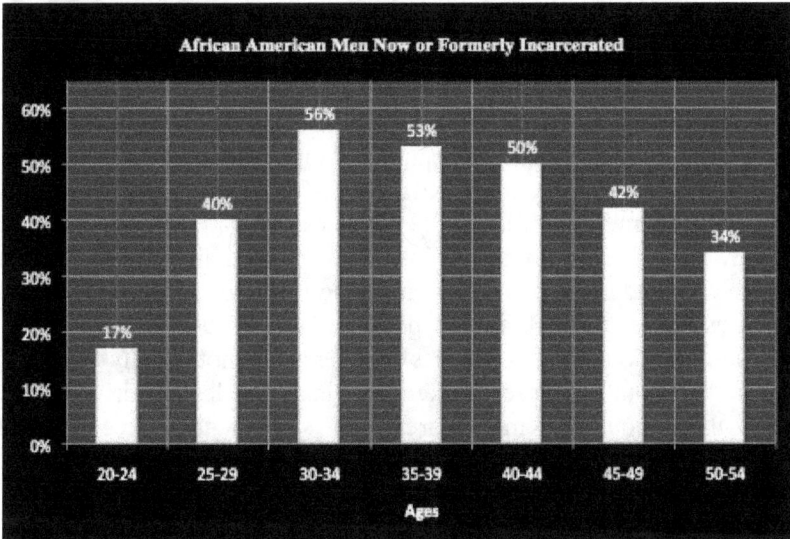

Two-thirds of Milwaukee County's incarcerated African American men come from—and ultimately return to—just six Milwaukee zip codes, among the poorest neighborhoods in the county.[36] In zip code 53206, highlighted by Pawasarat and Quinn, where nearly all the residents are Black, there is a notable gender imbalance: 55% of the residents are female, 45% are male. Between ages 25 and 50, in particular, women greatly outnumber men, as many of latter, presumably, are incarcerated. Three times as many family households in this zip code are headed by women as are headed by men. Just 38 of the 544 women who gave birth in 2011 in that neighborhood were married. The unemployment rate in the zip code is 28%. Median household income is $22,602, less than half the state average of $50,395 and only slightly higher than that of Greece. Half the residents have incomes below 50% of the poverty level. Educational attainment in the neighborhood is far below state averages. Nearly half of the neighborhood's adults have not attained a high school diploma, less than 30% have a high school diploma (or equivalent), 18% have some college or an Associate's degree, 3.5% have a Bachelor's degree and only 1% have Master's degrees (usually essential for teaching and administrative careers). Other hypersegregated Milwaukee neighborhoods have similar profiles.

Pawasarat and Quinn place a great emphasis on the importance of driver's licenses as a factor in this situation. The postwar relocation of employment opportunities to the suburbs with few public transportation facilities made it necessary for workers to drive private automobiles to work.[††] As a consequence, even in zip code 53206, three-quarters of those employed either drive alone or carpool to work. And yet in January, 2012 only 10% of the 26,000 formerly incarcerated men in Milwaukee as a whole had a valid driver's license without recent suspensions or revocations and a similar sized group who had not been incarcerated also were without valid driver's licenses. Given a working age population of 67,000 Black men in Milwaukee County, this implies that 75% cannot legally drive to work. "Without a license, workers are unable to legally drive to job sites throughout the metro area and subject to police arrests, particularly when driving through suburban communities."[37] The lack of a driver's license can lead to arrests, fines, and ultimately incarceration as well as unemployment. Fines for drivers license offenses mount up, warrants for unpaid fines lead to more fines, work is missed and jobs are lost.

Milwaukee's incarceration rates for Black males are the highest in the nation, multiples of others. Some significant amount of this is from police policies in regard to driver's licenses. Others, more common, are the result of police and prosecutor's racially-focused policies and practices concerning drug use and sales: what Michelle Alexander calls the late-twentieth-century substitute for Jim Crow vagrancy laws. Authorities in Milwaukee, as elsewhere, assert that policing follows crime: there are more arrests in Black areas than in White areas because there is more crime in Black areas. Of course, one could reverse that reasoning: there is more crime (that is, *reported* crime) in Black areas because there are more police there, looking to make arrests. Which argument is valid?

As a case in point, the U. S. Department of Health and Human Services National Survey on Drug Use and Health found that for

---

[††] The absence of regional public transportation in the Milwaukee area is not accidental. See, for example:
www.salon.com/2011/03/29/most_segregated_cities/slide?show/10

2012, among full-time college students aged 18 to 22, the rate of current illicit drug use was only slightly lower for White than for Black students: 23% for White, 26% for Black.[38] There are about 60,000 college students in Milwaukee, the great majority of whom are White. Based on the data cited above, we can estimate that 15,000 of these are illicit drug users. If we assume that, say, 10% of these sell drugs to the others, then there are currently something like 1,500 White, middle class, drug dealers on Milwaukee college campuses. It is, then, easy to identify some of the centers of criminal activity in Milwaukee: the University of Wisconsin-Milwaukee, with perhaps 7,500 illicit drug users and 750 dealers; Marquette University, with perhaps 4,000 illicit drug users and 400 dealers, and so forth.

It is unnecessary to belabor the point. The Milwaukee police arrest Black men nearly wherever they are found, often for trivial drug offenses. They do not show equivalent zeal in arresting White college students (or their middle class parents, or their professors). The result of inequitable drug and driver's license arrests is that in Milwaukee County in 2010 there were approximately twice as many descendants of enslaved Africans as Whites in Milwaukee County's correctional facilities both for adults and juveniles: 2,857 adults and 207 juveniles, as compared to 1,453 White American adults and 51 juveniles, even though the White population is twice that of the Black population. (These are highly conservative estimates, including only those incarcerated within the county limits.)

The rate of incarcerations of Black men from Milwaukee leads to an inversion of the intergenerational transfer of cultural and economic capital otherwise typical of the United States and other developed countries. The Bureau of Justice Statistics estimates that in 2007, for example, 53% of those incarcerated in the U.S. had minor children. If the Milwaukee situation follows that pattern, a minimum of 6,800 Milwaukee African American school children, 15%, have an imprisoned parent. But that is a minimum: the number of Milwaukee school children who have a parent who has been imprisoned could be as high as 27,280 (out of 44,000).[‡‡] Thus nearly

---

‡‡ According to the National Research Council 62% of Black children whose parents had not completed high school experience parental imprisonment by age 17.

every Black school child in Milwaukee either has a parent who is or has been in prison or has a friend or relative whose parent is or has been in prison. This in turn lowers household and community incomes and may be one explanation for the extreme poverty in Milwaukee's Black ghetto. It is more than sufficient to result in a culture where time in prison is an expected occurrence.

If we wish to present this situation even more starkly, Milwaukee can be compared with that usual exemplar of American segregation and poverty: Mississippi. As in Milwaukee, forty percent of Black families with children in Mississippi have incomes below the poverty line. The median household income of Black families in Mississippi is $24,609, comparable to that in Milwaukee. If an average Black family moved from Milwaukee to Mississippi, there would likely be no change in their income. Given that the cost of living in Mississippi is lower than in Milwaukee, they would probably be slightly better off. Mississippi is usually ranked as last or next to last in the quality of education it provides for its children. And yet the percentage of male Black students reading at the Below Basic level on NAEP in Mississippi is four points lower (that is, better) than that in Wisconsin. If an average Black family moved from Milwaukee to Mississippi, their children would probably have a slightly better chance of learning to read by the time they left school.

The graduation rate for male Black students in Mississippi is five percentage points higher than that for male Black students in Wisconsin. If an average Black family moved from Milwaukee to Mississippi, their children would be more likely to graduate from high school than if they had stayed up North in Wisconsin. Mississippi has a higher incarceration rate for White people than does Wisconsin: 503 compared to 415 per 100,000. Wisconsin's 2010 incarceration rate for Black people, as we have seen, is 4,042 per 100,000, ten times the rate at which it imprisons White people.[39] Mississippi's incarceration rate for Black people is 1,742, "only" about four times the rate at which it imprisons Black people.

Would it be better for a Black family to live in Milwaukee or Mississippi? In Mississippi they would be better off, or about the same, on average, financially than in Milwaukee. In Mississippi the children of the family would have a better chance of learning to read. In Mississippi the children of the family would have a better chance of graduating from high school. In Mississippi the young men of the family would be less than half as likely to spend time in prison. One could argue, insofar as Milwaukee was a destination, that the Great Migration was a mistake.

Modeling a More Equitable Milwaukee

At this point we can construct a hypothetical, more equitable, Milwaukee. While in most of these case studies, that modeling is approximately equally divided between improvements in the public school system and ending disparate arrests, prosecutions and incarcerations, that is not the case for Milwaukee. There is no city in the United States with racial disparities in incarcerations anything like those of Milwaukee. As a matter of fact, even the incarceration rate for Black males in South Africa under apartheid was dramatically lower than that of Milwaukee: "only" 831 per 100,000 as opposed to Milwaukee's 4,400 per hundred thousand.[40] Until its current policies and practices are changed the Milwaukee criminal justice system will continue to function more efficiently than that of apartheid South Africa in enforcing the rigidities of caste for those African Americans in its power.

The steps to be taken are not complicated. First, in Milwaukee as elsewhere, drug laws could be equally enforced throughout the county, with arrests brought into line with drug usage. This would result either in a very large increase in arrests of White residents of the county, or a very large decline in arrests of Black residents. After that, Milwaukee could follow jurisdictions like New York City and exchange arrests for citations for possession of small amounts of marijuana. Paralleling this change, stops and subsequent arrests for DWB ("driving while Black"), should come to an end. Here as with drug offensives, this could be monitored by simply tracking racial disparities. If a disproportionate percentage of traffic stops are of Black residents of the county, a change in policy would be in order. (Pawasarat and Quinn also make the commonsense recommendation for improvements in, and subsidies for, driver education programs.) A third measure, perhaps slightly less obvious, would be to bring to an end the current system in Milwaukee and elsewhere of court debt peonage. If someone who has been arrested cannot pay the fine levied, or the bail demanded, either other measures should be taken to serve the same purpose (aside from incarceration) or a system such as a revolving fund with installment payments could be created.

These actions would begin to lower the incarceration rate for young adult Black men, increasing their chances of employment, and generally increasing incomes in Milwaukee's Black community.

Once Milwaukee's criminal justice system ceases to be vastly inequitable, the next quantitative improvement would come from improving the school system. The path to improving school systems like Milwaukee's is also fairly straight-forward. First, children of parents who are not well-educated and who have incomes at or below the poverty level are to be provided with the type of pre-school educations routinely available to the children of prosperous, highly educated parents. This would include high-quality full-day pre-kindergarten[41] and full-day kindergarten preparing them for the routines of schooling and providing the basis for literacy. Their subsequent elementary and secondary education would include academic after-school and summer-school programs and challenging curricula. Their teachers would have continuing professional development, both for curriculum and teaching methods. School facilities would be comparable to those in the suburbs, school discipline would support, rather than terminate, academic achievement.

If the Milwaukee school system were as good as the school systems of the nearby suburban counties, college attendance rates would rise in parallel with high school graduation rates, as would college graduation rates and the numbers of Black graduate students. Projecting incomes for Milwaukee's Black community based on current educational attainment for the White community, we would find a significant increase, propelled, for the most part, by the superior incomes of college graduates (even when accounting for the lower incomes paid to Black workers at each educational level). When these things were done, the barriers of caste would be broken and Black residents of Milwaukee would begin to have the opportunities desired by all Americans.

These changes could be begun by the mayor, chief of police, district attorney and superintendent of schools any day they decide to do so.

Chapter Five: Notes

---

[1] Brown University. US2010.
www.s4.brown.edu/us2010/segregation2010/city.aspx?cityid=55530
00

[2] Statistical data is from the Bureau of the Census unless otherwise noted.

[3] http://www.nytimes.com/interactive/2012/01/15/business/one-percent-map.html?ref=economy. Nationally, 28,325,000 out of 116,000,000 households have incomes under $25,000 (24%). 5,062,000 (37%) out of 13,600,000 Black households. 18% under $25,000 Black while Black households are 12% of total. 23,263,000 non-Black households under $25,000 out of 102,400,000: 23%

[4] Social Science Research Council. Measure of America, 2014. http://www.measureofamerica.org/

[5] http://www.bls.gov/news.release/pdf/wkyeng.pdf, April 17, 2014. "Some college" not provided by BLS, estimated as mid-point between high school diploma and BA.

[6] Comparing the Census's 2012 median incomes for male workers gives a similar result: the White median income is 29% higher than the Black.

[7] Miner, Barbara J. Lessons from the Heartland: A Turbulent Half-Century of Public Education in an Iconic American City. New York: The New Press, 2013, p. 111.

[8] Oliver, Melvin L. and Thomas M. Shapiro. Black Wealth/White Wealth: A New Perspective on Racial Inequality. Tenth-Anniversary Edition. New York: Routledge, 2006, p. 5.

[9] U.S. Census Bureau, Survey of Income and Program Participation, 2008 Panel, Wave 10; Internet Release Date: 3/21/2013, Updated: May 13, 2013. Estimates for income quintiles were updated after correcting for an inconsistency in how the cut-off points for income quintiles were set, Updated: July 12, 2013. Estimates for Type of Household by Age of Householder were updated to maintain consistency with prior year tabulations.

[10] Census reports 1990 Black median family income of $21,000, equivalent to $36,000 in 2010. U.S. Department of Commerce, Economics and Statistics Administration, Bureau of the Census. We The Americans: Blacks, September, 1993. http://www.census.gov/prod/cen1990/wepeople/we-1.pdf

[11] New York Times, July 22, 2013:
http://www.nytimes.com/2013/07/22/business/in-climbing-income-ladder-location-matters.html?pagewanted=all&_r=2&#map-search
[12] Sharkey, Patrick. Neighborhoods and the Black-White Mobility Gap. Philadelphia: The Pew Charitable Trusts, 2009, p. 9. http://www.pewstates.org/uploadedFiles/PCS_Assets/2009/PEW_NEIGHBORHOODS(1).pdf. Sharkey has now further reported on this research in his book Stuck in Place: Urban Neighborhoods and the End of Progress toward Racial Equity.
[13] Sharkey, p. 11. Chetty et al add: "we show that upward income mobility is significantly lower in areas with larger African-American populations. However, white individuals in areas with large African-American populations also have lower rates of upward mobility, implying that racial shares matter at the community level" p. 3.
[14] Rank, Mark Robert. One Nation, Underprivileged: Why American Poverty Affects Us All. Oxford University Press, 2005, p. 74.
[15] Sharkey, p. 15.
http://www.pewstates.org/uploadedFiles/PCS_Assets/2009/PEW_NEIGHBORHOODS(1).pdf
[16] Massey, Douglas S. and Denton, Nancy A. American Apartheid: Segregation and the Making of the Underclass. Cambridge, MA: Harvard University Press, 1993, p. 144; 181.
[17] "A 1994 report by Wisconsin's nonpartisan Legislative Audit Bureau found that Milwaukee public school students transferring to the suburbs scored better than Milwaukee students who applied for but did not get into the program." Miner, p. 133.
[18] U.S. Department of Education Office for Civil Rights. Civil Rights Data Collection. Data Snapshot: School Discipline. Issue Brief No. 4 (March 2014).
[19] U.S. Department of Education Office for Civil Rights. Civil Rights Data Collection. Data Snapshot: School Discipline. Issue Brief No. 1 (March 2014).
[20] Lois Riley, quoted in Dougherty, Jack. More Than One Struggle: The Evolution of Black School Reform in Milwaukee. Chapel Hill: The University of North Carolina Press, 2004, p. 171.
[21] "37% of Black male 20 to 34-year-olds without high school diploma/GED were incarcerated in 2008." The Pew Charitable

Trusts, 2010. Collateral Costs: Incarceration's Effect on Economic Mobility. Washington, DC: The Pew Charitable Trusts.

[22] MPS Annual Report, December 2013.

[23] http://www.act.org/solutions/college-career-readiness/compare-act-sat/

[24] IPEDS.

[25] IPEDS.

[26] Miner, p. 160.

[27] Miner, p. 156.

[28] Miner, p. 215.

[29] As there is only the slightest of chances that a Black student in Milwaukee schools will graduate from high school, then gain admission to a four-year college and graduate from that, the already low percentage of adult Black residents of Milwaukee reporting to the Census that they have a Bachelor's degree or above clearly includes many who went to school elsewhere.

[30] Miner, pp. 146-7. Shared costs do not include state and federal special education and English language learner funds. Citing Michael Barndt and Joel McNally, "The Return to Separate and Unequal," Rethinking Schools report, Spring 2001.

[31] Wisconsin State Department of Corrections, Profile of Inmates in Prison on December 31, 2013, June 2014.

[32] Pawasarat, John and Lois M. Quinn, Wisconsin's Mass Incarceration of African American Males: Workforce Challenges for 2013. Employment and Training Institute University of Wisconsin-Milwaukee, 2013, p. 1. www4.uwm.edu/eti/2013/BlackImprisonment.pdf

[33] Pawasarat and Quinn, p. 3; 19.

[34] Pawasarat and Quinn, p. 2.

[35] Chart based on Pawasarat and Quinn, p. 12.

[36] Pawasarat and Quinn, p. 4.

[37] Pawasarat and Quinn.

[38] Substance Abuse and Mental Health Services Administration, Results from the 2012 National Survey on Drug Use and Health: Summary of National Findings, NSDUH Series H-46, HHS Publication No. (SMA) 13-4795. Rockville, MD: Substance Abuse and Mental Health Services Administration, 2013.

http://www.samhsa.gov/data/nsduh/2012summnatfinddettables/natio
nalfindings/nsduhresults2012.htm#ch2.9
[39] http://www.prisonpolicy.org/profiles/WI.html
[40] Mauer, Marc. Americans Behind Bars: The International Use of
Incarceration, 1992-93.
[41] Reynolds, Arthur J. et al. Association of a Full-Day vs Part-Day
Preschool Intervention With School Readiness, Attendance, and
Parent Involvement *JAMA.* 2014;312(20):2126-2134.

Chapter Six: New Orleans

New Orleans is a relatively small American city that sometimes seems not to be part of the United States at all. Or, rather, it is two small cities: one White and prosperous; the other Black and poor. Until Hurricane Katrina, New Orleans was glamorized with images of jazz and dissipation. After Katrina, as if a curtain had been ripped away, it was revealed as a particularly extreme example of the continuing subjugation of the descendants of enslaved Africans. These matters are presented in a most literal manner in New Orleans. Many of the White residents live on higher ground (for example in the Garden District) than the residents of the predominately Black neighborhoods of the city, such as the Lower Ninth Ward. This became a crucial difference after the hurricane, when the ill-constructed levees broke, as the authorities knew that they would, and the lowest-lying parts of the city were flooded 20 feet deep, many of their inhabitants drowned, others driven out of the city.[1] Reconstruction, as well, was conduced on racial lines, abetted by and abetting private profit, almost as if the ill-constructed levees, the botched emergency measures, and reconstruction were intended to alter the demography of the city.[2]

The population of New Orleans before the hurricane was close to 500,000, two-thirds of whom were Black. Post-Katrina there are fewer than 350,000 residents. Since the hurricane there has been considerable movement of groups into and out of the city. Half of the White residents in New Orleans in 2010 did not live there before Hurricane Katrina struck the area in 2005.[3] Just 30% of the Black population has moved there since the storm. The net White population declined 17% after the storm; the Black population decline of 37% amounted to 119,000 people, more than the current White population of the city.[4] The greatest change in the White population was a decline in the number of those over 65 years of age. On the other hand, there were increases in the number of White young adults, ages 20 to 30 and of White residents 55 to 64. The largest declines in the Black population were of those under 19 and from 30 to 49, but the decline in the Black population affected every age group except 55 to 64 and in each case was greater than that for the White population except for those 70 years of age and over.

New Orleans is a highly segregated city, with an Index of Dissimilarity of 65.5 (60 is considered very high), which can be interpreted to mean that two-thirds of the Black population would have to move in order for the city's neighborhoods to be integrated. As things now stand, there are fourteen census tracts where the entire population is Black.[5] The median age of the White population is 38 years. Families with children under 18 years of age make up 14.5% of this population. Just 2.5% of White households are defined by the Census as those of women raising their own children without a husband.[6] There are 207,000 people in post-Katrina Black New Orleans, with a median age of 33 years, much lower than that of the White population. Twenty-eight percent of this population live in families with children under 18 years of age, nearly double that of the White population. Seventeen percent of Black New Orleans families are those in which a woman is raising her own children without a husband, nearly seven times the figure for White residents of the city.

The population age-distribution in the city varies markedly by race. Compared to the Black population, there is a very small percentage of young and school-age White children in the city and a high percentage of college age White young adults. The percentage of the oldest Black residents of New Orleans is half that of the percentage of the oldest White residents of the city: Black residents of New Orleans, especially men, die much younger than White residents of the city. White life expectancy is 76.2 years; Black life expectancy is 67.4 years. In one of the zip code areas that is 80% or more non-white, life expectancy is 54.5 years.[7] These disparities begin early. In Louisiana, 20% of all Black infants are born pre-term, compared with 12% of non-Hispanic White births. Twice as many of Black infants, 15%, as White infants (8%) have low birth-weight. Within the Black population there is considerable population variation by gender. In the 20-24 age cohort, there are 1,400 more Black women then men. There are 18% more Black women than Black men in the 30 to 34 age cohort. The difference in proportions rises steeply from age 60 until for the oldest African Americans it reaches 60%.

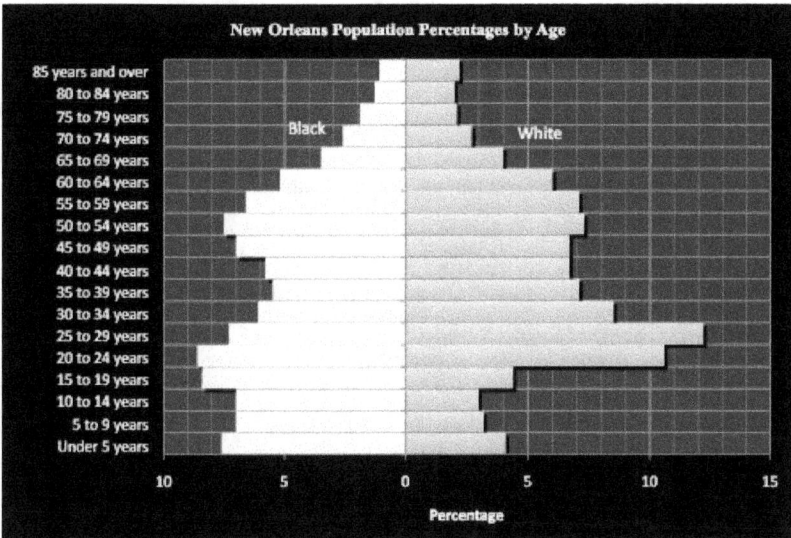

New Orleans Population Percentages by Age

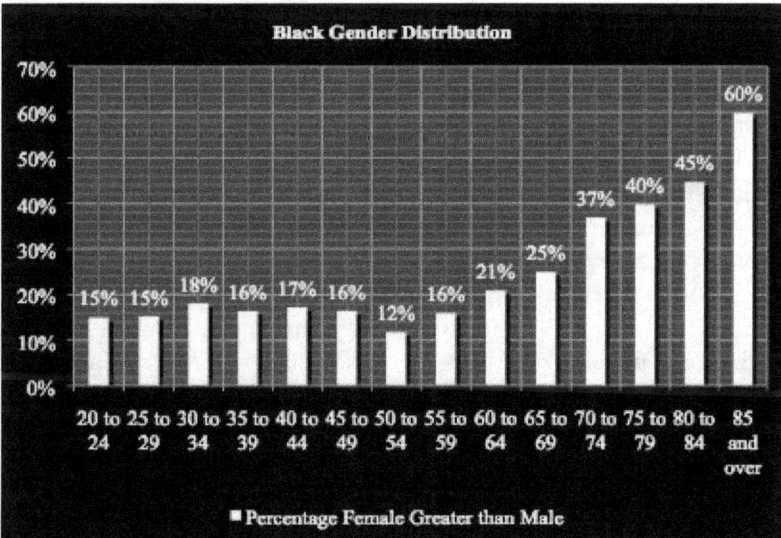

Black Gender Distribution

157

There are thousands of missing Black men in New Orleans. Some die violently. Some die from ill-health. Many, very many, are incarcerated.

Income

Racial income disparities in New Orleans are exceptionally extreme. Black per capita income in the city is $15,243; White per capita income in the city is nearly triple that: $43,022. The Black per capita income is lower than the national average ($18,257), while the White per capita income is much higher than the national White, non-Hispanic, average of $30,154. The percentage of Black families living on less than $10,000 a year (13%) is higher than the national average for Black families and more than four times that of White families in the city (3%). While a quarter of New Orleans White families have incomes over $150,000 a year, only 2% of Black family incomes reach that level. Fifteen percent of White families (3,154) have incomes over $200,000 per year (as compared to 6% nationally). The collective income of this top 15% of White families is probably in excess of $1 billion per year, a quarter of the city's White community's annual income of $4.3 billion and equal to nearly half of that of the Black community's aggregate income of $2.7 billion. Black family incomes in the highest income quintile would, if White, fall between the middle and fourth quintiles. Black family incomes in the fourth quintile are within the range of White family incomes in the second quintile. White family mean incomes in the lowest quintile are higher than mean Black family incomes in the third (middle) quintile of Black family incomes.

This extraordinary compression of Black incomes in New Orleans is a manifestation of the limited employment opportunities for African Americans in the city, where health and education employ a quarter of the working population and tourism is the next largest employer. Fifty-five percent of the New Orleans White civilian employed population are managers, business and professional people, 14% work in service occupations. In Black New Orleans, just 24% are managers, business and professional people and 28% work in service occupations. Black New Orleans serves White New Orleans.

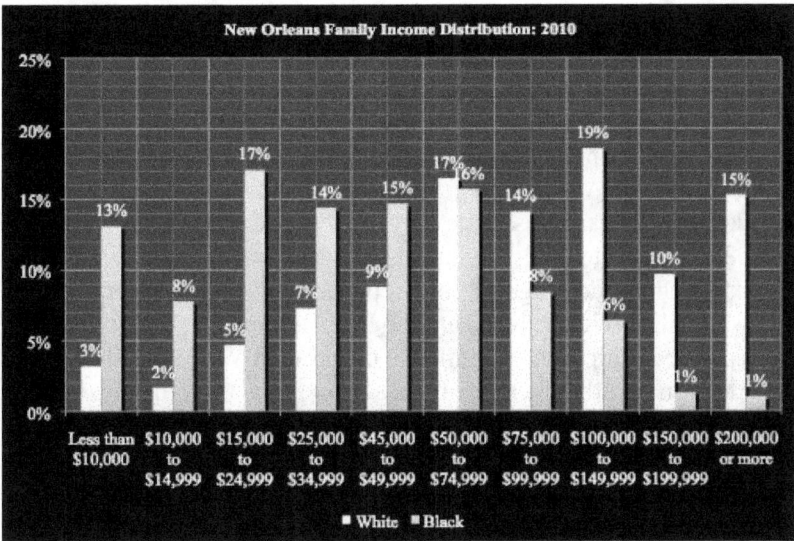

New Orleans Family Income Distribution: 2010

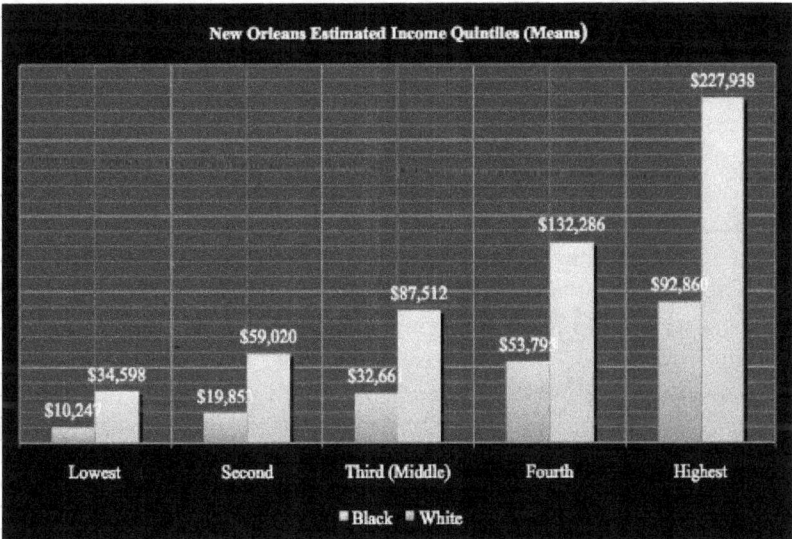

New Orleans Estimated Income Quintiles (Means)

The poverty rate for White people in New Orleans was 13.5% in 2010; the poverty rate for Black New Orleans people was more than twice that: 30.4%. (Both Black and White residents of New Orleans have slightly higher poverty rates than each group's national average.) Seven percent of White residents of New Orleans receive Food Stamp/SNAP benefits; four times that proportion, 28%, of Black New Orleans residents rely on Food Stamp/SNAP benefits. Just 8% of White children under age 18 live in poverty; 46% of Black children under age 18 live in poverty. More than half, 53%, of Black families with children and no husband present, live in poverty, as compared with 23% of similarly constituted White families in the city. Nationally, the averages for the groups are 43% for those Black families, 33% for those White families. In other words, while White women raising their children in New Orleans are much less likely to be impoverished than the national average, Black women in the city struggling to raise children without a husband present are much more likely to be in poverty than Black women in a similar situation nationally.[8]

Wealth

Wealth, financial assets and the "real" property of housing, is crucial to the well-being of people living in a non-socialist economy. Wealth is a cushion against adversity (such as a hurricane or unemployment) and is crucial for intergenerational economic mobility. As with incomes, there are stark disparities in wealth between the Black and White communities in New Orleans. More than one-third, 37%, of White households in New Orleans had interest, dividends, or net rental income in 2010, as compared to 7% of Black households. Nationally, the mean net worth of White households, excluding equity in their home) was $336,435 in 2011, compared to $49,119 for Black households.[9] The amounts for New Orleans are likely higher for White and lower for Black households. As there are 55,636 White households in the city, net worth of the households of the White community in New Orleans is at least $7 billion, as compared to $270 million for the 78,443 Black households.

The largest asset of most American families is an owner-occupied house. Vincanne Adams has documented the catastrophic effects of Katrina and the privatized "recovery" actions on Black home ownership in the city.[10] Nationally, the mean equity in their own home is $98,734 for White households, $35,258 for Black households. Average equity in the South is 87% of those figures: $86,376 and $30,845. In New Orleans there are 26,500 White owner-occupied units, and 28,300 Black owner-occupied units. Applying the regional mean equity factors, it would appear that the combined equity in housing for the New Orleans White community would be at least $2 billion, that for the Black community not more than $875 million.

We can then estimate that the total wealth of White New Orleans, approximately $9 billion dollars, is about 8 times that of the city's significantly larger Black community. To put this another way, the wealth of the average White household in New Orleans is more than 10 times larger than that of the average Black household. This is not a difference of class; it is a demarcation of caste.[11]

Mobility

As is the case nationally, in New Orleans Black and White children are raised in radically different environments. Most Black children grow up in highly segregated neighborhoods with high poverty rates, most White children grow up in very low poverty rate neighborhoods.[12] Researcher Patrick Sharkey found, perhaps unsurprisingly, that there are "extremely high rates of downward mobility among blacks raised in neighborhoods" with high rates of family poverty.[13] In New Orleans the Black distribution of family incomes is off-set from the White by two quintiles. That is, the mean Black family income of the richest 20% is approximately that of the average White family income of the middle 20% of White families, while the mean Black family income of the middle 20% is similar to that of the average of the lowest 20% of White incomes. The odds are two-to-one against a Black child in New Orleans doing much better in life than that child's parents.

New Orleans's Black community is a service caste where 60% of the children are born into the bottom national quintile in income, 80% in the bottom two. Two-thirds of New Orleans's Black Americans are at the poverty level in income with little wealth and little hope of improving their situation.

The Anvil of Caste: Education

Educational attainment is a crucial factor in socio-economic mobility or, alternatively, in the perpetuation of caste boundaries. Nearly a quarter of New Orleans Black adults do not have a high school diploma. The corresponding percentage for White residents is 6%. More than half, 56%, of adult White residents of the city have a Bachelor's degree or higher, as compared to 15% of Black residents. Levels of educational attainment are correlated with income, wealth, economic mobility and probability of incarceration. The correlation between levels of educational attainment and wealth, for example, are clear and particularly marked at the extremes. Median net household wealth of those where the householders is without a high school diploma is under $10,000, three-quarters of that being home equity. The median net household wealth of those where the householder has a Bachelor's degree or above is nearly $150,000, with a much higher percentage contributed by financial assets. The comparative lack of educational attainment of the New Orleans Black community is a limiting factor for the economic condition of that community and, given the unusually high degree of educational attainment of the White community in the city, is significant for disparities between the African American and White communities in New Orleans.

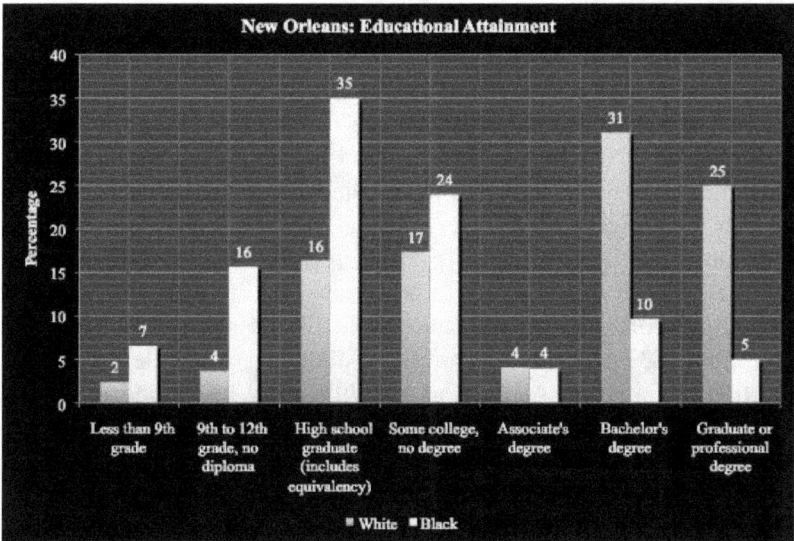

New Orleans: Educational Attainment

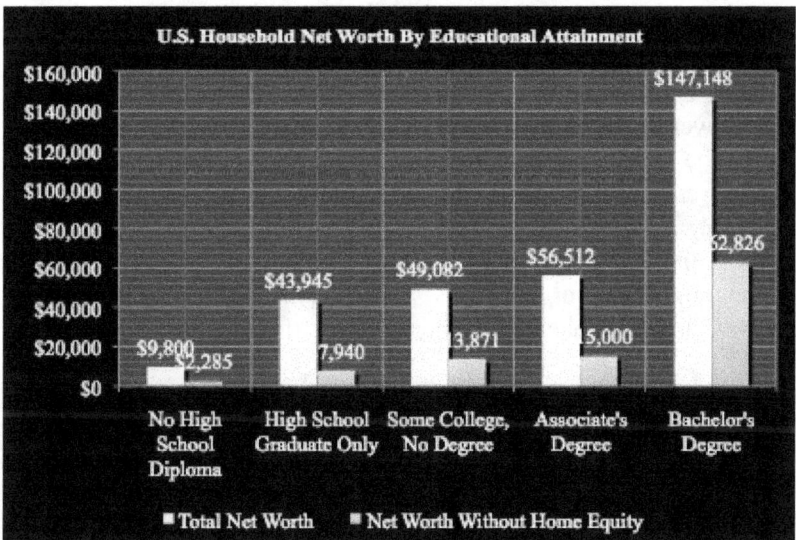

U.S. Household Net Worth By Educational Attainment

We have seen that the White population of New Orleans has a relatively small number of school-age children. As a consequence, the White school-age population in 2010 (ages 5 to 19 years) was 12,091, that of the Black community, 46,419. In the 2011-12 school year there were 43,166 children enrolled in Orleans Parish schools: 38,106 were Black, 2,577 were White, non-Hispanic. According to the Louisiana Department of Education there were 44,686 students enrolled in Orleans Parish public schools in 2013 and 20,039 students enrolled in private schools in the Parish.[14] It would seem, then, that 18% of New Orleans Black students are enrolled in private (including Catholic) schools, as are 79% of White students, which has left the public schools (including charters) 88% Black.[15] This situation is made all the more unusual by the provision of vouchers by the state, transferring funds to private schools, some of which are Catholic, many others of which are not recognized by the State's Department of Education.

The New Orleans public schools, like those of New York City, began as charity institutions for the poor, which in New Orleans meant, for the most part, the city's Black residents. Other children were sent to private schools among which those of the Roman Catholic Church were prominent. By the early twenty-first century the New Orleans public schools not only served a predominately African American student body, they employed large numbers of African American staff and teachers. After Hurricane Katrina the state government took the opportunity to introduce an experiment in which the majority of public schools were removed from the Orleans Parish School Board (OPSB) and placed under the supervision of a Recovery School District (RSD). Thousands of employees of the school district were fired, which undoubtedly had a significant economic effect on the city's African American residents.[*] Now "New Orleans is considered a portfolio district,

---

[*] In 1999 median household income for Black families in New Orleans ($21,408) was 54% of that for White families ($39,722). In 2010 median household income for Black families ($27,107) was just 47% of median household income for White families ($57,245). The increase for Black families ($5,500) was less than a third of that for White families ($17,000).

where the governing authority oversees a system of independent schools that operate under performance contracts. Charter schools, not directly run by the district, have autonomy to hire staff, allocate their budgets, and negotiate service contracts. OPSB and RSD act as the portfolio manager by closing low-performing schools and allowing the opening of new schools or the replication of successful schools.[16]

In addition, there is that controversial, but relatively minor, voucher program separately funded by the state.[†]

New Orleans is not a district for which there is National Assessment of Educational Progress (NAEP) data. However, NAEP does provide data for the state of Louisiana as a whole. In 2013 35% of White students in grade 8 in the state were Proficient or above in reading as were 12% of Black students (15% of female Black students and 9% of male Black students): nearly 90% of grade 8 Black students in Louisiana read below grade level. These numbers varied considerably by family income. While 25% of the state's White students who were eligible for the National Lunch Program (that is, their families were poorer than most) scored Proficient or above, 42% of White students from more prosperous families read at or above grade level. Among Black students, 10% of the lower income students scored at or above Proficient, but 24% of those from higher income families did so. In other words, the racial and income differentials are similar, within races, but less poor Black children only do as well as poorer White children.

The Louisiana Educational Assessment Program (LEAP) does provide some student achievement data for New Orleans. On the Spring 2014 LEAP Criterion-Referenced Test of English Language Arts at grade 8, results for the Orleans Parish district (enrolling 12,440 students), "without previously failing schools assigned to RSD" 11% were "Advanced" and 29% showed "Mastery." Results for the RSD schools, enrolling 30,100 students, were 2%

---

† The structure of public education in New Orleans is approaching the condition of the famously complicated Schleswig-Holstein Question in nineteenth-century European politics, of which, according to Lytton Strachey, the British statesman Lord Palmerston is reported to have said: "Only three men in Europe have ever understood it. One was Prince Albert, who is dead. The second was a German professor who became mad. I am the third and I have forgotten all about it."

"Advanced" and 11% showing "Mastery." We might estimate, for the two organizations combined, something on the order of 4% "Advanced" and 15% showing "Mastery," leaving 81% below grade level by the state's measure.[17]

In spite of the failure of the public schools in New Orleans to teach the overwhelming majority of students to read and write at grade level in grade 8, graduation rate estimates for the 2011-12 school year for all public schools in Orleans Parish together were 62% for Black males, 80% for Black females, 74% for White males and 104% for White females (showing some amount of inward transfers to the public schools of White females for the later high school years).[18] The Louisiana State Department of Education (which does not make data disaggregated by race, or gender within race publically available) reports that the Orleans Parish public schools graduated 1,137 students in 2011-12 and the Recovery School District graduated 1,134. Of those 2,271 graduates, the state reported that 1,306 (58%) enrolled in college the next semester, 438 (19%) in two-year colleges and 869 (38%) in four-year colleges.[19] Some of those are White, Hispanic, or Asian.

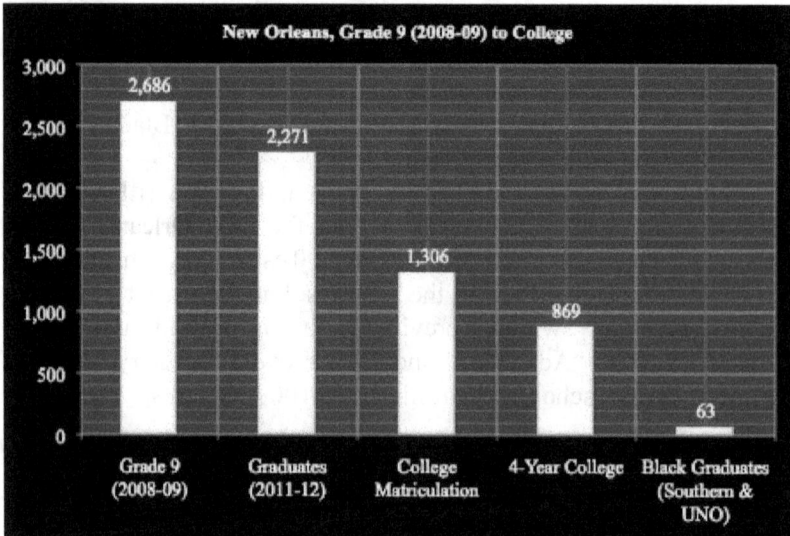

New Orleans, Grade 9 (2008-09) to College

There are many post-secondary institutions in the New Orleans area. Some, such as Tulane and Louisiana State University, have international catchment areas. We can look at two large schools with a more localized student body: Southern University at New Orleans and the University of New Orleans. Three-quarters of New Orleans high school graduates who enrolled in four-year colleges attended those two schools. Southern University at New Orleans in 2012 graduated 32 students within 150% of normal time, all of whom were Black, 10 of whom were men. The University of New Orleans graduated 328 students in 2012 within 150% of normal time, 31 of whom were Black, 6 of whom were African American men. The two institutions together graduated 360 students, of whom 63 were Black and 16 were men.

If the state's data on college attendance is accurate, it would appear that of the three-quarters of New Orleans high school graduates who enrolled in those four-year colleges, very few graduated within six years. This is consistent with the fact that 58% of Black New Orleans 25 years and over reported to the Census that they had gone no further in their educations than a high school diploma.

The Hammer of Caste: The Criminal Justice System

Cindy Chang, writing in *The Times-Picayune* in 2012, reported that "Louisiana is the world's prison capital. The state imprisons more of its people, per head, than any of its U.S. counterparts . . . Louisiana's incarceration rate is nearly five times Iran's, 13 times China's and 20 times Germany's . . .

Among black men from New Orleans, one in 14 is behind bars; one in seven is either in prison on parole or on probation . . . In Louisiana, a two-time car burglar can get 24 years without parole. A trio of drug convictions can be enough to land you at the Louisiana State Penitentiary at Angola for the rest of your life . . . About 5,000 black men from New Orleans are doing state prison time, compared with 400 white men from the city. Because police concentrate resources on high-crime areas, minor lawbreakers there are more likely to be stopped and frisked or caught up in a drug sweep then, say, an Uptown college student with a sideline marijuana business.[20]

An "Investigation of the New Orleans Police Department" of May 16, 2011 by the United States Department of Justice, Civil

Rights Division, had found that: "NOPD's failure to acknowledge the potential for stereotypes and bias to taint police work, on both an individual and an organizational level, and to take steps to prevent this, further cultivates an atmosphere in which discriminatory policing can occur unchecked . . .

> the ratio of arrest rates for both African-American males to white males, and African-American females to white females, was nearly 16 to 1. Although a significant disparity in arrest rates for this age group exists nationwide, it is not nearly as extreme as the disparity found in New Orleans . . . The level of disparity for youth in New Orleans is so severe and so divergent from nationally reported data that it cannot plausibly be attributed entirely to the underlying rates at which these youth commit crimes . . . NOPD use of force data also shows a troubling racial disparity that warrants a searching inquiry into whether racial bias influences the use of force at NOPD. Of the 27 instances between January 2009 and May 2010 in which NOPD officers intentionally discharged their firearms at people, all 27 of the subjects of this deadly force were African American.[21]

There are 26,000 Black male residents of New Orleans between ages 20 and 40. If we assume that about 60% of those graduated from high school, that leaves 10,400 who did not. This is the group, nationally, most likely to suffer incarceration "in their life course." One in seven of the 26,000 Black male residents of New Orleans between ages 20 and 40, who are at any one time incarcerated, on parole or on probation, would be about 3,700 men. As the average prison sentence in the U.S. is about five years, it would seem that over the twenty year span of that cohort, it is highly likely that *all* Black males in New Orleans who did not graduate from high school would at some point by age 40 have been incarcerated, on parole, on probation, with limited employment opportunities and greatly damaged social relations.

Modeling a More Equitable New Orleans

The task of modeling a more equitable New Orleans, a city where one's future is not determined by racist reactions to the color of one's skin, is unusually difficult because of the lack of transparency of education data. It is, for example, unclear how many of the high school diplomas issued and counted by the state are "LA Core 4 College and Career" diplomas or "Basic Core College and Career" diplomas, or just "Career" diplomas. A first step to improving education outcomes for the city's African Americans would be for the Louisiana State Department of Education to provide detailed data disaggregated by race, ethnicity and gender across all publically–funded schools in Orleans Parish.

In addition to this, because of the unusually high percentage of the area's students enrolled in private independent and religious schools, it would be good if similar data were collected from those entities. The voucher system might provide a means to that end if it was required that schools accepting vouchers provide appropriate information to the state. Until those things are done, all that can be said is the appropriate k-12 goals would include NAEP-equivalent scores indicating grade-level achievement for reading at grade 8 at 50% of all student sub-groups and "LA Core 4 College and Career" diplomas for the majority of students in each race, ethnic and gender subgroup. This would support a postsecondary goal of at least 50% of all New Orleans adults in each race, ethnic and gender subgroup attaining education to the level of Bachelor's degrees and above, as is now the case with White residents alone. That would more than triple the present educational attainment of New Orleans residents who are the descendants of enslaved Africans, bringing with it the concomitant advantages of income, wealth and socio-economic mobility.

If, for the sake of argument, we model the effects of improvements in the education of education in New Orleans for the Black community by setting educational attainment for Black adults ages 25 and over to the current distribution for the White community we find an increase of 23,000 with a Bachelor's degree and 21,643 with a graduate or professional degree and a decline of 17,000 in those without a high school diploma. Given current median earnings by educational attainment, this would result in an increase in total Black community income from $4.1 billion to $5.9 billion per year: 44%.[22] We can then make the same experiment with community wealth. If we set New Orleans Black educational attainment at the White percentages, we could anticipate an enormous increase in the total wealth of the Black community and of the city as a whole.

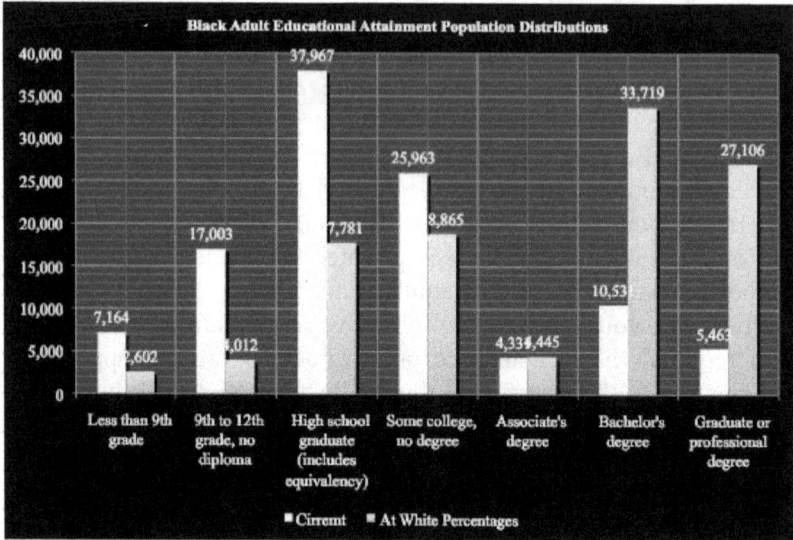

Black Adult Educational Attainment Population Distributions

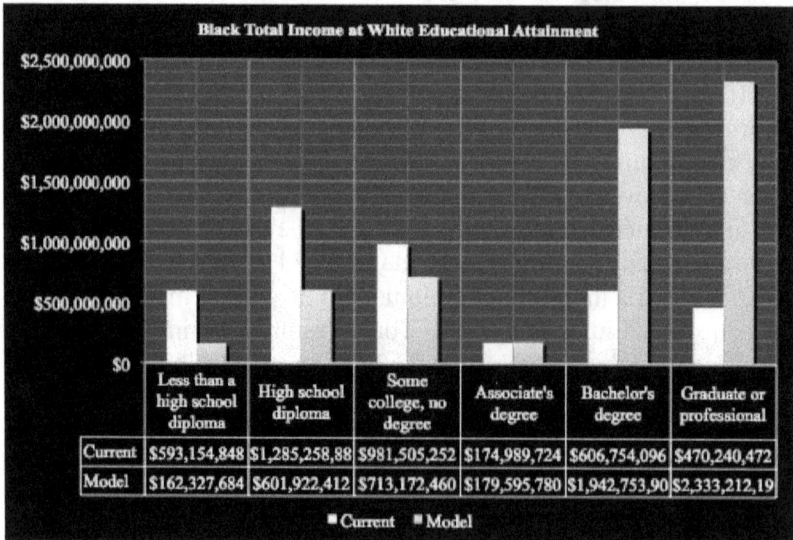

Black Total Income at White Educational Attainment

	Less than a high school diploma	High school diploma	Some college, no degree	Associate's degree	Bachelor's degree	Graduate or professional
Current	$593,154,848	$1,285,258,88	$981,505,252	$174,989,724	$606,754,096	$470,240,472
Model	$162,327,684	$601,922,412	$713,172,460	$179,595,780	$1,942,753,90	$2,333,212,19

■ Current ■ Model

All these factors—increased educational attainment and therefore increased incomes and increased wealth—would have positive effects on the educational achievement of the next generation, contributing to socio-economic mobility. As to reform of the New Orleans criminal justice system, little need be said beyond the statements in the U.S. Department of Justice report. The New Orleans police, prosecutors and judges must stop acting as if Black New Orleans were occupied enemy territory. The New Orleans Police Department, professionalized, operating without racial stereotyping and in accordance with normal rules and regulations of policing, would reduce inequities in contacts and arrests. The courts would eliminate inequities in prosecutions, incarcerations and sentences. In conjunction with improvements in the education system, the "missing" young adult male African Americans would cease to be missing, community incomes and wealth would increase, family life would become more stable, caste boundaries would disappear.

The mayor, chief of police, district attorney and chief state school officer could begin implementing these changes any day they decide to do so.

Chapter Six: Notes

---

[1] http://new.dhh.louisiana.gov/assets/docs/katrina/deceasedreports/
KatrinaDeaths_082008.pdf
[2] Adams, Vincanne. Markets of Sorrow, Labors of Faith: New
Orleans in the Wake of Katrina. Durham & London: Duke
University Press, 2013. Adams uses the term "philanthrocapitalism."
[3] Kaiser Family Foundation. New Orleans Five Years After the
Storm. 2010.
http://kaiserfamilyfoundation.files.wordpress.com/2013/02/8089.pdf
[4] Chart adapted from
http://censusviewer.com/city/LA/New%20Orleans
[5] Joint Center or Political and Economic Studies Orleans Parish Place
Matters Team. Place Matters for Health in Orleans Parish: Ensuring
Opportunities for Good Health for All, June 2012, p. 6.
[6] Data from U.S. Census, American Community Survey.
[7] Joint Center or Political and Economic Studies Orleans Parish Place
Matters Team, p. 21.
[8] U.S. Census, Selected Economic Characteristics, 2006-2010
American Community Survey Selected Population Tables, DP03.
[9] U.S. Census Bureau, Survey of Income and Program Participation,
2008 Panel, Wave 10, updated, Table 1. Median Value of Assets for
Households, by Type of Asset Owned and Selected Characteristics:
2011.
[10] Adams, 2013.
[11] It is likely that the wealth inequalities in New Orleans are far
greater than these estimates, due to the unusually high number of
White households in the highest income quintile, which, nationally,
holds a disproportionate share of wealth.
[12] Sharkey, Patrick. Neighborhoods and the Black-White Mobility
Gap. Philadelphia: The Pew Charitable Trusts, 2009, p. 9.
http://www.pewstates.org/uploadedFiles/PCS_Assets/2009/PEW_
NEIGHBORHOODS(1).pdf. Sharkey has now further reported on
this research in his book *Stuck in Place: Urban Neighborhoods and
the End of Progress toward Racial Equity.*
[13] Sharkey, p. 11. Chetty et al add: "we show that upward income
mobility is significantly lower in areas with larger African-American
populations. However, white individuals in areas with large African-

American populations also have lower rates of upward mobility, implying that racial shares matter at the community level" p. 3.

[14] Drellinger, Danielle. "Private school enrollment falls 5% in Louisiana, even more in New Orleans, Baton Rouge areas." The Times-Picayune, February 13, 2014. http://www.nola.com/education/index.ssf/2014/02/private_school_en rollment_fall.html

[15] National Center for Education Statistics (NCES).

[16] Sims, Patrick and Vaughan, Debra. "The State of Public Education in New Orleans: 2014 Report." New Orleans: The Cowen Institute for Public Education Initiatives at Tulane University, 2014, p. 2. http://www.speno2014.com/wp-content/uploads/2014/08/SPENO-HQ.pdf

[17] Sims and Vaughan, p. 21 gives the total Advanced and Mastery as 19%. http://www.speno2014.com/wpcontent/uploads/2014/08/SPENO-HQ.pdf

[18] U.S. Department of Education, Office for Civil Rights.

[19] Louisiana State Department of Education, College Going/Enrollment Data for 2011-2012 High School Graduates. http://educatenow.net/wp-content/uploads/2014/05/2011_2012CollegeEnrollmentPersistence Data_NO_only.pdf

[20] Chang, Cindy. "Louisiana is the world's prison capital." The Times-Picayune, May 13, 2012. http://www.nola.com/crime/index.ssf/2012/05/louisiana_is_the_worl ds_prison.html

[21] http://www.justice.gov/crt/about/spl/nopd_report.pdf, (pages ix-x).

[22] Earnings and unemployment rates by educational attainment, 2013. Bureau of Labor Statistics. http://www.bls.gov/emp/ep_chart_001.htm.

Chapter Seven: New York City

It could be said that the future of Black America is being forged in New York City. It is, and has been for a century or more, a center of African American success. It is a center of achievement for African Americans, financially and culturally. There are Black CEOs, actors, musicians, authors and scientists resident in the city. Harlem, famous for its Renaissance, is a by-word for Black cultural achievement. But Harlem, like other African American New York neighborhoods, is also a community of concentrated poverty, of trash-strewn streets and police helicopters just above the roof-tops, of drug addiction and failing schools. That poverty, that deprivation, the caste status of New York's African Americans, are the consequences of the institutional racism represented and applied by New York City's educational and criminal justice systems.

The city seems wonderfully diverse and integrated during the working day and into the evenings. At night, however, it is among the most segregated of American cities with a Black/White Index of Dissimilarity of an astonishing 81.4—nearly all Black residents of the city would have to move into new neighborhoods to balance its housing patterns.[1] African Americans are over 50% of the residents in Harlem, the Bronx and central Brooklyn, while large areas of the city have levels of Black residency below 10%. The city is also segregated in terms of incomes, with considerable overlap between its highly segregated Black neighborhoods and high poverty areas. There are median household incomes as low as $18,000 per year in Harlem and $15,000 per year in central Brooklyn. This compares with $240,000 in the Upper East Side of Manhattan, $105,000 in the Riverdale section of the Bronx and $170,000 in the Brooklyn Heights neighborhoods, which have relatively few African American residents.[2]

As the cost of living in New York City has risen during the New Gilded Age, the Black population has declined. It is not the impoverished African American residents who have left the city—they remain in their traditional enclaves, which, if anything, have expanded. It is the higher- (or formerly higher-) income Black New

Yorkers who have left for the suburbs. According to Raisa Bahchieva and her associates,

> The new trend towards the waning of the black population is evident in the contraction of areas dominated by Black/upper-middle-income/families and the moderate expansion of Black/low-income/families and singles areas, some of which occurred at the expense of wealthier black tracts becoming poor at the borders with the poor black areas . . . These results paint a picture of a hollowing out of the black middle class in New York City.[3]

One reason for this "hollowing out" was the foreclosure crisis. In a classic cycle, housing prices in New York City rose in the early 2000s, vastly increasing the price of housing throughout the city, including the traditional Black middle class neighborhoods. These neighborhoods were then targeted by banks and others offering complicated mortgages "to enable" owners to profit from increasing valuations. When the complications (e.g., steeply higher monthly payments) set in, the houses went into foreclosure.

Jerilyn Perine and her associates have conducted research which "highlights the damage of the recent foreclosure crisis on NYC homeowners.

> Southeast Queens [for example] shows high numbers of [legal] filings in neighborhoods, like Queens Village, with high homeownership rates that had transitioned from the [p]redominantly black/upper-middle income/families population cluster in 2000 to [m]ajority black/low-income/families & singles in 2010. This underscores the loss of wealth that many foreclosed households underwent in the past decade.[4]

The highly segregated neighborhoods of Woodlawn in the Bronx, Hollis and Jamaica in Queens and East Flatbush in Brooklyn, which have a majority of residents who are African American with low incomes, are contiguous with, and impinge on, neighborhoods that are equally segregated, but inhabited by predominately Black upper and middle income families. This is quite different from the situation of members of other racial and ethnic groups in the city, for whom where they live is by and large limited only by what individual families can afford.

Nor is the physical health of Black New York good. Overall, the death rate for Black residents of the City is nearly 40% higher than

175

that of White New Yorkers and the disparity is wider yet for Black residents of the city's poorest neighborhoods.[5] According to the New York City Department of Health and Mental Hygiene, "death rates are almost 30% higher in the poorest New York City neighborhoods than in wealthier neighborhoods." The infant mortality rate for Black New Yorkers is three times that for White, non-Hispanic, New Yorkers.[6] Diabetes is twice as prevalent among Black New Yorkers as White.[7] As a consequence, life expectancy at birth for Black New Yorkers is 77.2 years, while for White, non-Hispanic, New Yorkers it is 81.4 years.[8]

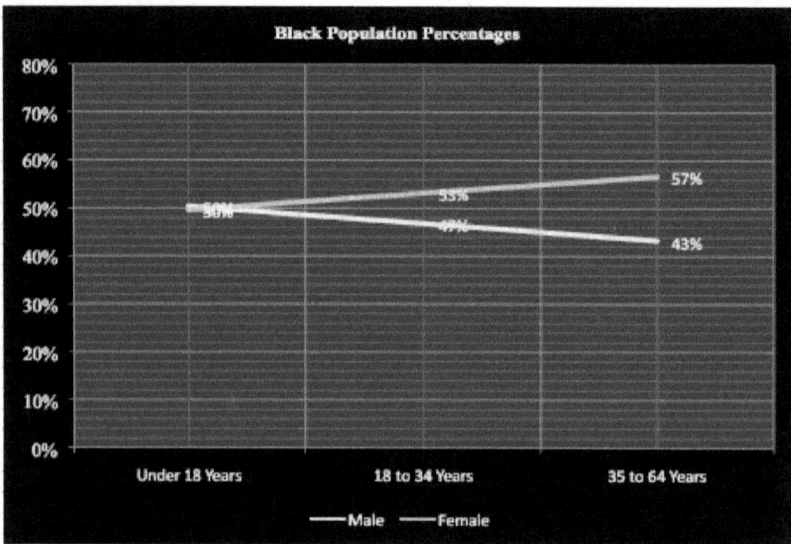

There are also great disparities in the population distribution by gender between Black and White, non-Hispanic, New Yorkers. While the gender percentages of the White, non-Hispanic, population are balanced until age 65, the male percentage of the Black population drops steadily through the age cohorts, beginning at 50% for those under 18 years of age and declining to just 38% for those 65 years of age and older. In other words, between 6% and 14% of the male Black working age population of New York is, as it were, missing. We will look at some of the reasons for this in this chapter's section on the criminal justice system.

Income

The median Black household income in New York City ($40,500) is just two-thirds that of median White income ($62,100) and mean Black income is barely more than half that of White residents of the city. The difference between the proportions of median and mean incomes indicates that White incomes are heavily weighted toward the top earners and that is indeed the case: 16.5% of White households have incomes of $150,000 or above, as compared to just 4.5% of Black households. This can be traced to the fact that half of the city's White workers are employed in management, business and finance, with just 15% in service occupations, while twice the White proportion, 30%, of Black employees are in service occupations. Black New Yorkers are disproportionately employed in comparatively lower paid occupations such as educational services and healthcare and government. And the unemployment rate of the Black workforce is nearly twice that of New York City's White, non-Hispanic, workforce.

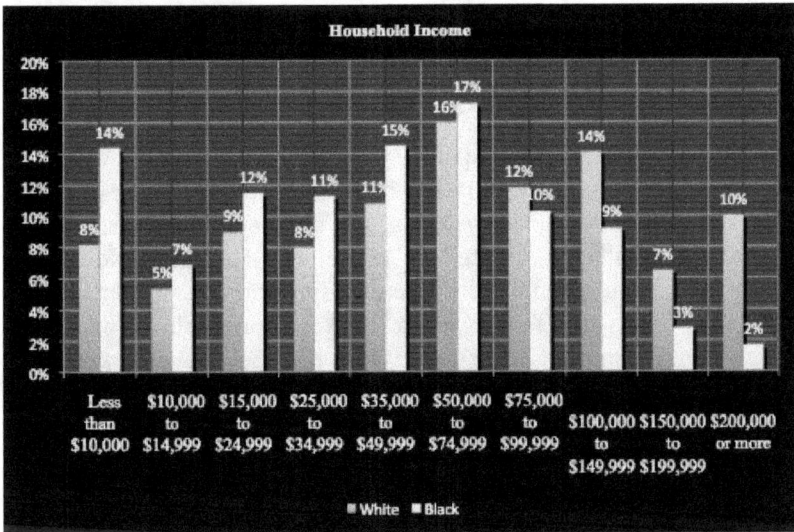

The very top of the income scale New York City is the home to the notorious 1% and few of those are Black. Laird Bergad found that "The upper 1% of non-Hispanic white households earned median incomes of $869,820 in 2010 compared with $327,224 among non-Hispanic blacks in the same year." The top 1% of New

York City Black household incomes would not even make it into the top 10% of New York City White, non-Hispanic, households, which had median incomes of $428,112 in 2010, while the wealthiest 10% of non-Hispanic Black households had median incomes much less than half that: $180,233. At the other end of the income scale "Poor non-Hispanic black households earned considerably lower median household incomes compared with non-Hispanic whites.

> The lower 10% of non-Hispanic white households earned medians of $12,553 in 2010 compared with $7,497 for non-Hispanic blacks. And, the lower 20% of non-Hispanic white households had median incomes of $18,783 in 2010 compared with $11,525 for non-Hispanic black households."[9]

A household income of $11,500 per year is less than half the poverty level for a family of four; a household income of $7,500 is deep poverty. We can note that the average rent for a two-bedroom apartment in New York City is now $48,000 per year.[10]

Finally, "Food Insecurity" is the ultimate definition of poverty. Approximately a quarter of the residents of New York City's Black ghettos are food insecure—from time to time they go hungry.[11]

Wealth

As we have seen, Black New Yorker's have lower incomes than the city's White, non-Hispanic, residents and even the richest African American New Yorkers have significantly lower incomes than the richest White New Yorkers. This disparity is also true of wealth. More than a quarter of White, non-Hispanic, New York households have income from interest, dividends or net rents, while less than 10% of Black New Yorker households have such investment income. In other words, 92% of Black New Yorkers have no wealth other than equity in their own homes and only 26% of Black New Yorkers own their homes (compared to 38% of White New Yorkers).

Few Black New Yorkers without income from interest, dividends or net rents are likely to be homeowners. Nationally, the mean net worth of Black householders, excluding home equity, is $49,199 (that for White, non-Hispanics, is $336,435). The national mean Black home equity is $35,258 (White home equity is $98,734). Working from 2006-2010 Census data, we can estimate the value of Black owner-occupied homes in New York City as approximately $6

178

billion and that of White, non-Hispanic, owner-occupied homes at something in excess of $57 billion. With Black investment income of $3 billion and White investment income of $148 billion, total Black NYC wealth is approximately $9 billion and total NYC White wealth in excess of $200 billion. On a per capita basis, White New York is about thirteen times as wealthy as Black New York, and quite possibly much more, given the city's attraction for the international 1%.

These disparities are worsening. The Federal Reserve calculates that nationally, median net worth of "nonwhite or Hispanic" families declined from $21,900 to $18,100 (17%) between 2010 and 2013 as White non-Hispanic family net worth increased from $139,900 to $142,000 (2%). And "nonwhite or Hispanic" *mean* net worth declined 2% from $188,500 to $183,900 as mean White non-Hispanic family net worth increased 1% from $701,400 to $705,900.[12] The situation in New York City is probably more extreme.

Mobility

The United States has the least intergenerational wealth mobility of any developed country,[13] perhaps because of the increasing concentration of wealth in the hands of 1% of the population and the extraordinarily little wealth held by the 13% of the population descended from enslaved Africans.

Intergenerational economic mobility is much more dependent on wealth than income. Wealth is either financial investments or property. We have seen the Black New York has relatively little of either. As elsewhere, New York City's Black income quintiles are shifted down one quintile from White income quintiles. That is, Black households with incomes in the highest 20% of Black incomes have incomes falling in the fourth quintile of White incomes, and so forth. It is unlikely a Black family will accumulate enough wealth from income to facilitate intergenerational economic mobility. Given this comparative lack of family wealth in New York City's Black community, downward mobility is more likely than upward mobility. This is exacerbated by the extraordinary segregation of the city's Black community. Both lower income and middle income Black families live in the same neighborhoods, neighborhoods with few cultural or educational resources. Lacking, as we will see, equal educational opportunities and lacking inherited capital, each generation of Black New Yorkers starts adult life from either the socio-economic position into which they were born, or below that.

The Anvil of Caste: Education

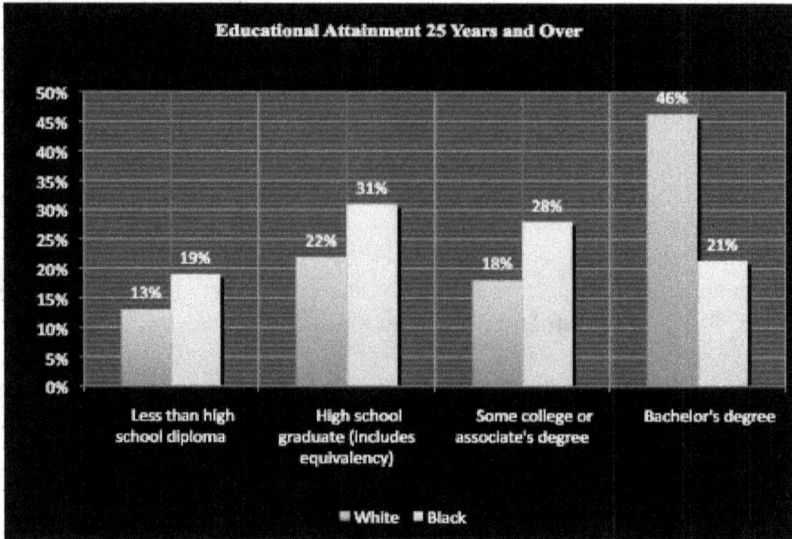

Income and wealth are directly related to educational attainment. Both median and mean net worth for families in which the head of the household has a college degree are ten times those for families in which the head of the household is without a high school diploma.[14] More than twice the percentage of White, non-Hispanic, adults in New York as African American New Yorkers have attained the crucial college degree leading to four times the median and five times the mean net worth of those with just a high school diploma. The stakes, in purely economic terms, are enormous. Why is it that higher educational attainment is so much less for New York's African American than White residents?

The key grade 8 reading results of the National Assessment of Educational Progress (NAEP) can throw some light on this issue. In 2013 nearly half (44%) of White, non-Hispanic, students in New York public schools scored at or above grade level, as compared to only 18% of Black students. (This was a six-point improvement for

White students and a two-point improvement for Black students from 2011 results, a net four-point widening of the gap.) Disaggregating the results by that proxy for family income, eligibility for the National Lunch Program, shows that the results for African Americans were dominated by those Black students whose family incomes were low enough to make them eligible—16% of these were at or above grade level. More than half again as many, 25%, of Black students from more prosperous families, those few who were *ineligible* for the National Lunch Program, read at grade level. White students from poorer families score higher than Black students from less poor families. Black students eligible for the National Lunch Program, with a parent who had some education after high school, and those *ineligible,* with a parent who graduated from college, had similar outcomes: 24% and 28%, respectively. (White students from prosperous families, those ineligible for the National Lunch Program, with a college graduate parent were at the 68% level. There are insufficient numbers of White students in the other categories for NAEP to report.)

The implication is that having a middle class family income or a highly educated parent are equally beneficial in raising outcomes by approximately ten percentage points. However, lower income Black students with a college-graduate parent still had just a 17% chance of reading at grade level. Why is that? It is likely that because of the city's extreme segregation most Black students attend poorly resourced schools, those in their neighborhood, while most White, non-Hispanic, students attend better resourced schools, those in *their* neighborhoods. Higher parental education in the absence of very high income is not an advantage in the situation of acute segregation prevalent in New York City, where Black families with incomes below the top quintile of White families in New York City cannot afford to live in neighborhoods with good schools.

The public schools in New York City are divided among 32 geographic districts. About one-third of these are acutely segregated with fewer than 100 White students enrolled in their high schools. Total Black enrollment varies from 2% in District 24 to 91% in District 18. Districts 5, 13, 16, 17, 18, 19, 23, and 29, each more than 50% Black, serve the most segregated of the city's neighborhoods

181

(those, as it happens, with the highest rates of food insecurity).* The results of the New York State English Language Arts test at grade 8 in 2014 showed 15% of Black students, city-wide, at level 3 and 3.7% at level 4, both improved from 2013. The middle class Black districts—18, 22 and 29—showed combined level 3 and 4 results as 23%, 17% and 19.1%, respectively, while the most deprived Black districts—5, 16, 17, 28 and 32—averaged 18%. Therefore there was not much difference between the outcomes reached by New York's most segregated schools serving impoverished and less impoverished Black students. On the other hand, integrated District 15 brought 33% of its relatively few Black students to levels 3 & 4; District 2 did so with 32% of its Black students and District 26 did so with 41% of its very few Black students.† The achievement levels of *all* Black students in these districts are much greater even than those for Black students whose family incomes are high enough to make them ineligible for the National Lunch Program, citywide. One possible reason for this is that their schools are oriented toward, and have the resources to serve, the more prosperous families of non-Black students.

The graduation rate for the city's White, non-Hispanic, students is 81%. It is 61% for Black students, although about half of the city's *male* Black students do not graduate four years after 9th grade. Given that only 18% of Black students in the city read at grade level on the grade 8 NAEP it is remarkable that 61% graduate. One reason for this has been the practice of awarding "local diplomas" to students who are deemed unqualified for college. In New York City more than 16% of graduates were given these second class diplomas in 2012.[15] Assuming that local diplomas were concentrated among Black and Hispanic students, it is likely that more than 20% of Black students in grade 9 received these diplomas at graduation, lowering the actual graduation rate to 41%.

How well does the New York City Department of Education prepare its students for careers and college after high school? New York City has a vast public postsecondary system: the City

---

* District 5 is in Harlem, Districts 13, 16, 17, 18, 19 and 23 are in Brooklyn. District 29 is in Queens.
† These districts had Black enrollments of 16%, 11% and 5%, respectively. The Free and Reduced Price lunch percentage of the students of District 2 was 61%, that of District 15 was 67% and that of District 26 was 48%.

University of New York (CUNY). CUNY has two-year community colleges, four-year colleges, a law school, a medical school and a graduate center. The community colleges admit nearly 40,000 first-time students, 80% of whom need remediation; the four-year colleges admit over 31,000. These are most of the graduates of the New York City public schools who go on to college. The four-year colleges graduate 21% of their students with Bachelor's degrees within 150% of normal time. The community colleges graduate 6% of their students with Associate's degrees within 150% of normal time. For Black students the graduation rates are 13% and 5%, respectively (and for African American men, 10% and 5%).

All things considered, the implication appears to be that the New York City public schools fail to adequately prepare more than 85% of their Black graduates for four-year colleges and 95% of those not qualifying for four-year colleges for the requirements of two-year colleges. As just 61% of Black students receive diplomas, and just 41% receive "Regents" diplomas, it seems that fewer than 10% of all Black students graduate prepared for college and, in today's economy, prepared for careers. (This is perhaps less surprising when we again recall once again that just 18% read at grade level in grade 8.) As this goes on year after year, it would be more reasonable to say that the implicit goal of the New York Public Schools has been to fail to educate Black students, something achieved 90% of the time, rather than to say that the system does not succeed 90% of the time in reaching its professed goal of educating Black students.

Remarkably, the New York City Department of Education seems to simply accept the fact that schools in impoverished areas of the city offer fewer educational opportunities to their students than schools in wealthier (whiter) areas of the city and has created institutional structures based on, and therefore validating, the inferiority of their secondary schools. The city allows, requires, its middle school students to compete for places in the city's high schools, rather than leaving them to attend their neighborhood high schools. In order to facilitate this it has implemented a sophisticated, literally Nobel-Prize-winning process for allocating students among the schools. "'It was an allocation problem,' explained Neil Dorosin, the director of high-school admissions at the time of the redesign.

The city had a scarce resource — in this case, good schools — and had to work out an equitable way to distribute it. "But unlike a scarce resource like Rolling Stones tickets, where whoever's willing to pay the most gets the tickets, here we can't use price," Mr. Dorosin said . . .

But, in a way, they did.

The allocation problem—the scarcity situation created by the system's toleration of inferior neighborhood high schools—was solved with a system adapted from that used by medical schools. High schools, in effect, list students in the schools' order of preference, students list schools in their order of preference, the lists are put into a black box and—abracadabra—matches are made. Some students end up in what the City, by the very existence of the allotment system, admits are schools where there are few opportunities for a good education, while others are able to make their way into schools that offer better opportunities for a good education. What determines the populations of the two groups? According to the *New York Times*, "low-income and low-performing children are . . . more likely to end up in underfunded schools.

> [Professor] Sean Corcoran . . . found that the algorithm matches low- and high-achieving applicants with their first-choice schools at roughly the same rate. But Professor Corcoran said, "Lower-achieving kids are applying to lower-achieving schools and ranking them as their top choices." It seems that most students prefer to go to school close to home, and if nearby schools are underperforming, students will choose them nevertheless. Researching other options is labor intensive, and poor and immigrant children in particular may not get the help they need to do it.[16]

That is clear enough: the New York City Department of Education distributes education opportunities in accordance with the educational and financial resources of the families of students. Those with greater resources are rewarded with greater opportunities. And the entire elaborate system of "school choice" is in effect a tax on the families of the city's school children and a diversion of resources that might be better spent on actually improving the city's neighborhood high schools.

That this system is not often questioned in principle, but only in technical detail, may be because it is typical of the way in which New York City's Department of Education allocates resources. The city's Gifted and Talented program is another example. Many school districts have special programs for students designated as gifted and talented. Students in these programs have greater resources devoted to their educations than other students: better, more experienced, teachers; more challenging curricula; higher expectations; challenging peers. There are various ways in which students may be placed in these programs. A common method, that followed by the New York City Department of Education, is a test, usually understood as a proxy for an intelligence test. This seems fair enough. Intelligence is evenly distributed throughout any large population, by definition, therefore an intelligence test or reasonable proxy should give all racial, ethnic and economic groups of students an equal chance of receiving the benefits of gifted and talented programs. New York City's 32 geographic districts, given housing patterns, vary by their proportions of students in each racial/ethnic group and by the economic status of their families. If the intention of the NYC Department of Education were to provide gifted and talented children with the enriched educational resources of these programs without regard to race, ethnicity or economic status, the outcome would be a relatively equal proportion of children qualifying in each of the 32 districts.

What do we find?

In District 2, 6% of students, k-3, were deemed qualified for admission to city-wide gifted and talented programs: the brass ring. This Manhattan district in multi-ethnic New York City is just 18% Black, while 59% of its students qualify for either free or reduced price lunch programs. As the city-wide average is over 70% qualifying for free or reduced price lunch programs, District 2 is unusually prosperous with an unusually low percentage of Black students. The runner-up was District 3, also in Manhattan, also at 6% gifted and talented, with 63% of its students Black or Hispanic but just 51% qualifying for free or reduced price lunch programs. After these, the percentage of students being admitted to city-wide gifted and talented programs declines steeply. The third place district was at 2%, the eleventh placed ranked at 1%, the 18th at one-half-of-one-percent qualifying for city-wide gifted and talented programs. The tenth-placed district and nearly all following enroll 75% or more of their students in free or reduced price lunch programs.

The three districts with the lowest percentages of students qualifying for admission to city-wide gifted and talented programs were Districts 23, 9 and 7, with free and reduced price lunch program enrollments of between 80% and 90% and Black and Hispanic enrollments of between 97% and 98%. The three together had 25 students designated as gifted and talented (about 0.12%), as compared to the 698 students in District 2 alone.

What can we conclude from this? There are two possibilities: either intelligence (giftedness and talent) in New York City is distributed by race/ethnicity and economic status, or the New York City Department of Education uses a method to allocate additional educational resources and opportunities that results in such outcomes. That method, like the that used for the allocation of places in "the scarce resource" of decent high schools, is to make the process depend on the educational and financial resources of parents, who must learn about the Gifted and Talented program and work with the bureaucracy to have their children tested for it. If they do not, then the children, no matter how gifted and talented, are not tested and, therefore, cannot have the opportunities offered by the program.

One more example:

The New York City Department of Education runs a number of specialized high schools. These are not vocational schools offering job training. They are the gate-keepers for privileged preparation for elite colleges, upper middle class careers, the perpetuation of class status and mobility. They have world-class facilities, teachers and curriculum. They have high graduation rates and close to 100% college admission success. The best known of these high schools are the Bronx High School of Science and Stuyvesant High School. In a recent year, the Bronx High School of Science admitted 968 new students: 50 were Hispanic and 18 were Black. Stuyvesant admitted 952 students: 21 were Hispanic and 7 were Black. Students are admitted to these schools by their scores on a test taken in grade 8. The test is basically a mathematics test. NAEP measures student achievement for grade 8 mathematics as well as reading. In 2013 18% of New York City's White, non-Hispanic, students scored at the Advanced level, necessary for admission to the specialized high schools, as did 26% of the Asian students. One percent each of the city's Black and Hispanic students scored at the Advanced level. The New York City Department of Education does not appear to be teaching mathematics to its Black and Hispanic students.

There is an additional barrier. It is generally acknowledged, even by the New York City Department of Education, that the test used for admission to the specialized high schools requires, in addition to "Advanced" mathematics achievement, extra-curricular instruction: cramming. Kaplan, Inc., a $2.2 billion company owned by Graham Holdings (the Graham family used to own the *Washington Post*), offers preparation for the test, "Premier Tutoring," at three price points: 16 hours, 24 hours and 32 hours. The 32-hour package costs $5,000 (payable in three installments). For this fee students receive (according to the Kaplan website), "proven, score raising strategies to help maximize . . . points on Test Day." A Kaplan "Premier Tutoring" course would cost an average White New York City family 7% of their annual income. It would cost a Black woman raising her children without a husband present 28% of her annual income, four times as much—in the unlikely event she had $5,000 after living expenses.

Any objective observer would find it unusual that NYC has a system of selective high schools with a gateway examination that cannot be passed without extra tutoring. The New York City Department of Education appears to believe that its middle schools are not good enough to prepare students for its own best high schools. Doesn't that seem a bit odd? Perhaps not when we know that many schools in the poorest parts of the city do not offer the courses, such as advanced algebra, necessary to even read the questions on the test.

The New York City Department of Education restricts educational opportunities for Black students (and not Black students alone) by providing resources to schools in proportion to neighborhood family incomes; by placing the burden for identifying gifted and talented students on families, by restricting admission to its best high schools to those students who live in privileged neighborhoods and whose families can afford specialized tutors. In this way Black educational achievement and attainment is limited, Black incomes are kept low, Black wealth and intergenerational mobility minimized by the actions of the education system's administrators.

Quite recently there appears to have been a change in direction. The city has vastly expanded the availability of pre-kindergarten classes and appears to be taking other measures to increase educational opportunities for African American students. One can only hope that changes of this nature will continue to be made and that they will be effective.

The Hammer of Caste: The Criminal Justice System

The racial inequities in the New York criminal justice system are hardly a matter of debate. Incarceration rates for African Americans in New York State are nearly ten times those for White residents of the state. The "Stop, Question and Frisk" activities of the New York City Police Department were only the most publicized instance revealing the racial basis for much of the Department's actions. In a city that is 33% White, non-Hispanic, 29% Hispanic and 23% Black, police stopped two to three times as many Black residents as Hispanic residents and five to seven times as many Black residents as White residents.[17] Further, according to the New York State Attorney General's office, "racial disparities documented in stops continue through arrest, disposition, and sentencing. This disparity is especially pronounced in marijuana arrests, in which white defendants charged with misdemeanor marijuana possession after a stop are nearly 50% more likely than blacks to receive an ACD [adjournment in contemplation of dismissal], and thereby avoid a conviction."[18]

And then, quite suddenly, the New York City Police Department stopped using what it had described as an essential law enforcement activity that was reducing serious crime. A judge ruled that the tactic is unconstitutional and a new mayor dropped the previous administration's appeal against that ruling. Stops dropped from more than 16,000 per week to fewer than 2,000 per week. The city government instructed the police department to issue tickets, rather than making arrests, for minimal marijuana possession. The then-Police Commissioner said "No question about it, violent crime will go up." It went down.[19] Serious crime in the city in 2014 was down 4.4% from a year earlier and nearly 5% from two years earlier. All categories of serious crime showed decreases, that for robbery was down 14% from a year earlier and 19% from two years earlier.[20] In an extraordinary development beginning the week of December 22, 2014, New York City police staged a work action for reasons that were not clear, but apparently part of labor contract negotiations. The police union stated that officers should not make arrests "unless absolutely necessary." Arrests overall declined by 66% from the same period the previous year, drug arrests declined by 84%, parking and traffic citations fell by over 90%, quality of life summonses declined 94%. One writer commented: "If the NYPD can safely cut arrests by two-thirds, why haven't they done it before?

The human implications of this question are immense. Fewer arrests for minor crimes logically means fewer people behind bars for minor crimes. Poorer would-be defendants benefit the most; three-quarters of those sitting in New York jails are only there because they can't afford bail. Fewer New Yorkers will also be sent to Rikers Island, where endemic brutality against inmates has led to resignations, arrests, and an imminent federal civil-rights intervention over the past six months. A brush with the American criminal-justice system can be toxic for someone's socioeconomic and physical health. [21]

What can we learn from this? With the stop-and-frisk program the New York City Police Department deployed enormous resources on activities that led to few arrests and fewer convictions and had no positive effect reducing levels of serious crime. There have been similar costs and consequences of "unnecessary arrests." These activities did, however, criminalize and alienate large numbers of young African American men. They became "known to the police." Their public lives were limited by the actions of the police or by their anticipation of those actions. It could be argued that the Police Department was well intentioned, but mistaken. However, that argument would not be convincing, given the number of years that the program was in place and the data that was available. It is more reasonable to conclude that the purpose of the stop-and-frisk program and those arrests that were "not absolutely necessary" were their outcomes: the removal of young adult, primarily African American, men from their families and neighborhoods, the enforcement of the caste status of New York City's African American residents.

Another indicator of the nature of the relationship between the criminal justice system in New York City and the Black community is the regular killings of unarmed African American men by police officers. Sometimes these killings take place when a Black man resists or objects to an arrest; sometimes they take place without any provocation. These killings are sufficiently common that they have resulted in an understanding in the Black community that all young Black men are at risk of their lives whenever they encounter the police. "What parents have done for decades, who have children of color, especially young men of color, is train them to be very careful when they have a connection with a police officer . . . "

> It's different for a white child. That's just the reality in this country. And . . . very early on with my son, we said, look, if a police officer stops you, do everything he tells you to do, don't move suddenly, don't reach for your cell phone, because we knew, sadly, there's a greater chance it might be misinterpreted if it was a young man of color.[22]

If the White mayor of New York City has this view of the New York City police's attitude toward the Black community, there can be little doubt about that community's understanding, and the reality, of the role of the police in the life of the city.

Modeling a More Equitable New York City

The Organisation for Economic Co-operation and Development (OECD) has found that "by hindering human capital accumulation income inequality undermines education opportunities for disadvantaged individuals, lowering social mobility and hampering skills development . . . Inequality significantly shapes the opportunities of education and upward mobility of disadvantaged individuals."[23] The way that this takes place in New York City is particularly clear. While the upper 10% in the city tend to invest in the education ("human capital" transfer) by sending their children to private schools, the remaining families in the upper two quintiles are able to purchase better educational opportunities for their children along with their housing in the city's low poverty neighborhoods.

The New York City Department of Education until quite recently has been peculiarly resistant to providing equal educational opportunities to Black students. It refers twice as many, proportionately, of its Black students to law enforcement as their share of the enrollment.[24] It supports schools in neighborhoods with middle class White, non-Hispanic, and Asian majorities more generously than schools in neighborhoods with Black majorities. It offers enhanced educational opportunities, such as gifted and talented classes, many times as often in non-Black as in Black neighborhoods and maintains specialized high schools from which, for all practical purposes, Black students are excluded. The results of neighborhood and school segregation, as we have seen, include the fact that even those Black students whose parents have college educations have trouble learning to read at grade level in New York City schools, that even the children of some Black officials at the highest levels of city government fail to finish high school and must settle for a GED.

The inequitable distribution of resources is particularly glaring in the system's Gifted and Talented and specialized high school programs. Entry to the Gifted and Talented system is by means of a test taken at the beginning of a student's education. However, the city tests only 21% of its kindergarten students for admission to its Gifted and Talented programs. The percentage of students in a neighborhood the New York City Department of Education tests varies by the income of their parents. In some community school districts 70% of the students are tested. In others, as few as 7% are tested. If, instead, say, 70% of ALL students were tested, we could estimate that there would be an additional 10,000 students qualifying for the city's Gifted and Talented programs. These additional students would mostly be Black, Hispanic and living in poverty. Providing these students with the educational resources devoted to the Gifted and Talented program would set them on track to higher levels of educational achievement and attainment.

The now radically inequitable system of selective high schools could be used as an instrument for fundamental change in the nation's largest school system. This process would begin by abolishing the current admissions test. That should be done for a number of reasons, not the least being that no child's future should be determined by a single, high stakes, standardized test, especially one that is admittedly not aligned with the curriculum of the schools and blatantly discriminates on the basis of family income. An alternative would be a system used for college admission in various places around the country: a quota, based on enrollment, from each middle and junior high school. If a school enrolls, say, 1% of the city's grade 8 students, then 1% of the pool of students admitted to the specialized high schools should come from that school. Each school should be permitted to set their own criteria for identifying those students, as who knows students better than their teachers?

What would be the consequences of this innovation? Some schools that now send many students to the selective high schools would send fewer. Every school that now sends no students to the selective high schools would send some. Every student in New York City would have a more equal opportunity to learn in some of the best high schools in the nation.

In addition to the benefits for individual students, a change of this type might well have systemic benefits. It is possible that parents now willing and able to pay large amounts of money for after-school and Saturday classes for their children from kindergarten through grade 8, and to pay for special "cramming" tutoring for the specialized high school test, would consider moving from neighborhoods where the competition for places is high to neighborhoods where the schools currently do not send students to the selective high schools. It is possible that those parents would put pressure on those schools—and the New York City Department of Education—to improve the schools in their new neighborhoods, so that, for example, the neighborhood middle schools offer courses leading to the Advanced level of achievement in grade 8 mathematics.

These changes in the operation of the Gifted and Talented and specialized high school programs might be accompanied by a change in the process for assigning children to the city's regular high schools. That change would be to abolish school choice, which would end the system's tacit acceptance of inequitable opportunities to learn in the city's high schools. Ending school choice would make the variations in school quality vividly apparent, paving the way to improvements in "drop-out factories" along the lines of the "Abbott" decision: full-day universal pre-school, full-day "academically" oriented kindergarten, high quality curricula k-12, after-school, weekend and summer classes, continuous teacher professional development, the assignment of teachers to schools by reference to the needs of students, not the preferences of adults.

According to Patrick Sharkey, "The evidence from the studies of school quality does reveal that when low-income students living in highly disadvantaged residential settings are able to attend high-quality schools, their academic performance improves substantially.

The studies offer tangible evidence that the explanations for persistence at the bottom of the academic distribution do not lie fully within low-income individuals or families. Instead, aspects of the residential environment surrounding such families, such as schools, can play an important role in facilitating, or impeding, economic mobility.[25]

We can model the long-term effects of giving Black students access to high quality schools by setting educational attainment of Black adults 25 years of age and older at the current level of White residents of the city. This would double the number of adult Black residents of the city with Bachelor's degrees and nearly triple the number with graduate degrees.

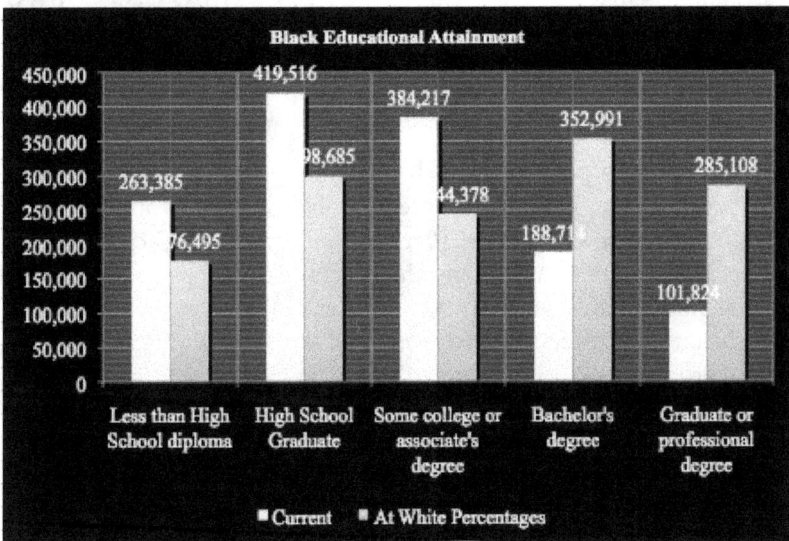

At current average national Black incomes at each level of educational attainment, increasing New York's Black educational attainment levels to the current levels for White residents of New York would increase the community's annual income by $14 billion as shown in the chart below. (The chart reads that, for example, as the number of Black New Yorkers with Bachelor's degrees goes from 189,000 to 353,000, the income of that group as a whole would increase from $10,873,000,000 to $20,338,000,000.) In a virtuous circle, other things being equal, this increase in college-educated adults, with its concomitant increase in family incomes, would increase Black student achievement levels.

Model Black Community Income Calculations				
Educational Attainment	Current (000s)	Model (000s)	Current Income ($000,000)	Model Income ($000,000)
Less than a high school diploma	263	176	6,465	4,332
High school diploma	420	299	14,201	10,111
Some college, no degree	384	244	14,525	9,238
Bachelor's degree	189	353	10,873	20,338
Graduate or professional	102	285	8,765	24,541
Totals	1,358	1,358	$54,829	$68,561

The changes posited by this modeling exercise are not utopian. They do not even include the effects to be expected from the recent reforms of police operations. If reform in New York City's criminal justice system continues, many thousands of "disappeared" working age African Americans will re-appear, as it were, resulting in significant socio-economic benefits to Black families and neighborhoods.

Improving the schools would be more difficult, in practice, as more complicated, but quite possible given the political will. Indeed, the new mayor and schools chancellor do seem to be moving matters in the right direction, but there is much more to be done.

Notes: Chapter Seven

[1] Brown University, US2010.

[2] WNYC. Median Income Across the US.
http://project.wnyc.org/median-income-nation/?#11/40.7306/-73.9866

[3] Bahchieva, Raisa; Du, Jingqiang; Popkin, Illene; Reilly, Neil; Shultz, Harold. Making Neighborhoods: Understanding New York City Transitions 2000-2010. CHPC New York City, p. 51.

[4] Perine, Jerilyn; Reilly, Neil; Bahchieva, Raisa. Making Neighborhoods: Study Summary and Highlights. CHPC Citizens Housing Planning Council, November 2014, p. 22.

[5] New York City Department of Health and Mental Hygiene. Health Disparities in New York City, April 2010, No.1.

[6] Zimmerman, R., Li, W., Gambatese, M., Madsen, A., Lasner-Frater, L., Kelley, D., Kennedy, J., Maduro, G., Sun, Y. Summary of Vital Statistics, 2012: Infant Mortality. New York, NY: New York City Department of Health and Mental Hygiene, Office of Vital Statistics, 2013.

[7] New York City Department of Health and Mental Hygiene. Epi Research Report, April 2013.

[8] New York City Department of Health and Mental Hygiene. Epi Research Report, March 2013.

[9] Bergad, Laird, W. The Concentration of Wealth in New York City: Changes in the Structure of Household Income by Race/Ethnic Groups and Latino Nationalities 1990-2010. CUNY: Latino Data Project, Report 56, January 2014, p. 23.
http://clacls.gc.cuny.edu/files/2014/01/Household-Income-Concentration-in-NYC-1990-2010.pdf

[10] *New York Post.* http://nypost.com/2014/06/18/4-nyc-neighborhoods-boasting-rentals-for-less-than-2k-a-month/

[11] 24% of residents in Congressional District 8, Eastern (Jamaica) Brooklyn, are food insecure as are 22% in the 9th District, Central Brooklyn. Congressional District 13, Harlem, has a 23% rate of food insecurity. The 15th Congressional District, the Bronx, has a 27% rate of food insecurity. In contrast, the oddly shaped District 10, including Brooklyn Heights, Tribeca and the upper West Side of Manhattan, has a food insecurity rate of 15%.

http://www.feedingamerica.org/hunger-in-america/our-research/map-the-meal-gap/2012/ny_allcdsmmg_2012.pdf

[12] Bricker, Jesse; Dettling, Lisa J.; Henriques, Alice; Hsu, Joanne W.; Moore, Kevin B.; Sabelhaus, John; Thompson, Jeffrey and Windle, Richard A. Changes in U.S. Family Finances from 2010 to 2013: Evidence from the Survey of Consumer Finances. Federal Reserve Bulletin.
file:///Files/Inequality%20and%20Race/U.S.%20Data/FRB%20%20Federal%20Reserve%20Bulletin%20Inequality%20cf.%20Yellen.html

[13] Sharkey, Patrick. Neighborhoods, Cities, and Economic Mobility. New York University, October 10, 2014, p. 14, citing Smeeding, Timothy M., Robert Erikson and Markus Jantti (Eds.) 2011. Persistence, Privilege, and Parenting: The Comparative Study of Intergenerational Mobility. New York: The Russell Sage Foundation.

[14] Bricker.

[15] New York State Board of Regents, June 2012 meeting, p. 11.
http://www.regents.nysed.gov/meetings/2012Meetings/June2012/GradRate.pdf

[16] *New York Times.*
http://www.nytimes.com/2014/12/07/nyregion/how-game-theory-helped-improve-new-york-city-high-school-application-process.html?ref=education&_r=0

[17] New York State Office of the Attorney General. A Report on Arrests Arising from the New York City Police Department's Stop-and-Frisk Practices, November 2013, p. 5.

[18] New York State Office of the Attorney General, p. 4.

[19] Bostock, Mike and Fessenden, Ford. "Stop-and-Frisk" Is All but Gone from New York. New York Times, September 18, 2014.

[20]
http://www.nyc.gov/html/nypd/html/crime_prevention/crime_statistics.shtml

[21] Ford, Matt. "The Benefits of Fewer NYPD Arrests. *The Atlantic*, December 31, 2014.
http://www.theatlantic.com/national/archive/2014/12/the-benefits-of-fewer-nypd-arrests/384126/

[22] http://www.motherjones.com/mojo/2014/12/bill-de-blasio-dante-son

[23] Organization for Economic Cooperation and Development, Directorate for Employment, Labour and Social Affairs. Focus on Inequality and Growth. 9 December 2014.
http://www.oecd.org/els/soc/Focus-Inequality-and-Growth-2014.pdf
[24] U.S. Department of Education, Office for Civil Rights.
[25] Sharkey, p. 11.
http://www.bostonfed.org/inequality2014/papers/sharkey.pdf

Chapter Eight: Philadelphia

"DuBois reduced the complexities of the 'Negro Problem' . . . to their social and economic underpinnings. It was white racism that made the black experience different and increasingly dysfunctional . . ." *David Levering Lewis, W. E. B. DuBois, Biography of a Race, 1868-1919, p. 208.*

Philadelphia, a city with more than 1.5 million residents, is a center of higher education, traditional cultural organizations, telecommunications, finance, insurance and manufacturing. But, as elsewhere in America, manufacturing in Philadelphia is in decline and nine of the ten largest employers in the city are universities or hospitals. Philadelphia also has the highest poverty rate (27 percent) among the ten most populous cities in the United States.[1] The city has an old, "Main Line," White class of inherited wealth and both a prosperous professional class and some new members of the one-tenth of one percent. There is a parallel distribution in the city's Black community: some families tracing their residence there to colonial times, some to the Great Migration, some professional, some unskilled, many unemployed.

Forty-two percent of the population of Philadelphia is African American, 36% White, non-Hispanic. Like the others we have reviewed, Philadelphia is a remarkably segregated city. In 2010 it had a White-Black/Black-White Index of Dissimilarity of 73.4, meaning that nearly three-quarters of the population of the city's Black districts would have to move in order for Whites and Blacks to be evenly distributed. There are, proportionately, many more Black school-age children (5 to 17 years of age) in the city than White school-age children: 19% of the Black population is of school-age, as compared to 11% of the White population. There is also a larger proportion of Black than White children five years of age and under, 7% to 5%. On the other hand, there is a smaller proportion of young adults, ages 18 to 34, in the Black community (25%) than in the White community (32%). These distributions may reflect decisions by members of the White community to live outside the city during their children's school years and the large number of college-age

White students who move to the city to study at the University of Philadelphia, Temple University and the city's other institutions of higher education.

There are also demographic disparities *within* Philadelphia's Black community. There are more male than female Black residents of Philadelphia in childhood, up to age 14, at which point the percentage of Black males drops, so that in the 25 to 39 cohorts, in which there are just under 100,000 Black women, there are 18,500 (20%) fewer, "missing," male Black residents of Philadelphia.[2] There is a leveling off from 40 to 60, then a steeper decline until from 80 there are just half the number of Black men as Black women in each age group, at that point presumably as a result of health issues. (The ratio of male White to female White Philadelphia residents is approximately 1:1 until age 60, when the number of White males also begins to fall.)

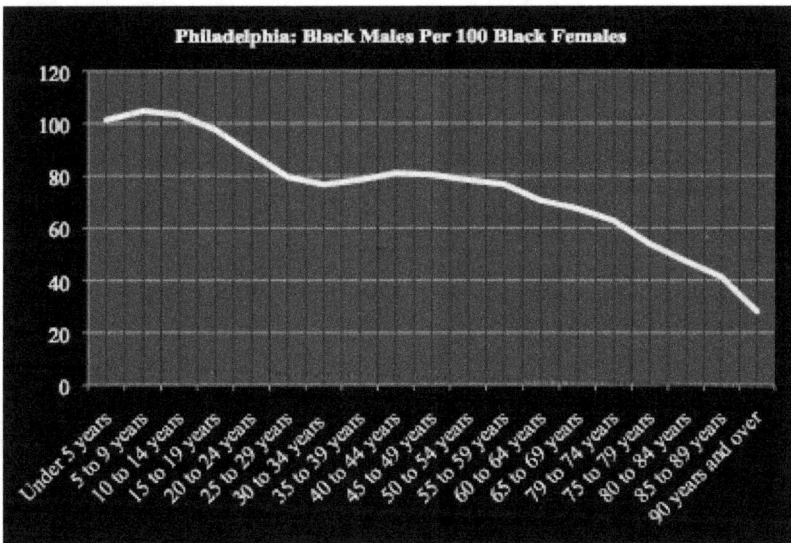

Poverty and deficient health care in Pennsylvania's Black community have resulted in 16% of all Black births in the state being premature, as compared to 10% of White, non-Hispanic, births. For the same reasons, twice the percentage of Black as White newborns have low birth-weight (14% vs. 7%). Twenty-six percent of Black women and 20% of Black men as compared to 16% of White women and 15% of White men report that their health status is poor or fair.[3] A Black woman in Pennsylvania is likely to die six years earlier than a White woman, a Black man is likely to die nine years earlier than a White man and sixteen years earlier than a White woman.[4]

Income Disparities

A quarter of Philadelphia's Black families had incomes below the poverty rate at the time of the 2010 Census. This was two and a half times the poverty rate for Philadelphia's White families. Similarly, the poverty rate for Black families with children, (34%), was approximately twice that of White families with children (18%). Forty-six percent of Black families in which a woman was raising her children without a husband had incomes below the poverty rate, as did 43% of such White families, but there were three times as many Black as White of these most economically insecure families in Philadelphia.

Philadelphia's Black family median income is $36,176; its White family median income is $62,339: 72% higher. Thirteen percent of Black families have incomes of less than $10,000 per year, as compared to 5% of White families. If we distribute Philadelphia family income into quintiles (groups of 20%) in accordance with national proportions based on mean incomes for each group, the second, third and fourth Black family quintiles correspond to the first, second and third White family quintiles, respectively, and the mean of the highest Black family income quintile is closer to that of the fourth than to that of the fifth White family quintile. Nearly 80% of Philadelphia's Black families have incomes below that of the average White family in the city.

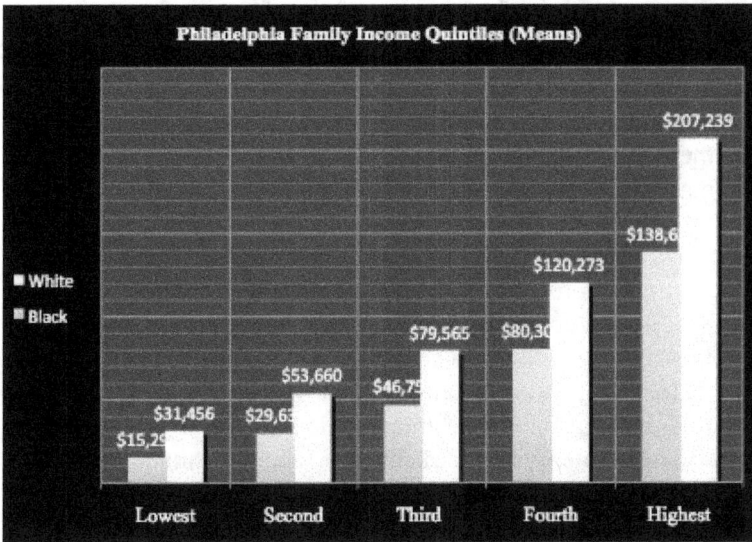

Philadelphia Family Income Quintiles (Means)

White
Black

	Lowest	Second	Third	Fourth	Highest
White	$15,29	$29,63	$46,79	$80,30	$138,6
Black	$31,456	$53,660	$79,565	$120,273	$207,239

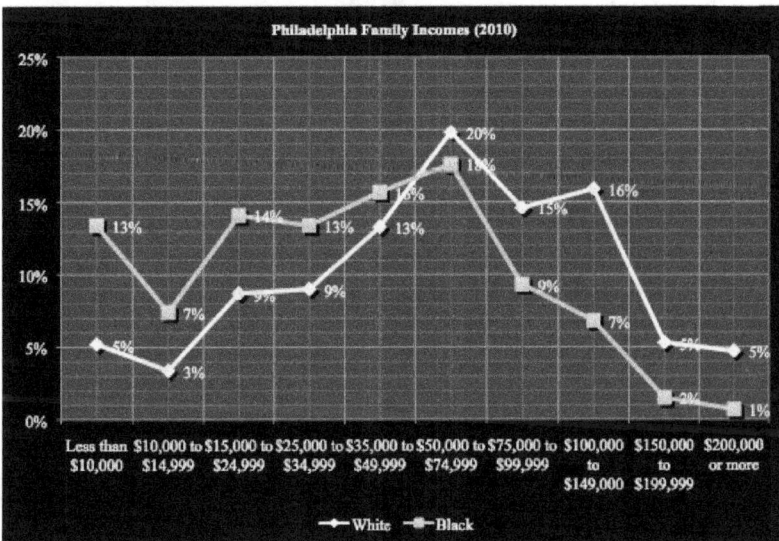

Philadelphia Family Incomes (2010)

	Less than $10,000	$10,000 to $14,999	$15,000 to $24,999	$25,000 to $34,999	$35,000 to $49,999	$50,000 to $74,999	$75,000 to $99,999	$100,000 to $149,000	$150,000 to $199,999	$200,000 or more
White	5%	3%	9%	9%	13%	18%	15%	9%	5%	5%
Black	13%	7%	14%	13%	16%	20%	16%	7%	2%	1%

White — Black

At the other end of the income spectrum, more than a quarter of Philadelphia's White families have incomes over $100,000 per year, as compared to just 10% of Black families. This may reflect the fact that of the non-military employed, close to half of White adults work in the managerial group of occupations, compared to a quarter of Black adults. Thirty percent of Black adults work in service occupations, twice the percentage of White adults.[5] The distribution between occupations and race is symmetrical: Whites manage, Blacks serve. As a consequence the Black community as a whole has an income of $10.8 billion, as compared to that of $19 billion for the slightly smaller White community: a 70% difference.[6]

That is the data for those Philadelphia adults who are employed. Unemployment rates vary markedly by race in Philadelphia, even when differences in education are taken into account. In 2010 the overall unemployment rate for Black Philadelphians was 17%, that for White Philadelphians was 8%. The Black unemployment rates for those without a high school diploma and for high school graduates were 27% and 22%; the White unemployment rates at those education levels were 19% and 12%. Black unemployment rates fell below those of the average unemployment rate for all White workers only for those Black Philadelphians with advanced degrees, for whom it was 6%, still twice that of White Philadelphians with advanced degrees. We can only conclude that the racial penalty for Philadelphia's Black workers is severe.[7]

Black Philadelphians are poorer than White Philadelphians; they work in less prestigious, less highly skilled employment; they are more often unemployed; they are less healthy, they live shorter lives. And 20% of young adult Black men are missing.

As the unemployment data above demonstrates, educational attainment is by and large determining for economic status. Nationally, 19% of African Americans over 25 years of age have graduated from college, as compared to the 30% of White American who have a Bachelor's degree or higher. In Philadelphia, just 13% of African Americans have graduated from college, as compared to 34% of White residents of the city. White Philadelphia residents are more likely to have advanced degrees than White Americans in the rest of the country, while Black residents of Philadelphia are not as well educated as White residents of the city, as the average non-Hispanic White adult, or as African Americans generally.

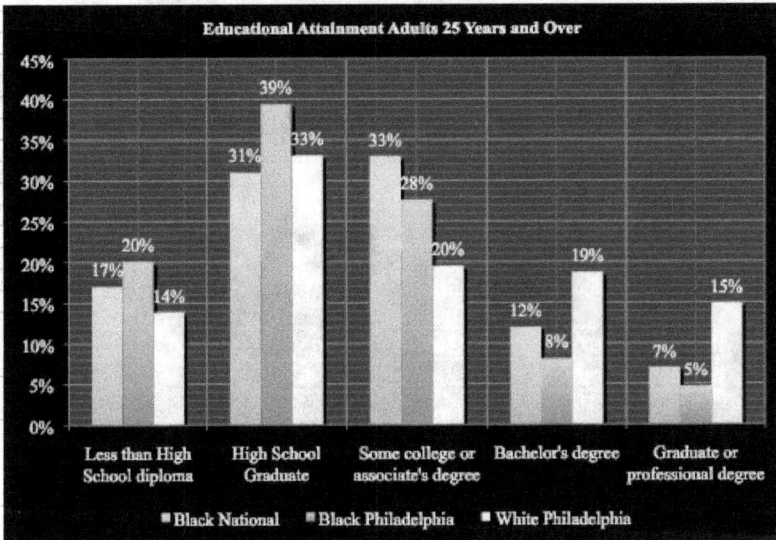

This has a direct effect on incomes. If we assume that wages in Philadelphia are in step with national averages, we would expect that the 20% of Black adults without high school diplomas, if they were in full-time employment, would earn about $20,000 per year; the 39% with high school diplomas and no further education would earn, on average, $27,000 per year, the 28% with some college $23,499, and the 13% with Bachelor's degrees would earn $46,000 per year. With those assumptions we can make a comparative community income calculation: 100 White, adult, full-time wage earners in Philadelphia would together bring home $4,169,980. One hundred Black, adult, full-time wage earners in Philadelphia would bring home $2,892,972: 69% of that of the White group. The difference of educational attainment, and the lower wages paid to Black workers at every educational level, produces a 31% "race-based" reduction in the community's income as compared to the White community.[8] The superior earning power of college graduates is particularly crucial for aggregate community incomes.

Combined Income of 100 Workers

	Less than high school diploma	High school graduate (including GED)	Some college or associate's degree	Bachelor's degree	Total
Black	$400,000	$1,072,500	$822,472	$598,000	$2,892,972
White	$349,440	$1,132,560	$734,340	$1,953,640	$4,169,980

■ Black ■ White

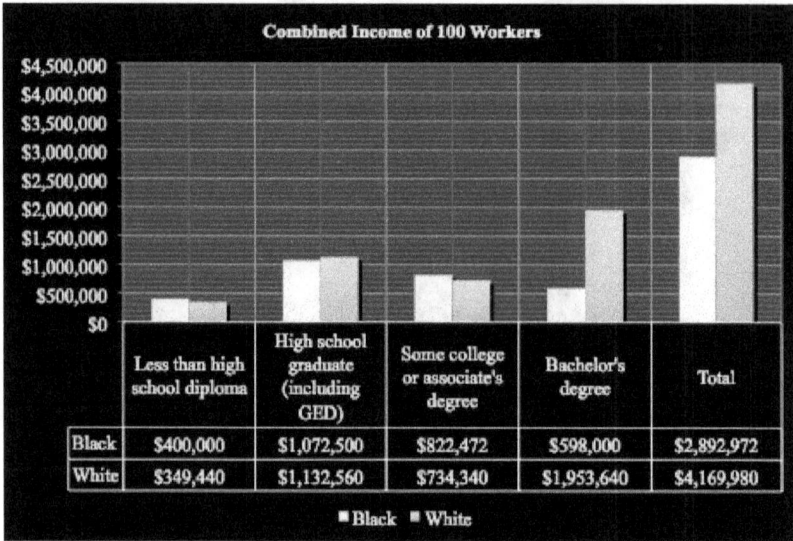

There are other factors that lead to further deficiencies in the income of Philadelphia's Black community as compared to that of the White population. The unemployment rate and the percentage of adults not in the labor force at all are much higher for Black adults than for Whites. Philadelphia's Black adult unemployment rate between 2010 and 2012 averaged 21% of those in the labor force in 2012, while 45% of African Americans over 16 years of age were not in the labor force: two-third's of the city's African-American adults have no regular incomes. The comparable figures for the county's White, non-Hispanic, adults were 12% unemployed and 38% not in the labor force: 50% as compared to 66%—sixteen percentage points.* Looking at it another way, there are 32% fewer adult full-time wage earners in the Black community as compared to the White community in Philadelphia, and, as we have seen, those who are full-time wage earners make, collectively, 31% less than their White counterparts. We find, including these factors, that Black aggregate income is 61% of that of White aggregate income, even

---

* For both groups, those not in the labor force as defined by the Census include homemakers, the disabled and those living on investment incomes, among others.

though the Black population is slightly larger than the White population.

These income disparities naturally result in great differences in what members of each community can afford. Black residents of the city are half as likely to own their own homes, more likely to pay more than 30% of their gross income in rent, less likely to own cars and more than twice as likely to be dependent on public transportation to get to work. Even these data minimize the economic disparities in Philadelphia, as much of the middle class and wealthy, largely White, workforce lives outside the city limits, in suburbs segregated both by income and race.

Disparities of Wealth

There are many people with relatively high incomes with relatively little wealth. There are a few people with relatively large amounts of wealth and relatively low incomes (for example, long-time homeowners in parts of Los Angles). These distinctions have become more visible as inequities in income and wealth have become more extreme during the twenty-first century. Incomes at the mean of the highest quintile are now just equivalent to beginning salaries in parts of the financial industry, while the top 1% and the top one-tenth of one percent of the population absorb rapidly increasing disproportionate amounts of the wealth of the world.

Although positive changes in income are the motor for individual economic mobility, wealth is crucial for intergenerational mobility. For many people, wealth begins with the inheritance of a home, for a few people wealth begins with the inheritance of, say, much of a large corporation, but without inherited wealth at some level, each generation begins at zero, with only social capital, such as higher education, available as a basis for socio-economic mobility.[†]

There are stark disparities in wealth between the Black and White communities in Philadelphia. More than one-quarter, 26%, of White households in Philadelphia had interest, dividends, or net rental income in 2010, as compared to 6% of Black households. This implies that 94% of Philadelphia's Black households have no financial (non-home) assets. Nationally, the mean net worth of White

---

[†] Philadelphia's Pew family, for example, had wealth sufficient to necessitate founding its own investment trust to handle it.

households, excluding equity in their home, was $336,435 in 2011, compared to $49,119 for Black households.[9] As there are 265,000 White households in the city, net investment wealth of the households of the White community in Philadelphia would appear to be approximately $23 billion, as compared to the $719 million net investment wealth of the 244,000 Black households. The largest asset of most American families is an owner-occupied house. Nationally, the mean equity in their own home is $100,000 for White households, $35,000 for Black households. In Philadelphia there are 155,000 White owner-occupied units, and 121,000 Black owner-occupied units. Applying the national median equity factors, it would appear that the combined equity in housing for the Philadelphia White community would be at least $15 billion, that for the Black community one-fourth of that, approximately $4 billion. We can then estimate that the total wealth of White Philadelphia as in excess of $38 billion dollars, at least 8 times that of the city's similarly sized Black community. However, these calculations do not account for the city's (White) billionaires, of whom there are at least four, with a collective net worth of approximately $18 billion. There are no Black billionaires in Philadelphia (because the only African American billionaire, Oprah Winfrey, does not live in Philadelphia).

There is no need to take these calculations further: the financial wealth of Philadelphia's Black community is, as they say, a rounding error compared to that of the city's White community. When we look at this together with the income disparities, particularly at the extremes, it is apparent that from an economic point of view Black Philadelphia does not participate in the same society as White Philadelphia. It is a caste apart.

Mobility

Philadelphia is markedly segregated both racially and by income. Since 1970 it has experienced the greatest increase in income segregation among American metropolitan areas. "Philadelphia was the 43rd most segregated metropolitan area in 1970 and the 3rd most segregated by 2007. In 1970 only 16 percent of Philadelphia families lived in poor or affluent neighborhoods; in 2007, 43 percent of families lived in such neighborhoods."[10] That is, increasing numbers of Philadelphia families live in neighborhoods that are either entirely poor or entirely affluent. As there are very few affluent neighborhoods within Philadelphia's city limits, this trend serves primarily to isolate impoverished city residents, who are overwhelmingly African American. The poverty rates of those predominately Black neighborhoods correspond to Patrick Sharkey's definition of neighborhoods in which there is little chance of upward mobility: their schools are ineffective and they are besieged by violent crime on the one hand and, as we will see below, by the police and courts on the other. Because of these conditions, few Black children in Philadelphia will grow up to have incomes much greater than that of the family into which they were born and many will have lower incomes.[11] This lack of intergenerational upward income mobility is illustrated by the fact that median family income for Black families in Philadelphia in 2010 was $36,152, the same as, or just 10% higher, at most, than that a generation earlier in inflation-adjusted dollars.[12]

Intergenerational wealth mobility, or the lack thereof, is even more of a problem for Philadelphia's African Americans than intergenerational income mobility. Less than a quarter of African Americans raised in the middle quintile of national wealth distribution achieve greater wealth than their parents. On the other hand, 68% of African Americans raised in the middle quintile of wealth end up in the bottom two quintiles as adults.[13] Only African Americans raised in the poorest households exceed their parents' "wealth," which in any case is likely to be barely existent or negative.[14] It is therefore unlikely that there is much intergenerational family wealth upward mobility in Philadelphia's Black community. As Alice Goffman's stories tell us, there is, on the contrary, much intergenerational *downward* mobility in both income and wealth in Philadelphia's Black neighborhoods.[15]

The Anvil of Caste: Education

The Philadelphia City School District now enrolls 146,500 students, 56% of whom are Black;[16] 79% of the district's students are eligible for the National Lunch Program, that measure of poverty.[17] Approximately three-quarters of all in-school and out-of-school suspensions and arrests are of Black students. The average teacher's salary is $67,500, typical among large cities but rather high for the region.[18] 35% of those teachers are absent ten days or more each year and just 38% meet all state licensing and certification requirements.

(These are both highly unusual metrics. Pittsburgh, for example, has a teacher absentee percentage of 21% and 93% of its teachers meet state requirements.) The district has a long history of conflicts between the teachers' union and the district administration, as well as between teachers and school-site administrators. In the last few years the state government has intervened in the city, cutting budgets, closing schools and introducing policies to increase the number of charter schools. In the 2013-14 school year there were 57,181 general education students and 9,788 special education students in Philadelphia's charter schools (up from 31,264 and 4,126 in 2009-10).[19] The city's non-charter-school unusually high student-teacher ratios is partially a result. While spending on instruction has shown a steady increase, from approximately $1.1 billion in 2000-01 to $2 billion in 2011-12, spending on support services has trailed inflation.[20] Non-teaching staff, such as counselors and librarians, has been severely cut.[21] The gap between what nearby wealthy districts spend on education and that spent in Philadelphia doubled between 2010 and 2014.[22]

The budgetary issues and administrative policies of the district are highly controversial, but there is little controversy about the fact that the ability of the Philadelphia school district to teach its students to read is far less than that of the national average for public schools. While nationally nearly half of White, non-Hispanic, students in grade 8 read at grade level—Proficient or above on the National Assessment of Educational Progress (NAEP) examination—and 17% of Black students do so, in Philadelphia only a quarter of White students and 12% of Black students read at grade level in grade 8 in 2013.[23] This was actually an improvement for Black students, from 9% in 2009, but a marked decline in scores of White students, from 33% in 2009 and 37% in 2011. (It is notable that only 5% of Black students in Pennsylvania charter schools test at or above Proficient in reading at grade 8.)

Matters are even worse for students from lower income families (those eligible for the National Lunch Program). Just 19% of White students in Philadelphia in this category and 9% of Black students eligible for the National Lunch Program read at grade level in grade 8 (as compared to 28% and 12% of each group nationally). Black students whose parents had some education after high school match the national average for all Black students, 21% at or above

Proficient, and those whose families have incomes too high to be eligible for the National Lunch Program, exceed it, at 30% Proficient or above. Perhaps these children learn to read at home.

We can look at this another way by calculating the *numbers* of students reading at grade level (Proficient and above) whose parents are at various educational attainment levels by aligning NAEP and Census data. Twenty percent of Philadelphia' Black adults over 25 years reported to the Census that they had less than a high school diploma, equivalent to NAEP's "Did not finish high school."[24] Thirty-nine percent said that they were high school graduates with a diploma or GED, equivalent to NAEP's "Graduated high school." Twenty-eight percent reported some college or associate's degree, equivalent to "Some education after high school" and 12% of African Americans reported attaining a Bachelor's degree or higher: "Graduated College."

Given that, we find that *no* grade 8 students in Philadelphia schools reporting that both their parents are without a high school diploma are able to read at grade level or above. Eight percent of Black students reporting that at least one of their parents completed high school read at grade level. Seventeen percent of Black students read at or above grade level in grade 8 and have at least one parent who had some college. And 9% of Black students at grade 8 read at grade level and report that at least one of their parents has a college degree. There are approximately 6,000 Black students in grade 8 in the Philadelphia public schools. If we assume that the percentages of Black adults 25 years of age and over reporting the various levels of educational attainment to the Census is approximately the same as that of the parents of students, then we find there were 1,200 Black students whose parents did not complete high school, of whom none read at grade level; 2,400 whose parents graduated from high school, of whom 200 read at grade level; 1,600 whose parents had some education beyond high school, of whom 300 read at grade level and 800 with a parent who had attained a Bachelor's degree, of whom less than one hundred read at grade level or above by NAEP's standards.

A consequence of these and similar failures of the school system is an estimated high school graduation rate of 45% for Black students and 63% for White students in the 2011-12 school year, both far below national averages. If those students attended schools in neighboring Delaware County, they could expect graduation rates of 66% for Black students and 88% for White students. In nearby Montgomery County, Pennsylvania, the expectation would be for graduation rates of 82% and 92%. That the Philadelphia public schools do not bring half of their students to graduation does not bode well for the next generation, given the NAEP assessments just described. The children whose parents were poorly educated have little chance of significant educational achievement themselves.

The Philadelphia public schools do not educate any of their students as well as national averages for each group. They fail to come anywhere near to providing the quality of education given to students in nearby districts. Although family income and parental education levels have some effect on student achievement, defining the task of the schools, the extent of these failures is too great to be attributed to anything other than the quality of the schools themselves.

Further education outcomes for Black residents of Philadelphia are consistent with this record. Just 13% of Black adults (10% of the men) in the city have attained a college degree and 20% tell the Bureau of the Census that they are without a high school diploma. The 39% of Black residents of Philadelphia who report that they do have high school diplomas include an unknown number who have a GED or equivalent, rather than having graduated from the city's high schools. Just 13% of the Black residents of Philadelphia report to the Bureau of the Census that they have attained a Bachelor's degree or education beyond that point, as contrasted with 34% of White residents of the city.

We can estimate a flow through the city's educational institutions that would contribute to that outcome. In addition to its distinguished arts and music schools, Philadelphia has two major national research universities: the University of Pennsylvania and Temple University. In a recent year the University of Pennsylvania admitted 2,400 first-time undergraduate, degree-seeking students, 200 (8%) of whom were Black and less than half of those were male African Americans. Temple University admitted 4,200 first-time students, just over 600 (14%) of whom were Black. Less than a third of those were male African Americans.[25] Temple graduated 2,500 students, 400 of whom were Black, slightly over a quarter of the Black graduates were male. Penn graduated 2,200 students with

Bachelor's degrees, fewer than 200 of whom were Black, 80 of whom were Black males. This gives us 800 Black students entering our sample of 4-year colleges (250 of whom were male), 600 (200 male) graduating with Bachelor's degrees.

Not all of the students of these universities are graduates of the Philadelphia schools, but it is perhaps not greatly out of line to take their data as standing for the four-year portion of the postsecondary sector as a whole.

The major local two-year institution, the Community College of Philadelphia in a recent year admitted about 4,000 first-time, degree-seeking students, 1,700 of whom were Black; slightly more than one-third of those were men. In 2012, fewer than 200 students received their Associate's degree at the Community College of Philadelphia; 49 of those were Black, 17 of the Black students were men.[26] This is a graduation rate of 3% for Black students at the College, hardly distinguishable from complete failure.

We can now make a rough estimate of the typical educational progression of Black students in Philadelphia. There were approximately 10,000 Black students enrolled in grade 9 in the Philadelphia public schools in the 2008-09 school year; half of whom were male.[‡] There were 5,400 Black students enrolled in grade 12 four years later, 2,500 of whom were male. An estimated 4,300 Black students received regular diplomas, 2,000 of whom were young men. If we assume that all the Black students enrolling in the Community College of Philadelphia and the two universities were graduates of the Philadelphia schools (the over-estimation of Philadelphia residents in those numbers balancing the neglect of possible college placement among other postsecondary institutions), 800 went to four-year colleges and 1,700 went to two-year colleges. (This would be a matriculation rate of 57% for all Black students, 48% for men, which seems quite high, but we are only attempting a rough estimate here.) Out of this group, there were 49 (17 male) graduates with Associate's degrees from the Community College of Philadelphia and 600 with Bachelor's degrees (200 male) from the two research universities. This output, as it were, happens to be 15% of the estimated postsecondary "input" of high school graduates,

---

[‡] Philadelphia is similar to other urban districts in that its grade 9 enrollment is increased by a "gate" test.

which corresponds well with the self-reported educational attainment data from the Census.

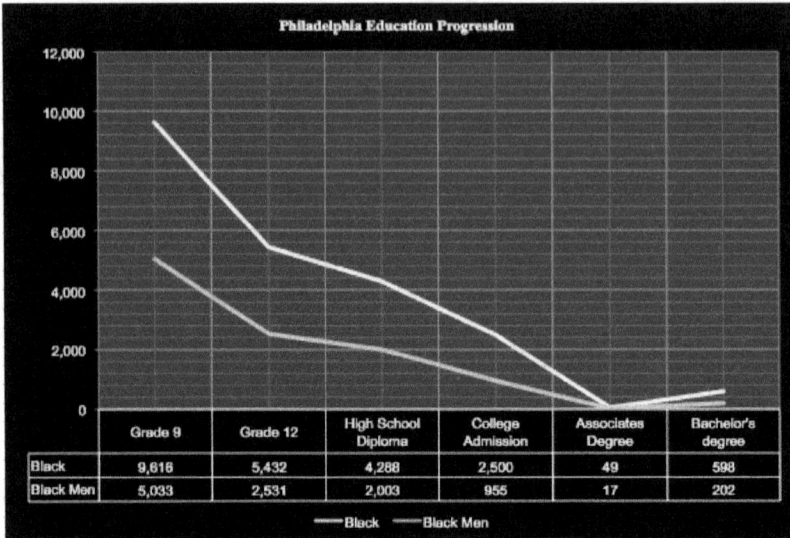

	Grade 9	Grade 12	High School Diploma	College Admission	Associates Degree	Bachelor's degree
Black	9,618	5,432	4,288	2,500	49	598
Black Men	5,033	2,531	2,003	955	17	202

Philadelphia Education Progression

Black — Black Men

White students in Philadelphia, following the same path, were much more than twice as likely to reach the same goal. Of course they were also twice as likely to be taught to read at grade level by the time they were in eighth grade.

The Hammer of Caste: The Criminal Justice System

In 2001 the Justice Policy Institute of the National Center on Institutions and Alternatives found that: "While the White incarceration rate in Pennsylvania is in line with the more modest use of incarceration seen in Western Europe and Canada, the African American and Hispanic incarceration rates are amongst the highest in the world . . ."[27] The State of Pennsylvania incarcerates African Americans at nine times the rate at which White residents of the state are incarcerated. Statewide, nearly 30% of those incarcerations are for violations of drug laws. In Pennsylvania, as elsewhere in the United States, the drug laws are a primary vehicle for the enforcement of the lower caste position of the Black community: they are dramatically differentially enforced, even though it is well-established that the level of illicit drug use is similar in the Black and

White communities. The Prison Policy organization found that "Between 1986 and 1996, the rate at which Whites entered Pennsylvania prisons for a drug offense declined slightly (from 4.48 to 4.44 per 100,000). Meanwhile, the rate at which African Americans entered Pennsylvania prisons for a drug crime grew five fold (26 to 148 per 100,000)."[28] The most common sentence for drug crimes in Pennsylvania is five years.[29] In an illustration of the common "revolving door" prison experience, nearly as many Black prisoners in the state (3,800) are incarcerated for parole violations as for drug offenses (5,000). The average sentence for parole violations was four to eleven years.[30] A Black resident of Pennsylvania, particularly a young adult male, is at great risk of a five-year jail sentence, extendable by another five years or more, for behaviors that are not illegal in, say, Colorado, behaviors that are ignored in White neighborhoods of Philadelphia.[31]

If we estimate the currently incarcerated number of Philadelphia's Black males between the ages of 18 and 64 at 12,000, and use the common estimate of three times the number incarcerated as the number under the control of the criminal justice system, including those on parole and probation, we arrive at a figure of approximately 20% of the city's working age African Americans either not in the community or not able to fully participate in the life of the community.[32] To this group should be added those, predominately young African American men, who are "on the run," not currently either incarcerated, on parole or on probation, but living the hunted life described by Alice Goffman in her book of that title, always a few minutes from a chance encounter with the police that will lead to incarceration, or with one of those violent deaths common in Black ghettos.

Goffman's description of the relationship between the inhabitants of a particularly impoverished and violent Black section of Philadelphia and the criminal justice system reads like a description of a city occupied by a hostile army. The keystone element, as it were, is the drug trade and the laws prohibiting it. As they operate outside the law, business disputes among dealers and customers are dealt with in an extra legal fashion, often by violence. In so far as the drug trade involves a large proportion of the people in the community, the police can find violators of the drug laws nearly at will on any Black neighborhood's street corner. This dynamic is gendered: while anyone may be a user of drugs, the selling of illicit drugs is predominately a male occupation and therefore the involvement with the criminal justice system is predominately a male hazard. One outcome of this is that many Black girls finish school and go on to college, while their male peers go to jail.[33]

There is, then, the structural racism of the criminal justice system, embodied in the inequitably applied drug laws, and then there is the racism that manifests in the concentration of police activities in Black neighborhoods (justified by the drug law violations found there, rather than in, say, the housing of students attending the University of Pennsylvania or Temple University). All this is exacerbated by a culture within the Philadelphia Police Department itself that appears to partake of (if not to encourage) the destructive culture of those whom they are policing. Karen Heller, a reporter for the *Philadelphia Inquirer,* would have us "Imagine if coworkers allegedly violated rules again and again, not over a year, but sometimes for more than a decade . . .

> Imagine if they allegedly committed acts of violence, and stole money and drugs, and their reckless behavior resulted in $500,000 in settlement payouts . . . And imagine if these employees were never fired or appropriately disciplined and, in some cases, collected substantial overtime and commendations. What sort of business would tolerate such behavior? Welcome to the Philadelphia Police Department.[34]

Defenders of the status quo, such as chiefs of police, point to the comparatively higher level of violent crimes in Black communities as a reason for the concentration of police activity there. But as Goffman makes clear, in Philadelphia much of that violence is part and parcel of the drug economy and policing practices in regard to it. It arises from the illegality of commonly used drugs, from the scarcity of other means of obtaining an income in a community where the usual avenues to careers are constricted by a dysfunctional school system. If the schools of Philadelphia functioned as well for African American children as for White children (or as well as the suburban schools function for Black children) and if drug law enforcement were equitable, life in and for the city's Black community would be quite different. However, the values of the Pennsylvania state government have run in the other direction. It could not find adequate funding for Philadelphia's schools, but it has begun building a new $400 million prison outside Philadelphia.[35]

Modeling a More Equitable Philadelphia

The task of modeling a more equitable Philadelphia, a city where young Black men would not spend their youth on the run or incarcerated, requires that criminal justice system policies and practices must be reformed and the public school system improved. As noted above, the city's incarceration rate disparities are driven both by the irrationality of drug laws and their inequitable application. The sale and use of marijuana is now legal in a few states and many localities. Penalties in regard to the use of the powder and crystal forms of cocaine are being equalized. If the will for wholesale reform is absent these and similar matters could be attended to step-by-step. If it appeared that a fifth to a quarter of students at the University of Pennsylvania were likely to be arrested for possession of marijuana (to use the common estimate of marijuana use among White college students), it is possible that possession of marijuana would become a ticketing offense, as is becoming the case in many other localities, or less. If recreational use and sale of marijuana were legalized, as in Colorado and other states, a large part of the city's drug economy would disappear and along with it its associated violence and police corruption.

School improvement begins with adequate funding, challenging goals, professional development of teachers and careful planning. The nearby Maryland school districts of Montgomery and Baltimore counties are models for such efforts. The graduation rate for African American students in the Baltimore County district (which is 40% Black) has now reached 80%, on a $15,000 per student revenue. Montgomery County, Maryland, the pioneer in these matters, has a graduation rate over 85% for the 20% of its students who are African American, on a $19,000 per student revenue. (These revenue figures bracket the 2010-11 figure of $17,400 for Philadelphia). Baltimore City, with many of the same issues as Philadelphia, has a graduation rate of 70% for its Black students, much higher than that of Philadelphia. The strategies used to accomplish this are well-known: universal pre-kindergarten (preferably full-day); literacy-oriented early childhood education; extended school days and school years;

intensive professional education for teachers and sharing of best practices.

Within 24 months of high school graduation, more than 60% of Baltimore County's African American students are enrolled in college. Matching this would easily support a postsecondary goal of at least 40% of all Philadelphia adults in each race, ethnic and gender subgroup attaining education to the level of Bachelor's degrees and above. That would more than triple the present educational attainment of Philadelphia residents who are the descendants of enslaved Africans, bringing with it the concomitant advantages of income, wealth and socio-economic mobility.

If, for the sake of argument, we model the effects of improvements in the education of Philadelphia for the Black community by setting educational attainment for Black adults ages 25 and over to the current distribution for the White community we find an increase of 43,400 with a Bachelor's degree and 41,700 with a graduate or professional degree and a decline of 25,400 among those without a high school diploma. Given current median earnings by educational attainment, this would result in an increase in total Black community income from $14.5 billion to $18.6 billion per year: 28%.[36] It is clear that the bulk of this increase would come from the increased income flowing from the achievement of a college degree. We can then make the same experiment with community wealth. The increase in tax revenue from these changes in income and wealth would be a good source for the funds needed for the improvement of the education system.

These changes could be begun by the governor, mayor, chief of police, district attorney and superintendent of schools any time they decide to do so.

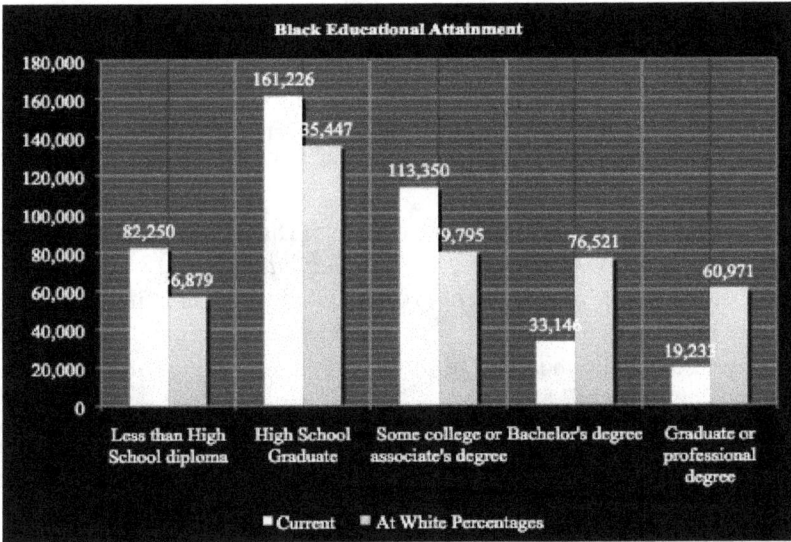

Black Educational Attainment

	Less than High School diploma	High School Graduate	Some college or associate's degree	Bachelor's degree	Graduate or professional degree
Current	82,250	161,226	113,350	33,146	19,231
At White Percentages	56,879	135,447	79,795	76,521	60,971

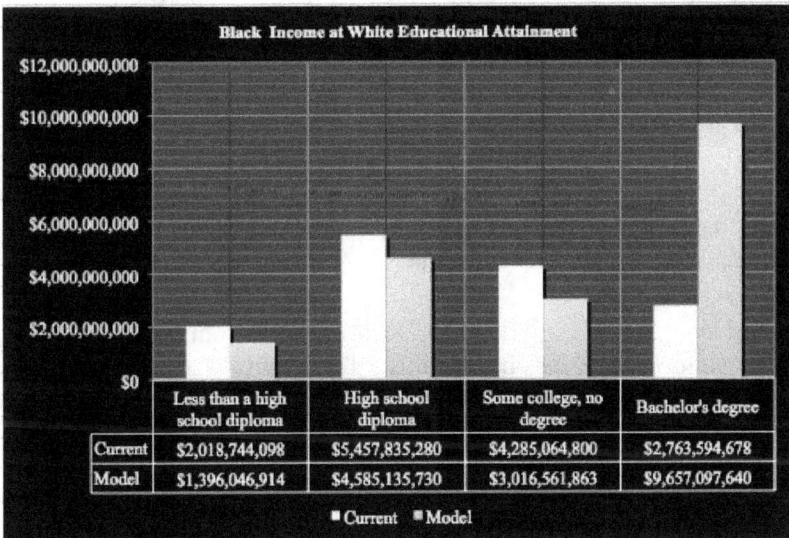

Black Income at White Educational Attainment

	Less than a high school diploma	High school diploma	Some college, no degree	Bachelor's degree
Current	$2,018,744,098	$5,457,835,280	$4,285,064,800	$2,763,594,678
Model	$1,396,046,914	$4,585,135,730	$3,016,561,863	$9,657,097,640

217

Notes: Chapter Eight

---

[1] Eichel, Larry. Philadelphia: The State of the City, A 2014 Update. Philadelphia: The Pew Charitable Trusts, April, 2014. http://www.pewtrusts.org/~/media/Assets/2014/04/05/PhiladelphiaSt ateofCityreport2014.pdf?la=en

[2] The disproportion between the genders in Black Philadelphia was noted by W. E. B. DuBois in *The Philadelphia Negro* (1899). He attributed it to the employment difficulties of Black men in the city at that time.

[3] Kaiser Family Foundation, http://kff.org/state-category/minority-health/?state=PA

[4] www.census.gov/ compendia/statab/cats/births_deaths_marriages_divorces/life_expect ancy.html

[5] Bureau of the Census, Selected Economic Data 2006-2010, American Community Survey, Table DP03.

[6] U. S. Census Bureau, 2012 ACS 1-year survey, tables B19313A&B.

[7] Loprest, Pamela and Mitchell, Josh. Labor Market and Demographic Analysis: A Metro-Level Picture of Short-term Employment Growth by Skill in Philadelphia. The Urban Institute, Washington, D.C., May 2012.

[8] Comparing the Census's 2012 median incomes for male workers gives a similar result: the White median income is 29% higher than the Black.

[9] U.S. Census Bureau, Survey of Income and Program Participation, 2008 Panel, Wave 10, updated, Table 1. Median Value of Assets for Households, by Type of Asset Owned and Selected Characteristics: 2011.

[10] Reardon, Sean F. and Bischoff, Kendra. Growth in the Residential Segregation of Families by Income, 1970-2009. US2010, November 2011, p. 20. https://dl.dropboxusercontent.com/u/9108869/RussellSageIncomeSe gregationreport-1.pdf

[11] Patrick Sharkey and his colleagues have found that even for "children whose family income is in the top three quintiles, spending childhood in a high-poverty neighborhood versus a low- poverty neighborhood [say, experiencing a poverty rate of 25 percent

compared to a rate of 5 percent] raises the chances of downward mobility by 52 percent." Sharkey, Patrick. Neighborhoods and the Black-White Mobility Gap. Philadelphia: The Pew Charitable Trusts, 2009, p. 9. http://www.pewstates.org/uploadedFiles/PCS_Assets/2009/PEW_NEIGHBORHOODS(1).pdf.

[12] The 1990 census gives national Black median family income as $21,110. Multiplying this by the inflation factor of 1.71 to get 2010 dollars gives us $36,098. The 2010 median Black family income for Philadelphia was approximately 90% of the national figure.

[13] Pew, p. 20.

[14] Pew, p. 19.

[15] Goffman, Alice. On the Run. Cambridge, Massachusetts: Harvard University Press, 2014.

[16] There has been a sharp decline in Black enrollments, less severe declines in the numbers of students from other groups.

[17] U. S. Department of Education, Office for Civil Rights, 2011 Survey.

[18] The average teacher salary in Baltimore is $60,126; in Newark, $61,566.

[19] Pennsylvania Department of Education Charter School Annual Reports and Enrollment Data. http://www.portal.state.pa.us/portal/server.pt/community/annual_rep orts_and_enrollment_data/7357

[20] Commonwealth Foundation. openPAgov.org. http://www.openpagov.org/education_revenue_and_expenses.asp

[21] "On September 9, 2014, Philadelphia parents and the advocacy organization Parents United for Public Education filed "Allen v. Dumaresq", asking the Commonwealth Court to order Pennsylvania's Education Secretary to do what the law requires: investigate hundreds of parent complaints of massive deficiencies in city schools . . . Problems alleged by parents include alarming levels of overcrowding such that teachers can no longer walk between desks to interact with individual students, increasingly limited curricular offerings, a distressing and dangerous lack of counselors and school nurses, and squalid and insufficient toilet facilities." Education Law Center, September 14, 2014.

[22] McCorry, Kevin. "Widening Equity Gap?" WHYY News, NewsWorks. January 5, 2015. http://www.newsworks.org/index.php/local//item/76981-widening-equity-gap-corbett-administration-advocates-differ-on-ap-education-funding-report/

[23] The state test (Pennsylvania Standards School Assessment) results indicate 60% of Black students achieving Proficient and Advanced scores in reading at grade 8. See: www.openpagov.org/school-performance/sdefault.asp. The NAEP results show unusual year-to-year variability for all sub-groups.

[24] A caution: the numbers of adults in these categories, as reported by their children, are not necessarily the same as those self-reported to the Census or those that might be obtained from school and college records.

[25] U.S. Department of Education, National Center for Education Statistics, IPEDS.

[26] U.S. Department of Education, National Center for Education Statistics, IPEDS.

[27] http://www.prisonpolicy.org/scans/keystone.shtml

[28] http://www.prisonpolicy.org/scans/keystone.shtml

[29] Pennsylvania Department of Corrections, Annual Statistical Report, 2011. 2011%20Annual%20Statitstical%20Report.pdf

[30] Pennsylvania Department of Corrections, Annual Statistical Report, 2011. 2011%20Annual%20Statitstical%20Report.pdf

[31] An indication of the race/ethnicity distribution of drug use in Philadelphia can be obtained from the number of drug deaths. In Philadelphia County between 2009 and 2013 there were 659 drug deaths, 461 of which were of White, 93 of Black and 100 of Hispanic men and women. (Pennsylvania State Coroners Association, Heroin Overdose Death Report, 2009-2013.) http://www.co.westmoreland.pa.us/Archive/ViewFile/Item/495

[32] These estimates are in line with the gender disparities found by the Census in this age group of Philadelphia's Black community.

[33] The percentage of Black females with a Bachelor's degree or higher (14%) is nearly forty percent higher than that of Black males (10.6%). There are nearly twice as many Black females enrolled in college or graduate school than Black males (31,000 as compared to 16,000).

[34] Heller, Karen. "Another Philadelphia police scandal, right on schedule." Philly.com, The Inquirer, August 7, 2014.

http://articles.philly.com/2014-08-07/news/52519336_1_six-narcotics-officers-philadelphia-police-department-narcotics-bureau
[35] Stroud, Matt. "Philadelphia Schools Closing While a New $400 Million Prison is Under Construction: Could It Be Worse Than It Sounds?" Forbes, June 17, 2013. http://www.forbes.com/sites/mattstroud/2013/06/17/philadelphia-schools-closing-while-new-400-million-prison-under-construction/
[36] Earnings and unemployment rates by educational attainment, 2013. Bureau of Labor Statistics. http://www.bls.gov/emp/ep_chart_001.htm.

Chapter Nine: Rochester, New York

"In the manufacture of photographic apparatus and materials and optical goods Rochester easily holds first place in the world . . . For many years before the Civil War it was a busy station of the "Underground Railroad," by which fugitive slaves were assisted in escaping to Canada. *The Encyclopedia Britannica, Eleventh Edition, 1911.*

The long trains loaded with Pennsylvania coal that used to go right into the basements of the Kodak plant no longer arrive. The workers, from the sledgehammer wielding laborers who in the winter broke up the frozen carloads of coal to the scientists working in the laboratories, refining Kodachrome, are no longer there. And Rochester, today, is in many ways the opposite of a station on the Underground Railroad. Instead of a welcoming place of safety, which the descendants of enslaved Africans pass through on their way to freedom in Canada, it is a city where they are kept firmly in their place by the forces of institutionalized racism.

Demographics

Rochester's population in 2010 was 210,585, less than in 1910. The City of Rochester, and its metropolitan area, primarily suburban Monroe County, are quite segregated, with a Index of Dissimilarity of 63 for the metropolitan area, where 60 (or above) is considered very high.[1] Areas of central Rochester are nearly completely African American, areas of the surrounding Monroe County are as completely White.

The median age of the White population of Rochester in 2010 was 36, that of the Black population, 28. The percentages of Black children in the cohorts from birth to 19 years of age are twice as great as those of White children in those cohorts. The percentages of young adult Black residents of Rochester then drops below that of White residents, which peaks in the cohorts 20 to 34 year of age. One explanation of this might be that while the city's Black population is reproducing itself, the White population of the city is maintained only by immigration of young adults, students at the University of Rochester, the Rochester Institute of Technology and other local institutions of higher learning.[*]

The infant mortality rate for Black residents of Monroe County is four times that for White residents of the county. Twice as many African Americans as Whites in the county report that their health is only "fair" or "poor" (24% and 12%).[2] Sixteen percent of adult African Americans in the county have diabetes and 43% have high blood pressure as compared to 9% of White residents with diabetes and 31% with high blood pressure.[3] The percentage of deaths in New York State that were "premature," before age 75, was 60% among Black, non-Hispanics, as compared to 34% among White, non-Hispanics.[4]

The percentages of each gender in the Black population of Rochester are approximately balanced in childhood, with a slight preponderance of males to age twenty, at which point the percentage of males in the Black population declines, from 85% of the female percentage in the 20 to 24 age-bracket to 72% in the 30 to 34 age bracket. For the population over 70 years of age the Black gender ratio is slightly over one man for every two women. In the four cohorts between 20 and 40, there are 3,174 fewer Black men than Black women, a number approximately equivalent to one of those 4-year cohorts. Or, in other words, a quarter of Rochester's young adult and half of its elderly Black men are missing.

Income

Racial segregation in the City of Rochester and Monroe County coincides with income segregation. White Monroe County's poverty rate, including Rochester, is 10%. Black Monroe County's poverty rate, including Rochester, is 37%. White Monroe County's median income is $72,078; Black Monroe County has a median family income of $33,720 (and Black Rochester has a median family income of only $28,870, just above the poverty line). Only eleven percent of Monroe County's White families with related children under 18 years of age have incomes under the poverty line, as do 33% of those of White women raising their children with no husband

---

[*] There were 11,500 White students in college housing in Monroe County, according to the 2010 U.S. Census (table PCO8).

present. In contrast, 45% of Monroe County's Black families with related children under 18 years of age have incomes below the poverty line, as do 54% of those of Black women caring for their children without a husband.

Although Kodak filed for bankruptcy in 2012, Bausch & Lomb continues to prosper, as does the University of Rochester, its medical system, and the Rochester Institute of Technology. Forty-one percent of White Rochester's civilian employed adults work in these and similar institutions in management, business, science and arts occupations. On the other hand, 33% of Black Rochester's civilian employed adults are in service occupations. These are quite remarkable disparities: White Rochester comprises a managerial, professional and scientific class, which is served by Black Rochester. The following table compares data for the Black and White populations of the City of Rochester alone.

Rochester (Census, 2010)	White	Black
Population	93,932	86,078
Median Family Income	$48,626	$28,870
Unemployment Rate	7.4%	17.4%
Poverty Rate	23%	37%
Management Occupations	41%	23%
Service Occupations	16%	33%

The disparities are even greater for Monroe County as a whole.

Monroe County	White	Black
Population	570,608	112,789
Median Family Income	$72,078	$33,720
Unemployment Rate	5.8%	15.4%
Poverty Rate	10%	37%
Management Occupations	44%	25%
Service Occupations	15%	34%

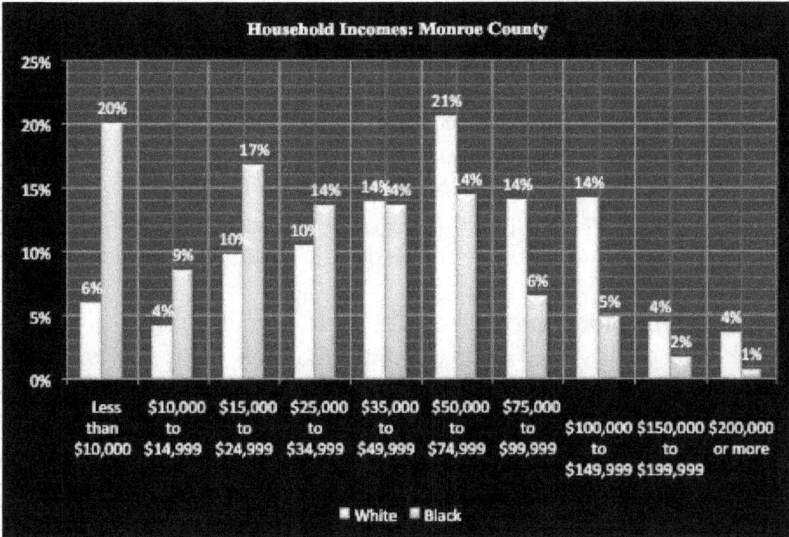

Household Incomes: Monroe County

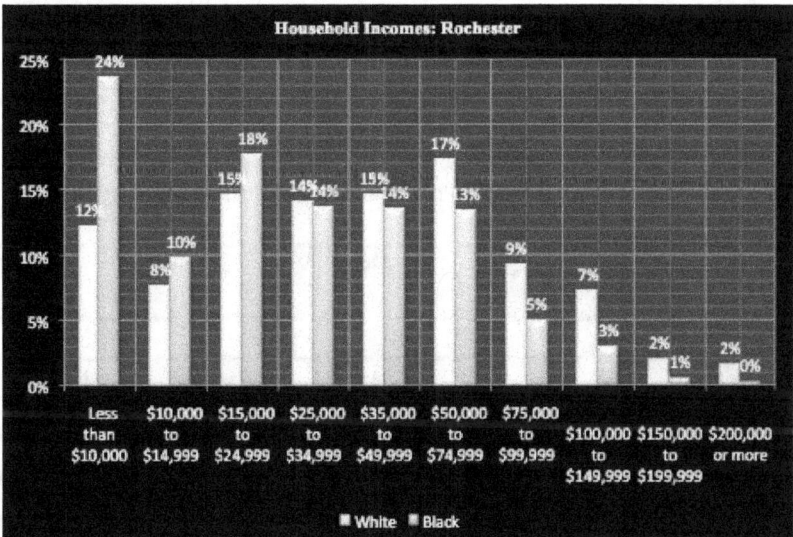

Household Incomes: Rochester

The distribution of household incomes in Monroe County, including Rochester, shows great contrasts between Black and White households.[5] In 2010, while over half of Black households in the county had incomes under $25,000 per year, just 20% of White incomes were in that category. At the other end of the income distribution, nearly a quarter of White households had incomes over $100,000 per year, compared to just 8% of Black households. White per capita income ($30,236) was double Black per capita income ($15,099).

In the much less prosperous city of Rochester itself, a quarter of Black households had incomes under $10,000 per year, twice the percentage of White households in that category. Twenty percent of White households had incomes over $75,000 per year, compared to only 9% of Black households. Just 29 Black families in the city had incomes over $200,000 per year, as compared to 464 White families (and over 7,000 in Monroe County). White per capita income ($24,389) in Rochester was double Black per capita income ($12,493). The Black poverty rate of 37% was 50% higher than that of Whites (23%). Half of Rochester's Black women raising small children alone lived in poverty. In other words, it is "normal" in the City of Rochester for Black children to grow up in poverty.

Rochester City's mean White family income is $63,044, while the city's Black mean family income is just over half of that: $37,372. These are much lower than the national averages in each case. We can produce an approximation of Rochester income quintiles (means) by assuming that the proportions between them are those of the national figures. This gives us the following distribution:

Family Mean Income (est.)	Rochester	White	Black
Top 5%	$272,878	$338,864	$207,536
Highest	162,299	193,537	126,612
Fourth	73,943	92,918	60,937
Third (Middle)	48,377	63,044	37,372
Second	29,573	40,316	21,526
Lowest	12,031	17,939	7,494

It can be seen that in Rochester, as nationally, Black family incomes (below the very few in the highest quintile) are, in effect, shifted down one quintile from White, non-Hispanic, family incomes, particularly for the lower three Black quintiles. The average (mean) income of Rochester's poorest 20% of Black families is less than half that of the lowest quintile of the city's White families. When Rochester's estimated Black income quintiles are compared with the income quintiles for all Americans, we see that the mean income of the highest quintile of Rochester's Black community is close to the fourth quintile, nationally, that the average income of the middle quintile of Rochester's Black community is in the second quintile of all Americans and that the average income of Rochester's lowest Black quintiles is less than half of that of the average American in the lowest quintile.

Mean Family Incomes	U.S.	Rochester Black
Top 5% Mean Income	$352,338	$207,536
Highest	209,559	126,612
Fourth	95,474	60,937
Third (Middle)	62,464	37,372
Second	38,184	21,526
Lowest	15,534	7,494

The lower two quintiles of Black Rochester families—40%—have an average income lower than the average for any country in the developed world, less than half that for Turkey, the poorest Organization for Economic Cooperation and Development (OECD) country.

Wealth

The economic stability and mobility of families is as much, if not more, dependent on wealth than on income. According to the OECD "wealth makes up an important part of a household's economic resources, and can protect from economic hardship and vulnerability.

For example, as should be obvious, a low-income household having above-average wealth will be better off than a low-income household with no wealth at all. Across the OECD, the average household net financial wealth per capita is estimated at $42,903.[6]

Wealth is conventionally divided between financial assets and houses (or as the Bureau of the Census has it, "owner-occupied units"). In Rochester in 2010, 10,037 of 46,396 White Rochester households and 1,533 of Black Rochester's 32,449 households had interest, dividends, or net rental income.[7] The rest of Rochester's Black households did not even have interest income from bank accounts. We can take it, then, that the combined financial assets of Rochester's Black community is a relatively trivial amount held by the highest quintile of Black households.

The mean net worth (excluding equity in their own home) of White, non-Hispanic, households in 2011 was $336,439, indicating a combined net worth for White Rochester of $15 billion.[8] The mean net worth (excluding equity in own home) of African Americans in 2011 was $49,119, indicating a combined net worth for Black Rochester of a tenth of that, $1.5 billion. We can then add in that quintessential American asset, the owner-occupied home. The mean value of a White owner-occupied home in 2010 was $100,000. The mean value of a Black owner-occupied home in 2010 was $35,000. There are 21,000 White owner-occupied units and 10,000 Black owner-occupied units in Rochester. Although the value of housing in Rochester is probably somewhat lower than the national average, a reasonable estimate of the home equity of the 21,000 White owner-occupied units is about $2.1 billion, that of the 10,000 Black owner-occupied units about $350 million. Totaling these approximations, it appears that the net worth, *including houses,* of White Rochester is approximately $17 billion, that of Black Rochester less than $2 billion.

We can take it, then, that the per capita wealth of the city's Black population is on the order of $23,000, that of the city's White population at least $185,000. The latter is close to the OECD average. The former is not in the same category as the average wealth of a resident of any developed country.

Mobility

There is a growing consensus that there is too little economic mobility in the United States. According to Raj Chetty and his colleagues (whose data is not disaggregated by race), the chances of a child brought up in a family with an income of $66,000 reaching the top quintile is 20%; the chances of that child falling to the bottom quintile was nearly the same, 19%. On the other hand, the chances of a child brought up in a family with an income of $40,000 reaching the top quintile is 9%, of falling to the bottom quintile, 25%.[9] Applying these figures to the Rochester family income distributions, we see that about 80% of the city's Black families are accounted for by the second example: it is nearly three times as likely that their children will fall to the bottom income quintile group as to rise to the top. This appears to indicate that for most Black families in Rochester, there is little upward economic mobility from one generation to the next.

We have seen that most of each generation in Black Rochester grows up in poverty or close to it, with little or no family net worth and little or no chance of improvement for themselves or their children. Why is this? There are two institutions enforcing the lower-caste status of the descendants of enslaved Africans in Rochester as elsewhere: the school district and the criminal justice system.

The Anvil of Caste: Education
Approximately three times as many African Americans as their White neighbors in the county have not graduated from high school; three times as many White as Black residents of the county are college educated. Ninety-two percent of the White adult population of Monroe County have at least high school diplomas or the equivalent; 39% have Bachelor's degrees or higher qualifications. Just 7% have not graduated from high school. Seventy-two percent of the adult Black population of Monroe County have high school diplomas or the equivalent; 10% have Bachelor's degrees or higher qualifications. Twenty-five percent have not graduated from high school—more than triple the White percentage.

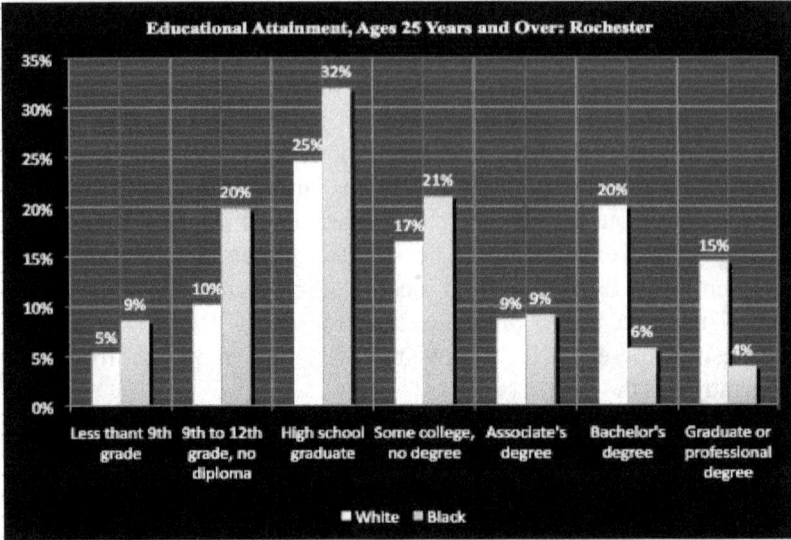

Educational Attainment, Ages 25 Years and Over: Rochester

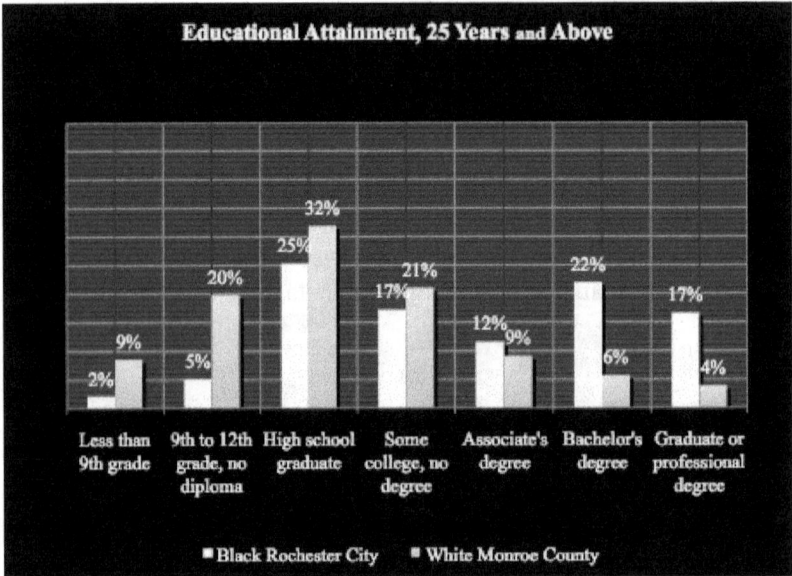

Educational Attainment, 25 Years and Above

The Rochester City School District has an enrollment of 29,197 students, 17,946 (61%) of whom are Black or African American, 7,208 (25%) of whom are Hispanic or Latino and 2,957 (10%) of whom are White. (There are approximate 10,000 school-age White residents of the city; two-thirds of these are not enrolled in the city's public schools.)[10] Eighty-five percent of the district's students are listed as "economically disadvantaged." In 2012-13 there were approximately twice as many students enrolled in grade 9 as in grade 12 as a consequence of a "gate" assessment at grade 9. The large number of children spending more than one year in grade 9 can both be attributed to a lack of academic achievement in earlier years and be said to be a factor leading to the absence of a high school diploma four years later. It is common among schools and districts serving children living in poverty, nearly unknown in wealthy communities.

In a typical Rochester school, comparatively few teachers are highly educated, few teachers new to teaching are in the classroom after their second year, few, if any, teachers are in the classroom after their fourth year. In the 2011-12 school year, only 16% of the district's teachers had a "Master's Degree Plus 30 Hours or a Doctorate," the standard designation for the best-qualified teachers. The state-wide average is 38%. The average salary of teachers in the district (2011) was $55,602. The turnover rate of teachers with fewer than five years of experience was 51%. The turnover rate of all teachers was 28%, double the state-wide average. (Nationally, 80% of teachers with 1 – 3 years experience and 84% of all teachers remain in the same school from one year to the next.[11])

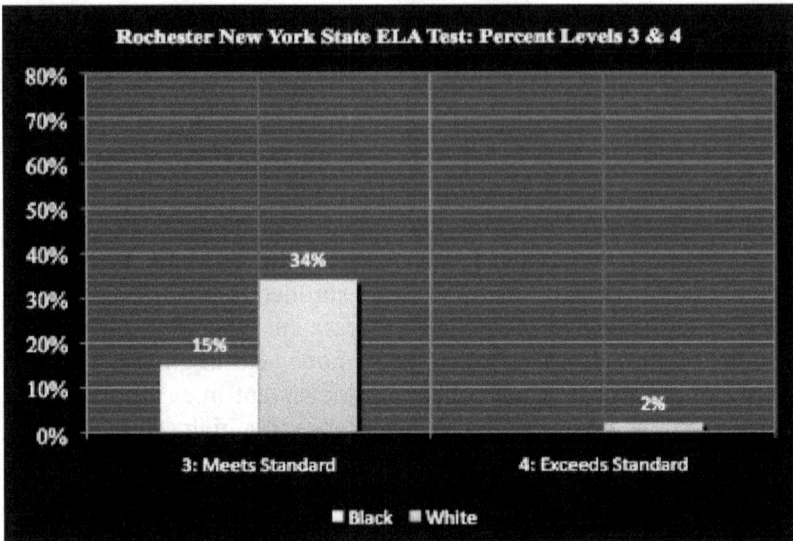

Rochester New York State ELA Test: Percent Levels 3 & 4

Statewide, 31% of New York students reach the National Assessment of Educational Progress (NAEP) Proficient (grade level) status in grade 8 reading, and 4% reach the Advanced level. White students score at Proficient or above 46% of the time; Black New York State students reach Proficient or above 18% of the time. As Rochester is not one of the urban school districts for which there are NAEP results, we turn to the New York State testing program, which also uses a four-point scale. The results in Grade 8 English Language Arts for the state are reported as 48% reaching level 3 ("meets standard") and 2% reaching level 4 ("exceeds standard"). A 2011 NAEP report, "Mapping State Proficiency Standards Onto the NAEP Scales" finds that the New York State testing program's proficiency level, that is, level 3, is equivalent to the NAEP Basic level, that is, level 2. We can then make a conservative estimate by averaging levels three and four on the New York tests, so that 25% of grade 8 students would be at grade level, slightly lower than the NAEP findings: call it a range from 25% to 28%.

Looking at New York State testing results for Rochester in the 2011-12 school year we find that 18% of all students reached the state's level 3 and 0% reached level 4, which would give us an estimated 9-12% at grade level by NAEP standards. Among Black students, 15% reached level 3 on the New York State test (and none at level 4), as compared to 34% of White students at level 3 and 2% at level 4. This translates as 7%-9% NAEP-equivalent Black students at grade level, 18% to 21% for White students. If comparisons of NAEP and New York State testing results are interpreted in this way, which seems reasonable, it would appear that 90% or more of Rochester's Black grade 8 students did not read at or above grade level in 2011-12.

The New York State Department of Education believes that the New York State "common core" tests, begun in 2013, are now aligned with NAEP. In the 2014 administration of these tests, 5.7% of all Rochester grade 8 students scored at level 3 or above (up from 5.6% the previous year).[12] This was the lowest percentage at grade level of any of the state's large cities. Among White students, 12% reached level 3 and 8% reached level 4. Among Black students, 4% reached level 3 and none reached level 4 (due to rounding, the combined levels 3 and 4 totaled 5%). For Black male students, 3% reached level 3 and none reached level 4.[13]

The failure of the district to teach its Black students to read and write by grade 8 is nearly total.

There are many ways to calculate high school graduation rates, some more exotic than others. There is little difference in results among them for successful districts. On the other hand, they can produce widely differing results for less successful districts because of the grade 9 "gate test" issue. If we wish to focus on the record of the school in educating its students, rather than, say, the "resilience" of individual students to the effects of an inadequate education, the commonsense method of dividing the number of diplomas by the number of students enrolled in grade 9 four years earlier will tell us what we want to know. There were 2,505 Black students in grade 9 of the Rochester public schools in the 2008-09 school year. There were 671 Black recipients of New York State's standard, Regents, diplomas in 2011-12, a graduation rate of 27%. There were 1,330 Black *male* students in grade 9 of the Rochester public schools in the 2008-09 school year. There were 323 Black male recipients of New York State's Regents, diplomas in 2011-12, a graduation rate by this method of 24%.[14]

The New York State Department of Education calculates an "Aspirational Performance Measure," in effect its judgment of whether students are well-prepared for careers and college.[15] The state judged 5.1% of Rochester graduates in June 2013 as satisfying this measure. The percentage of Black students was 2.9%.[†] As, according to Bruce Western and his colleagues, the lifetime chances of incarceration for a young adult African American man without a high school diploma is as high as 60%, more—many more—male Black students are being prepared by the Rochester schools for jail than for good jobs or college.

Rochester's education results can be compared to those in a nearby working-class suburban district, Greece, which has a k-12 enrollment of 11,281, 13% of whom are African American and 72% of whom are White. In 2012-13 there were approximately equal numbers of students in all high school grades, that is, the grade 9 "gate" was open. The district's average teacher salary (2011) was $60,870 (9% higher than that of Rochester) and the teacher turn-over rate was 13% (half of that of Rochester). The district's grade 8 English Language Arts outcomes for 2014 were that 32% of the district's students scored at levels 3 and 4 in the state English Language Arts test; 15% of the district's Black students did so, nearly four times that of Black students in Rochester. The district's "four-year graduation-rate total cohort for accountability" was 84%, 76% for Black students.

Black students in the Greece public school district are as likely to graduate from high school as the national average for White students. Black students in the Rochester school district have about one-third that chance. As with many districts like Rochester, a Black student can double his or her chance of learning to read and write and graduate from high school by taking the bus to a nearby suburban district.

How well-prepared are these Rochester school district graduates? We have seen the state's judgment in regard to its "Aspirational" measure. There are other ways to look at it.

We might first look at Monroe Community College for an indication of the postsecondary preparation and success of Black students graduated from the Rochester schools. Eighty-two percent of Monroe Community College's 50,000 credit and non-credit students are Monroe County residents; 4,328 are listed as Rochester

---

[†] The corresponding number for the nearby suburban Greece district were 43.4% for all graduates and 18.9% for the district's Black graduates.

residents (which of course does not necessarily mean that they are graduates of the city school district). The U.S. Department of Education's Integrated Postsecondary Education Data System (IPEDS) counts 4,119 first-time students in fall 2006, 670 of whom were Black, 296 were Black men. Completers within 150% of normal time (2012) total 938, 62 of whom were Black. Fourteen of those were men. Approximately 9% of Black students enrolling in Monroe Community College and 5% of Black men graduate within 150% of normal time. Not all of those graduates attended Rochester city schools.

At the University of Rochester, by way of comparison, we find that in 2006 there were 1,219 first-time, undergraduate, degree-seeking students, 50 of whom were Black. Each year the University enrolls, on average, four Black students from the Rochester school district, one of whom is male.[16] In 2013 the University awarded 1,441 Bachelor's degrees, 59 of which went to Black students. It is possible that two or three of these were from the Rochester school district. In 2006 there were 2,368 first-time, undergraduate, degree-seeking students at the Rochester Institute of Technology, 108 of whom were Black, 32 of those had transferred into the school. In 2013 the University awarded 2,478 Bachelor's degrees to students, 102 of whom were Black. Perhaps some of them were graduates of the Rochester schools.

It appears likely that only about one or two dozen male Black Rochester school district graduates go on to receive Associate's degrees each year and something on the same order, at most, receive Bachelor's degrees.

As a check on these estimates, we can look again at the educational attainment of Rochester city's adult population. This shows that 10% of those who are Black have Bachelor's or higher, about 5,000 people. With the 2,505 membership of the grade 9 class used for the calculations above, we would expect about 250 annually to eventually receive Bachelor's degrees or higher, which would over, say, forty years, provide twice the number of Black adults in Rochester educated to that level as is now the case. Given conditions in Rochester and American geographical mobility, the estimates above of the record of the Rochester school district appear reasonable. If we compare these educational outcomes for African American residents of Rochester to those for White residents of

Monroe County (including Rochester) we can see that nearly four times the proportion of the latter as the former have attained education to the Bachelor's degree level or above and that the proportions reverse for the populations without high school diplomas. It is not too much to say that a college education for Rochester and Monroe County residents is a White privilege.‡

These disparities have strong effects on the income of Rochester's Black community, its economic mobility and other factors, such as incarceration rates. Looking first at incomes, the Bureau of the Census has calculated the relationship between educational attainment and earnings. These vary by race and gender, but those variations are overwhelmed by the education-dependent income variations. Therefore unsatisfactory educational outcomes for Black students in the Rochester schools have an important effect in limiting their incomes. Thirty percent can look forward to incomes under $20,000 per year. Only 10% can expect incomes over $50,000, that is, above the median national income for all Americans. Sixty percent can expect incomes below the poverty level. An African American living in Rochester who has attained the Master's degree level of education (e.g., a school teacher) can expect to earn three times the income of a Black Rochester resident without a high school diploma. If African American educational attainment in Rochester were similar to that of White residents of Monroe County, more than four times as many as is now the case would have incomes at the level of that teacher.

Ron Haskins's widely cited report on "Education and Economic Mobility" examines the effect of a college degree on the potential of Americans to move among household income quintiles.[17] As we have seen, just 10% of Rochester's Black residents ages 25 and over have a college degree. This is equivalent, in Haskins's calculations, to the percentage expected of those in the bottom income quintile for all Americans. (The others increase from 20% in the second quintile to 53% of those in the top quintile having Bachelor's degrees or higher.) At that level, 68% of adults would be expected to remain in the bottom two quintiles and only 5% would have a chance of

---

‡ It is likely that of those White residents of Rochester listed as "some college, no degree," many are undergraduates who have not yet finished their studies.

reaching the top quintile.

The Rochester school district brings relatively few of its Black students to grade level in reading in grade 8. It graduates just over a quarter of them. A few dozen earn Associate's degrees, a few dozen more Bachelor's degrees and above. Without those qualifications the vast majority of graduates of the school district find that their opportunities for successful careers are quite limited, their chances of economic mobility beyond the station in life of their parents scant.

The Hammer of Caste: The Criminal Justice System

The Rochester Chief of Police has stated that in Rochester, "Despite still being a minority, blacks [sic] are more likely to be victims of violent crime,

> are twice as likely to be arrested, almost four times more likely to be arrested for a violent crime,[§] and more than twice as likely to be stopped and interviewed during an investigation [than White, non-Hispanic residents] . . . violent crime is about 10% more concentrated in majority black neighborhoods than would be expected in majority black neighborhoods if violent crime was randomly distributed across all census tracts regardless of racial composition."[18]

That is the presentation from the side of the criminal justice system. It can be slightly rephrased as it might be seen from the point of view of the Black community: *Although violent crimes are just 10% more frequent in Black Rochester, African Americans are twice as likely to be stopped and "interviewed" by the police and four times as likely to be arrested for violent crimes.*

In the United States as a whole, 1% of White, non-Hispanic, men, 18 to 64 years of age were incarcerated in 2012. Six times as many, proportionately, of Black men in that age group were incarcerated. The incarceration rate for Black men in Monroe County is ten times that for the county's White men. As the arrest rate for violent crimes (and thus, most probably, the incarceration rate) for African Americans in Rochester is four times that of Whites, it follows that the arrest rates of African Americans for non-violent

---

[§] "Violent crimes" in Rochester average about 13,000 per year, 10,000 or more of which are various forms of theft (robbery, burglary, larceny, auto theft).

crimes must be extraordinarily higher than those of White residents. Under Jim Crow, those arrests would have been for vagrancy. Today they are usually for violations of the drug laws (or for "trespassing," driving without a license, "defiant attitudes" during "interviews" with the police, parole violations—such as staying out late at night). In any case, the much higher incarceration rate for Black Monroe County residents than for White is most likely largely attributable to policing practices and the policies of the local criminal justice system.

A case in point is drug offenses. Research sponsored by the U.S. Department of Health and Human Services (HHS) has found that illicit drug usage is approximately as prevalent among White, non-Hispanic, Americans as in the Black community.[19] In testimony before the New York State Assembly, Gary Pudup, Director of the Genesee Valley Chapter of the New York Civil Liberties Union, stated that "If the drug laws were being applied evenhandedly [in Monroe County], we would expect that many more whites than blacks would be admitted to prison for drug offenses.

> But that is not the case. In fact, only six out of every 100,000 white county residents [0.06%] are in prison for a drug offense compared to 175 out of every 100,000 black county residents [1.75%]. This represents a ratio of 29-to-one . . . Twenty-five percent of adults sent to prison from Rochester come from areas with just 7 percent of the city's adult population. Almost one in three is admitted for drug offenses and 92 percent are black or Latino . . . Just 24 percent of the population in Sector 9 [a Rochester neighborhood] is non-Latino white . . . In 2006, at least 204 residents of the district were incarcerated; 61 of those individuals (30 percent of the total) were sent to prison for drug offenses . . . The demographics of Sector 6 are quite different: 65 percent non-Latino white. In 2006, just 19 persons living in the sector were sent to prison. Of those, only three — or 16 percent — were sent to prison for drug offenses.[20]

It is difficult to align the NYCLU and Rochester Police Department numbers, but it may be the case that as many as 80% of the arrests and incarcerations of Rochester's African Americans are for drug offenses, as compared to 30% of those of Rochester's White, non-Hispanic, population.

One would expect that in a city with a large, and largely White, college-age population that arrests for violations of the drug laws would reflect that. In the fall of 2012 there were approximately 25,000 White students enrolled in the University of Rochester, the Rochester Institute of Technology and Monroe Community College. Based on HHS surveys, at least a quarter of those, say 6,000, are probably users of illicit drugs. This is more than ten times the number of White prisoners incarcerated in the county. But the Police Department does not concentrate its activities among this group. Instead, Black residents of Rochester are disproportionately arrested and incarcerated. As the title of Michelle Alexander's *The New Jim Crow* suggests, the effect of this is to perpetuate the caste status of the descendants of enslaved Africans in Rochester. Young Black men are continually taken from their neighborhood into the custody of the criminal justice system, often repeatedly, and when released remain under the control of the criminal justice system, on parole, on probation, or simply watched and occasionally "interviewed." Under-educated by the Rochester school district, they have few opportunities for employment, few opportunities to contribute significantly to the incomes of their families, to the lives of their children.

Modeling a More Equitable Rochester and Monroe County

Black residents of Rochester and Monroe County form what is in effect a service caste for the White community. Few are managers, few are professionals, many are employed as home healthcare workers, paraprofessional school workers and the like. Many are unemployed. Many of the men are or have been incarcerated. Most Black children are raised in or near poverty levels.

There are two forces maintaining this situation: the education and the criminal justice systems. How can they be changed so as to free Rochester's African American community from its current position, locked below the class system of the rest of the area's residents?

The needed reforms in the criminal justice system are obvious and some have been implemented elsewhere. The police can—any day they wish—introduce equitable enforcement of the drug laws. This is not to say that there should be mass arrests on the campuses of the University of Rochester, Monroe Community College and the

Rochester Institute of Technology (or among the high-tech workers in the suburbs). If possession and sale of marijuana is now legal in an increasing number of states, if possession is a ticketed misdemeanor in other locations, why not in Rochester? But drug laws are simply a means to the end of the enforcement of caste. More generally, the disproportionate arrests and incarcerations for non-violent offenders should stop. If this were done, life in Rochester's Black community would change. The state of siege described by Alice Goffman in *On the Run* would be lifted. This would have the effect, over a relatively short period of time, of increasing the number of employable young adult Black men in the community, increasing per capita income, decreasing the rate of child poverty.

The needed reforms of the schools are equally obvious. Some are already being put into effect. Optimists would point to the fact that the graduation rate for male Black students in the Rochester schools has approximately doubled in recent years. (Pessimists would observe that the glass is now only a quarter-filled.) To build on this progress, it is necessary to implement something like the remedies mandated in New Jersey's "Abbott" rulings. "The Abbott rulings directed implementation of a comprehensive set of improvements, including adequate K-12 foundational funding, universal preschool for all 3- and 4-year old children, supplemental or at-risk programs and funding, and school-by-school reform of curriculum and instruction."[21] David L. Kirp, James D. Marver Professor of Public Policy at the University of California at Berkeley, has written a book about one of New Jersey's Abbott Districts. *Improbable Scholars: The Rebirth of a Great American School System and a Strategy for American Education.* The book describes how one of the Abbott districts, Union City, "has transported Latino immigrant children, many of them undocumented, into the education mainstream: 90 percent of those youngsters are graduating from high school and 75 percent are going to college . . . The book also shows how the lessons from this school district can be applied nationwide."[22] In other words, the education provided to impoverished students in Union City is similar to that provided to students from prosperous families in the Monroe County suburbs.

The Abbott program, its basis, prescription and outcomes, have been made highly controversial. That is inevitable. Some believe that public funding for education should be minimal. Others believe that public education should be funded so as to provide a "thorough and efficient" education for all students. The cost of Abbott-type remedies was estimated as a 20% increase in funding for the affected districts.

What might we reasonably expect from these possible actions?

Initially, there would be fewer African Americans incarcerated in Monroe County, fewer "not in the labor force." Gradually, employment would increase, as then would family incomes. As family incomes increased, home ownership would increase, as would the value of those homes and other investments. Children, less likely to be brought up in poverty, would be more likely to do well in school. As educational attainment of adults increased, so, again, their children would be more likely to do well in school. As high school graduation rates increased, violent and property crime rates would fall and, once again, incarceration rates would decline, and family incomes would increase. Finally, the economic mobility characteristic of the White community would take hold in the Black community.

All would not be roses and strawberry ice cream. American society, in general, is in a crisis of rising inequity. But, at least, Rochester's Black community would be part of that society, rather than as it is now, kept down and to one side, walled off by the forces of institutional racism.

These changes could be begun by the mayor, chief of police, district attorney and superintendent of schools any day they decide to do so.

Notes: Chapter Nine

[1] Brown University, Project US2010.

[2] Miller, Dana K. (editor). The State of Black Rochester 2013. Rochester, New York: Rochester Area Community Foundation African American Giving Initiative, 2013.

[3] Community Health Needs Assessment; Community Health Improvement Plan for Hospital Systems Serving Monroe County, New York, 2013. http://www.urmc.rochester.edu/community-engagement/documents/2013-Monroe-CountyCHNA-and-CHIP.pdf

[4] New York State Department of Health. Prevention Agenda 2013-2017. Description of Population Demographics and General Health Status, New York State, 2012. https://www.health.ny.gov/prevention/prevention_agenda/2013-2017/docs/general_description.pdf

[5] U. S. Census: DPo3: Selected Economic Characteristics 2006-2010 ACS.

[6] OECD Better Life Index. http://www.oecdbetterlifeindex.org/topics/income/

[7] Bureau of the Census, Table B19054, ACS 2006-2010.

[8] Bureau of the Census, U.S. Wealth Tables 2011, Table 1.

[9] *New York Times*, July 22, 2013: http://www.nytimes.com/2013/07/22/business/in-climbing-income-ladder-location-matters.html?pagewanted=all&_r=2&#map-search

[10] Data from New York State Department of Education, 2012-13 and reportcards.nysed.gov/files/2011-12.

[11] Goldring, R., Taie, S., and Riddles, M. (2014). Teacher Attrition and Mobility: Results From the 2012–13 Teacher Follow-up Survey (NCES 2014-077). U.S. Department of Education. Washington, DC: National Center for Education Statistics. Retrieved [date] from http://nces.ed.gov/pubsearch.

[12] New York State Department of Education, "Measuring Student Progress in Grades 3-8 English Language Arts and Mathematics, August, 2014, page 32. http://www.p12.nysed.gov/irs/ela-math/2014/2014Grades3-8ELAMath-final8-13-14.pdf

[13] http://data.nysed.gov/assessment.php?year=2014&instid=800000050065

[14] Data from the U.S. Department of Education National Center for Education Statistics and from the Rochester City School District, courtesy of Dr. Jing Che, to whom I am much indebted.
[15] New York State Department of Education, Public School District Total Cohort Aspirational Performance Measure (APM): 2009 Total Cohort as of June 2013, pp. 103-4.
http://www.p12.nysed.gov/irs/pressRelease/20140623/District-APM-June-23-2014.pdf
[16] Data from Kristen Balonek, Director of Special Projects, Provost Office, University of Rochester, to whom I am also much indebted.
[17] Haskins, Ron. "Education and Economic Mobility" in Isaacs, Julia B; Sawhill, Isabel V. and Ron Haskins. Getting Ahead or Losing Ground: Economic Mobility in America. The Brookings Institution, 2008.
http://www.brookings.edu/~/media/research/files/reports/2008/2/economic%20mobility%20sawhill/02_economic_mobility_sawhill
[18] Sheppard, James M. "Criminal Justice," in Miller, Dana K. (ed.). The State of Black Rochester 2013, Rochester, Rochester Area Community Foundation's African American Giving Initiative, 2013, p.54.
[19] United States Department of Health and Human Services. Substance Abuse and Mental Health Services Administration. Center for Behavioral Health Statistics and Quality. National Survey on Drug Use and Health, 2011.
http://www.icpsr.umich.edu/quicktables/quickoptions.do
http://doi.org/10.3886/ICPSR34481.v3
[20] Pudup, Gary, "Rockefeller Drug Laws Create Racial Disparities in Rochester," May 15, 2008. http://www.nyclu.org/content/rockefeller-drug-laws-create-racial-disparities-rochester Map: Siegel, Loren; Perry, Robert A.; Carey, Corinne. NYCLU, March 2009. The Rockefeller Drug Laws: Unjust, Irrational, Ineffective.
http://www.nyclu.org/files/publications/nyclu_pub_rockefeller.pdf
[21] Education Law Center. Abbott v. Burke Overview.
http://www.edlawcenter.org/cases/abbott-v-burke.html
[22] http://gspp.berkeley.edu/directories/faculty/david-kirp.

Chapter Ten: Prince George's County

The Armed Forces of the United States were desegregated by President Truman's Executive Order 9981 in 1948: "It is hereby declared to be the policy of the President that there shall be equality of treatment and opportunity for all persons in the armed forces without regard to race, color, religion or national origin." The Army ceased to maintain segregated units in 1954. In July, 1963, President Kennedy's Secretary of Defense, Robert McNamara, issued Defense Directive 5120.36, stating, inter alia, that

> Every military commander has the responsibility to oppose discriminatory practices affecting his men and their dependents and to foster equal opportunity for them, not only in areas under his immediate control, but also in nearby communities where they may live or gather in off-duty hours.

Finally, the Civil Rights Act of 1964 ended discrimination in the Federal Government.

These actions of Federal Government had particularly strong effects in the Washington, D.C., suburb of Prince George's County, Maryland, which became one of the nation's most significant concentrations of college-educated, managerially employed, African Americans with family incomes above the national median.

*   *   *

Prince George's County does not have a good reputation in its region. The school system is often described as "troubled," the county has "a drug problem," the incarceration rate for Black men is many times higher than that for White men. However, the county's Black population is not subjected to anything like the entrenched institutional racism described in earlier chapters. Prince George's County is, then, interesting in comparison not to neighboring, wealthy, White, Montgomery County, but to, say, Cleveland and New York.

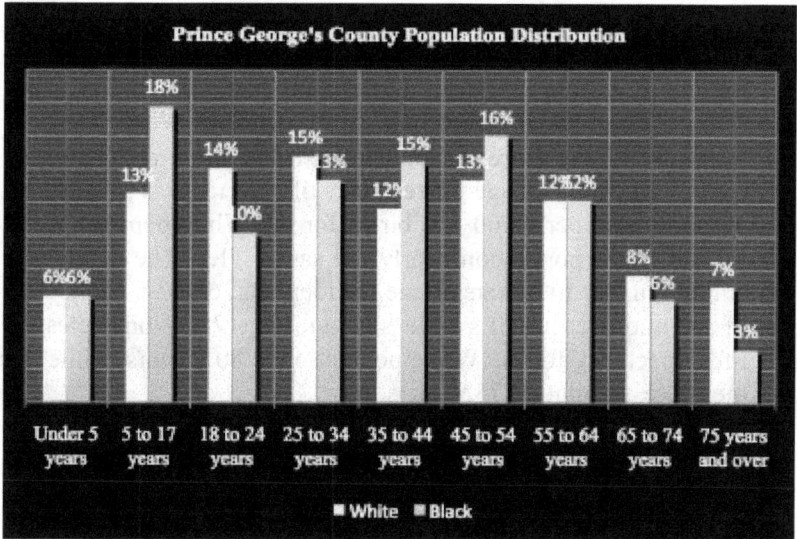

Prince George's County Population Distribution

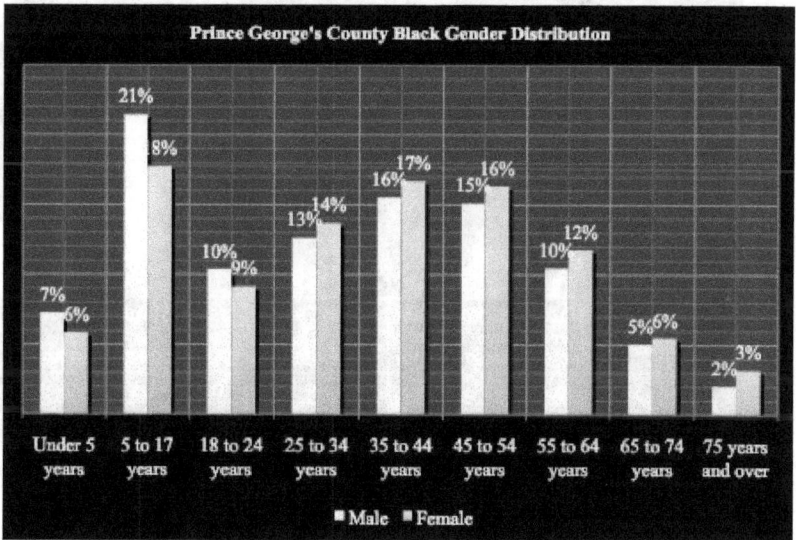

Prince George's County Black Gender Distribution

The Chains of Black America

Demographics

Prince George's County has a population of 863,000; the majority, 561,000, are Black. Despite legislative and other efforts, "White flight" and Black immigration have left Prince George's County significantly segregated, with majority White census tracts restricted to the extreme southeastern and northern sectors of the county. The median age for residents of both races is 37 years. Infant mortality rate per 1,000 live births for the White population is 10.2, for the Black population nearly the same: 11.5. The percentages of children under five years of age are identical, 6.4%. Cohorts 35 years of age and over are of similar size until age 75.[1] Nonetheless, while life expectancy for the White population is 80.2 years, while that for the Black population 75.9 years.[2]

There are 40,000 more working age Black women than Black men in Prince George's County, with the differences concentrated in the cohorts from age 25 to 59 years, which may in part reflect gender disparities in government employment in Washington, D.C.

Income

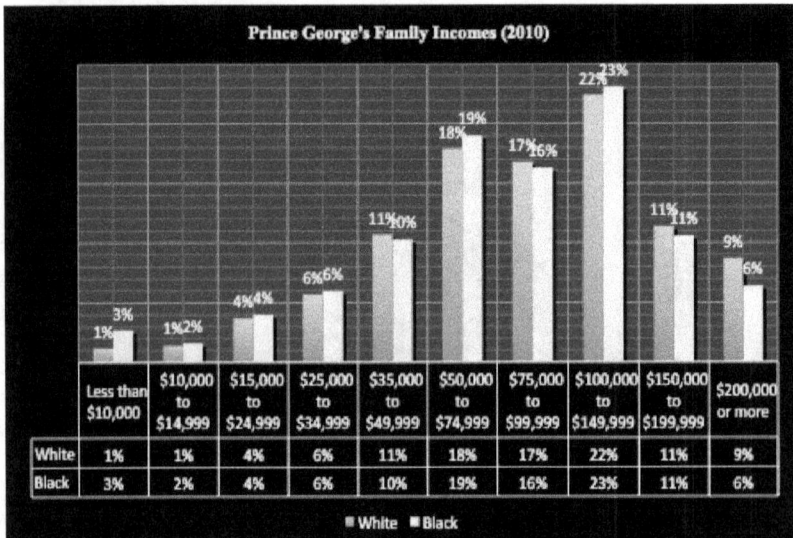

Prince George's Family Incomes (2010)

	Less than $10,000	$10,000 to $14,999	$15,000 to $24,999	$25,000 to $34,999	$35,000 to $49,999	$50,000 to $74,999	$75,000 to $99,999	$100,000 to $149,999	$150,000 to $199,999	$200,000 or more
White	1%	1%	4%	6%	11%	18%	17%	22%	11%	9%
Black	3%	2%	4%	6%	10%	19%	16%	23%	11%	6%

■ White ■ Black

Prince George's County's Black family median income of $84,121 is more than twice the national average for Black families and only slightly lower than the county's White family median income of $87,966. The only important differences in the racial income distributions are at the highest and lowest income levels and even those are relatively minor.

If we compare the range of income quintiles (groups of 20%), each Prince George's County quintile is higher than the national average and each Black income quintile is displaced *upward* by one rank in comparison to national averages for African Americans. In other words, the 20% of Prince George's families with the lowest incomes have higher incomes than the lowest 40% of African American incomes, nationally; the lowest 40% of Prince George's incomes are higher than the lowest 60% of African American incomes, nationally.[3]

Just 5% of Prince George's County Black families had incomes below the poverty rate in 2010, which is only slightly above the poverty rate for the county's White families (3%) and approximately one-fifth the rate for Black families nationally. Similarly, the poverty rate for Black families with children, (7%), was approximately the same as the national average poverty rate for White families (6%) with children and again approximately one-fifth of the Black national figure. Just thirteen percent of Black families in which a woman was raising her children without a husband, had incomes below the poverty rate, as compared to 22% of such White families in the County and 47% of all such African American families in the U.S. At the other end of the income spectrum, only 34% of Prince George's White families have incomes over $100,000 per year, as compared to an extraordinary 40% of Black families.

Forty percent of both Black and White civilian employed adults in the county work in the managerial group of occupations, compared to 17% of both groups who work in service occupations.[4] As a consequence the Black community as a whole has an income of $18 billion, as compared to that of $6 billion for the smaller White community, which is proportionate to the relative sizes of the two communities.[5]

In sum, by and large, the incomes of Black residents of Prince George's County are approximately the same as those of White residents of the county, higher than the national averages for all Americans, and much higher than the national averages for African Americans.

Disparities of Wealth

We have seen that in Prince George's County there are only minor differences between the incomes of Black and White residents and that by many measures the incomes of Black residents of the County are slightly higher than those of the White residents. We now turn to an analysis of the comparative *wealth* of Black and White residents of the county.

We must keep in mind the crucial difference between income and wealth. Some people have relatively high incomes with relatively little wealth; others can have relatively great wealth and relatively lower incomes. For example, young workers in the financial sector can have incomes at the upper 10% or even upper 1% level, while not yet having accumulated significant financial or property assets. And retirees who have paid off their mortgages in cities like Los Angeles or San Francisco may have significant wealth in the value of their homes, but relatively small incomes from pensions and Social Security. Although changes in income are the motor for individual economic mobility, wealth is crucial for intergenerational mobility. For many people, wealth begins with the inheritance of a home, for a few people wealth begins with the inheritance of, say, DuPont, but without inherited wealth at some level, each generation begins at zero, with only social capital, such as higher education, available as a basis for socio-economic mobility.

While average incomes are similar, there are stark disparities in wealth between the Black and White communities in Prince George's County. Approximately equal numbers of Black and White households had income from interest, dividends or net rents in 2010—24,000 White households, 23,000 Black households—but as the number of Black households is three times that of White households, there is a marked difference in the percentages of the county's Black and White households with such investment income. The implication of these figures is that while 35% of the county's White households have wealth in the form of more or less liquid financial assets, just 11% of the county's Black households have wealth in that form.

We can also calculate wealth differentials in the form of owner-occupied homes. The median value of owner-occupied units in Prince George's County is $332,200 for White households and

$324,400 for Black households: substantially the same. However, Black households in the county are more likely to have mortgages on their houses than White families (92% to 70%), have slightly more monthly costs on mortgaged properties ($2,219 to $1,995) and on unmortgaged properties as well ($626 to $608). Let us assume, for the sake of this exercise, that all county residents with mortgages have paid down half their mortgages. In that case, the 51,144 White owner-occupied unites would have a net value to their owners of $11 billion as would the 125,590 Black owner occupied units. In Prince George's County the two communities have approximately the same net worth, including both financial assets and home equity; however, because the Black community is larger, the per capita net worth of the county's Black community is one-third that of the county's White community.

It is likely that the reason for this dichotomy between comparative Black income and Black wealth is that there is little inherited wealth among the Black population. Prince George's County's Black residents have incomes equal to or greater than that of their White neighbors, but in most cases their parents did not, which would have made it more difficult to gain that first step toward wealth: a home.

Mobility

Oliver and Shapiro found a tale of "two mobilities." Upper-middle class Whites had intergenerational mobilities such that 60% of their children remained in that class and others showed high rates of upward mobility. But "only a little over one-third" of upper-middle class Black families maintained that status in the second generation and the chances of downward intergenerational mobility are twice as great for Black and for White families.[6] Oliver and Shapiro concluded that "No matter how high up the ladder blacks climb, they accumulate very few assets . . . Asset poverty is passed on from one generation to the next, no matter how much occupational attainment or mobility blacks achieve."[7]

Many Black residents of Prince George's County are in the fortunate position of living in middle class and upper middle class neighborhoods. Their children will have a better chance than most Black children of remaining in the middle class or even rising to higher quintiles. But for significant intergenerational mobility, it is wealth, not income, that counts. Mobility rates for Prince George's County's financially successful Black families will not equal those of their White peers until their wealth—houses and investments—are also equal. This will take some time.

Education

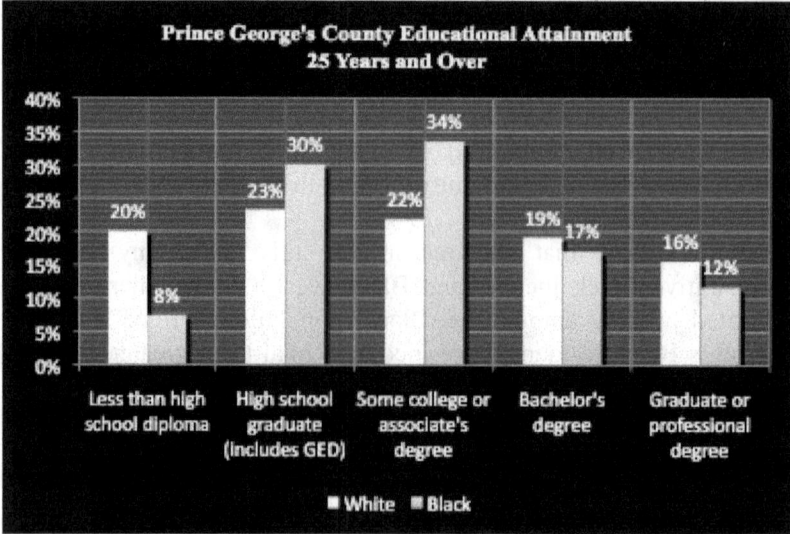

Prince George's County Educational Attainment
25 Years and Over

Given the demographic changes over the past generation, it is likely that many adults in Prince George's County were educated elsewhere.[*] The region, offering non-discriminatory employment, has attracted many of the nation's highly educated African American population. All but 7% of Black county residents have graduated from high school. Thirty-five percent of White residents and 29% of Black residents have a Bachelor's degree or above. An unusual 20% of White adult residents, but just 8% of the Black Prince George's County residents have not obtained a high school diploma. This distribution is unusual in two ways: Black educational attainment is higher than national Black averages and much more similar to local White educational attainment than is usually the case.

---

[*] In 1980 the Black population of the county was 250,000; in 1990 it was 370,000; in 2000 it was 500,000 (Maryland Planning Department historical census data).

The Prince George's County school district enrolls 125,136 students, 80,821 of whom are Black, 5,643 of whom are White, most of the remainder are Hispanic. Fifty-two percent of high school students, 64% of middle school students and 70% of elementary school students receive free or reduced price meals. As there are approximately 23,000 school-age White, non-Hispanic, children in the county, most White children are probably in private or religious schools. The district has a low student-teacher ratio of 14:1. Over 90% of the system's teachers have state certifications, 66% have Advanced Professional Certification. The average teacher salary in 2011 was $62,000.[8]

The Prince George's County district is not one of those assessed by the National Assessment of Educational Progress. Maryland has a state testing program with notably detailed and transparent data reporting. In the state of Maryland as a whole 42% of students score at or above Proficient, grade level, in grade 8 reading NAEP, as do 25% of Black and 53% of White, non-Hispanic students. The Maryland State Assessment program reported that 77% of all students in the state read at Proficient or Advanced in grade 8 reading, 40% of whom were at the "Advanced" level. Statewide results for Black students were that 65% read at Proficient or Advanced, 24% at the Advanced level. We will interpret this to mean that the state's "Advanced" score is the equivalent of NAEP "Proficient."

Neighboring Montgomery County arguably has the best large district in the country. Montgomery County's outcomes are the benchmark for district efforts to close the gap between Black and White achievement. Its schools brought 37% of their Black students to the Advanced level on the state tests for grade 8 reading, close to the state's outcomes for all students. In Prince George's County, 27% of all students scored Advanced, that is, grade level, on the state test for grade 8 reading, including 26% of Black students. The district, therefore, was in line with state achievement levels for Black students, levels that were significantly lower than those for all students in the predominately White state, and lower than those for Black students in neighboring districts, but significantly higher than national averages.[9]

The graduation rate for Black students who were first time freshman in the Fall of 2009 in Prince George's County was 76%. By way of comparison, the graduation rate for African American students in the same cohort in Montgomery County was 84% and state-wide 78%. These rates are considerably higher than national graduation rates for African American students, but once again the Prince George's County district lags behind its high achieving, predominately White, neighboring districts.

In 2011 65% of Prince George's County's Black students and 68% of White students who were 24 months post-high school were enrolled in college. Progression from grade 9 to college for the district's Black and White students was virtually identical.

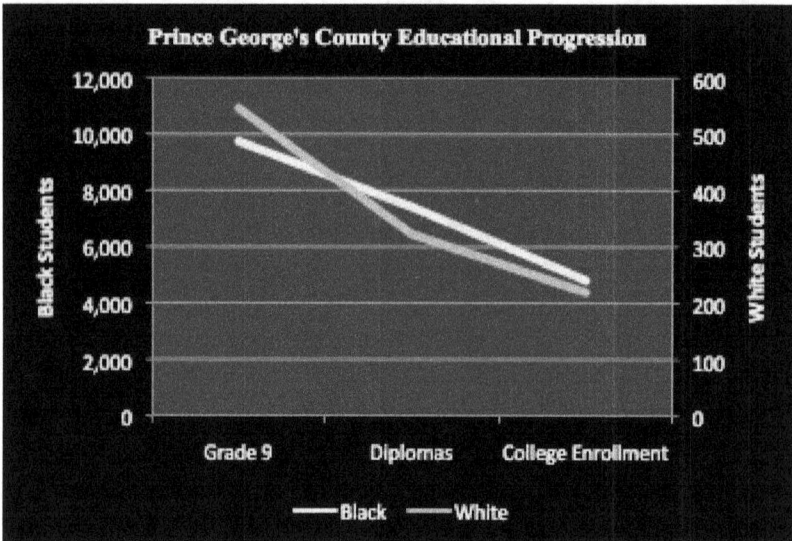

Prince George's County Educational Progression

The Prince George's County schools bring 60% more of its grade 8 Black students to grade level in reading than the national average. Its graduation rate for Black students is similar to that of the national average for White, non-Hispanic, students. It prepares nearly equal percentages of Black and White students for college. It could do better for its African American students, as does Montgomery County, but by national comparisons it does very well. It is not in itself an institution maintaining caste.

The Hammer of Caste: The Criminal Justice System

There are disparities in the enforcement of drug laws in Prince George's County, but they are relatively small compared to national and state averages and those for such cities as Milwaukee and Chicago.

As the percentage of the Black population rose since the turn of the century, violent crime in Prince George's County fell, from 1,000 per 100,000 residents in 2006, for example, to half that by 2013. Between 2010 and 2013 murder, rape and aggravated assault fell by a quarter, property crime by 17%, motor vehicle theft by nearly half.

The marijuana arrest rate in Prince George's County was 2.77 per 1,000 residents in 2010. Other Maryland marijuana arrest rates varied from 1.8 in Montgomery County to 11.36 in the city of Baltimore: Prince George's County was fourth from the bottom among the state's jurisdictions.[10] Although Black residents of Prince George's County were two-and-a-half times as likely to be arrested for marijuana possession as White residents, this was a differential in the lower half of those of the state's counties (differentials which vary from 1.35 times in Dorchester County in the rural Eastern Shore to 5.63 in the city of Baltimore).[11]

In Prince George's County, as elsewhere in the country where marijuana possession remains illegal, the burden of the enforcement of those laws falls more heavily on African Americans than on White, non-Hispanics. However, in general, the criminal justice system in the county appears to be a relatively benign force, professional and unlikely to preside over racialized enforcement.

Factors Promoting Equity in Prince George's County

Half a century of non-discrimination by the armed forces and the Federal Government have had particularly strong effects in Prince George's County, the home of many Black employees of federal departments in Washington, D.C. Hardly any generalizations about the socio-economic condition of African Americans apply in Prince George's County. The percentage of Black adults with Bachelor's degrees or higher in the county is the same as the national average for White Americans, while that for adults with graduate degrees is slightly higher. African Americans in Prince George's County are more likely than White Americans, nationally, to have managerial occupations. Median household income ($73,000) is much higher than the White national average ($56,000), and poverty rates are lower. (Less than half the percentage of Black women in Prince George's County as White women nationally raising children without a husband live in poverty.) The houses of Black residents of the county have a much higher value than the national average for houses owned by White Americans.[12] Although there are disparities in arrests and incarcerations for drug offenses, these are much smaller than usual in this country. The criminal justice system's comparatively light hand on the county's Black population could serve better yet if the drug laws were reformed, which would free resources for community policing and similar efforts serving the community.

In sum, the lesson of Prince George's County is that the caste-status, poverty, excessive incarceration rates and lack of educational attainment of the descendants of enslaved Africans are not "natural," "to be expected," or in some way the consequence of the lack of effort or desired by African Americans: they are the effects of institutional racism and where crucial institutions do not function in a racist manner, caste barriers fall.

There is still work to be done in Prince George's County. The district's schools have a poor reputation both within the county and in general. The school system, although showing better results for its Black students than national averages is still in need of improvement. There has been a lack of stable leadership and a degree of disorganization and lack of coordination both in the central office and among the schools themselves. A new planning document accepts these evaluations and lays out some commonsense actions to improve matters. Neighboring Montgomery County is within seven percentage points of closing the gap between the percentage of its Black students reading a grade level in grade 8 with the national average for White students. This is an attainable benchmark for improvement efforts in the Prince George's County schools.

These reforms of the schools and the criminal justice system are similar to those needed in many parts of the country. They are not unique to Prince George's County. The issues in Prince George's County are those of class, not caste. In the absence of institutionalized racism even the descendants of enslaved Africans can participate in the American Dream of a better life for their children.

Notes: Chapter Ten

[1] U.S. Census, Selected Population Profile, 2010-2012.
[2] Prince George's County Health Department, Public Health Quick Stats, August 2012.
http://www.princegeorgescountymd.gov/sites/Health/Resources/Plan ningHealthStats/Statistics/Documents/Quick+Stats_8-12-1.pdf
[3] United States income quintiles are for families:
http://www.census.gov/hhes/www/income/data/historical/families. United States Black income quintiles are for households, as are Prince George's County income quintiles:
http://factfinder2.census.gov/faces/tableservices/jsf/pages/productvie w.xhtml?fpt=table. Although Black income quintiles for Prince George's County households are not available, those for the County as a whole are a reasonable approximation.
[4] Bureau of the Census, Selected Economic Data 2006-2010, American Community Survey, Table DP03.
[5] U. S. Census Bureau, 2012 ACS 1-year survey, tables B19313A&B.
[6] Oliver, Melvin L. and Thomas M. Shapiro. Black Wealth/White Wealth: A New Perspective on Racial Inequality. Tenth-Anniversary Edition. New York: Routledge, 2006, pp. 159-60.
[7] Oliver and Shapiro, p. 173.
[8] U.S. Department of Education Office for Civil Rights.
[9] 2014 Maryland Report Card.
[10] Kumar, Sonia. The Maryland War on Marijuana in Black and White. American Civil Liberties Union of Maryland, October 2013, p. 20.
[11] Kumar, p. 20.
[12] U.S. Census, American Community Survey 2011-2013 3-Year Estimates, table S0201.

Chapter Eleven: Modeling Democracy

Prince George's County, as imperfect as it may yet be, points the way to the possibility of better lives for all African Americans. However, the lives of most American descendants of enslaved Africans living in other parts of the country are shorter than those of White Americans; their health is worse, infant mortality higher, incomes and wealth lower and economic mobility virtually non-existent. Median family incomes of African Americans in the cities we have reviewed vary from $33,000 in Rochester to $58,000 in New York (where median White, non-Hispanic, family income is $80,700). Nationally, the median Black family income is $42,000, compared to $64,000 for White, non-Hispanics: a 50% race-based "tax." The percentage of African American adults with Bachelor's degrees in the cities we have reviewed vary from 12% in New Orleans to 22% in New York. Nationally, the percentage of Black adults with Bachelor's degrees is 19%, compared to 30% for White, non-Hispanics. These health, demographic, wealth, income and educational attainment indicators define African Americans as a group by and large outside the American class system, barred from the American Way of Life by the everyday decisions of those in charge of basic institutions, living instead an isolated existence as a caste.

The caste boundaries of the descendants of enslaved Africans are to a large extent policed by the policies and practices of school authorities and by those of the criminal justice system. Hypersegregated schools with their often inexperienced and (or) ineffective teaching staffs and decaying facilities, failing to educate their students, contribute to low levels of educational attainment, low incomes and unusually high incarceration rates. Egregiously high incarceration rates for young adult Black men impoverish them and their children and the mothers of those children, causing them to have little choice other than to live in hypersegregated neighborhoods.

The caste status of the descendants of enslaved Africans are the result of the decisions and actions of individuals, not vague "conditions." Institutional racism is the racism of individuals operating through public institutions. Dealers in real estate, pursuing profit, have created and maintained segregated housing. State legislators and governors have created and maintained school finance systems that provide greater funding to the children of wealthier families than to those of poorer families. Members of boards of education, district superintendents and, in some cases, mayors, create and maintain budgeting and personnel policies that fund schools within districts in proportion to the financial (and sometimes racial and ethnic) status of residents: more resources, better-maintained facilities, more experienced, talented and highly educated teachers going to schools attended by students from wealthier, and usually whiter, families. District attorneys, prosecutors, police chiefs and individual law enforcement personnel enact and maintain policies that criminalize African Americans. In some cases these policies and practices generate profits on which local criminal justice systems are dependent.

Let us now conduct a thought experiment. We will imagine that the American criminal justice system functioned equitably and that the public schools also did so. The incarceration rate for African Americans would then not differ from that of their economic peers, Hispanic Americans, and the educational opportunities offered by suburban schools to White students would be available to students in all schools. What effect would this have on the socio-economic status of the descendants of enslaved Africans?

We will begin our calculations with the consequences of the creation of an equitable education system, one in which the allocation of resources is based on educational need, not race. The data from the National Assessment of Education Progress shows that this is not a single generation process. Parental education attainment influences student educational achievement. We will, therefore, set our imaginary democracy-creating machine in motion by making the grade 8 literacy level for the Black children of college educated adults, whose families are not eligible for the National Lunch Program, the grade 8 reading scores for all Black children. That is 32% at or above Proficiency rather than 17%. Assuming, for the sake of argument, a one-to-one correlation between grade 8 reading proficiency and high school graduation rates, this would result in an improvement in Black male high school graduation rates from approximately 60% to 75%, reducing the percentage of those not receiving a high school diploma from 40% to 25% with concomitant changes in outcomes for female Black students—a high school graduation rate of, say, 85%.

What then?

One result would be an increase in Black incomes. If we adjust the data for annual earnings for full-time workers by education level by taking 80% of the figures to account for the "racial tax" (we are modeling, not asking for miracles), we find that a high school diploma is worth close to $8,000 a year for Black workers, that is, nearly 40% more than the income of Black workers without a high school diploma. If 15% of a cohort experiences this increase in graduation rates and the associated increase in income, there will be a 6% increase in total income for that cohort of the Black community. There will be additional increases from the presumed increases in college attendance, graduation and advanced degree acquisition. Let us, for the sake of the model, sum all these, including high school graduation rate changes, at 12%. This would raise median Black incomes from about $35,000 (the mid-point of male and female median earnings of full-time, year-round workers) to $39,200, cutting in half the gap between Black incomes and the national average at each education attainment level.

These increases in Black educational attainment and incomes would have the effect of further increasing the educational achievement of Black children, partly by improvements in the quality of education on offer and partly by increasing the percentage of Black children whose parents themselves have higher educational attainment and higher incomes. (For example, as we have seen, Black students ineligible for the National Lunch Program whose parents have graduated from high school have twice the chance of reading at or above Proficient at grade 8 as those who are eligible for the National Lunch Program and whose parents have not graduated from high school.) Once this process is in motion, it would move forward with increasing effect with each generation, just as it did with classical immigrant groups.

Eliminating discriminatory practices in the criminal justice system is another point at which caste barriers could begin to be dismantled.

Assuming that much of the difference between the incarceration rates for male White Americans and male Latino Americans is economic in origin, we might realistically model a changed incarceration rate for male Black young adults on the Latino level.[*] This would cut the incarceration rate in half for young adult Black men, from 9% to, say, 4% of the cohort, from 120,000 of the 1.3 million African American males between 25 and 29 to 60,000, or from 360,000 of the four million between 20 and 34 to 180,000. There would be similar effects in regard to the numbers of young adult Black men virtually unemployable because they are on parole or probation. If the percentage of the working age male Black population who are not in a position to contribute to the income of the Black community because of the discriminatory practices of the criminal justice system, were reduced from 20% to 10%, we would expect to see a proportionate increase in the general income of the Black community and, perhaps, a decrease in the percentages of unmarried Black women with children.

A simultaneous increase in the high school graduation rate and decrease in the incarceration rate of American descendants of enslaved Africans would have a mutually reinforcing effect. As educational attainment rates increased, incarceration rates, which disproportionately affect those without high school diplomas, would decrease. Rising parental education levels and falling parental incarceration rates would raise the achievement and graduation rates of the next generation of Black children. Dismantling caste barriers can begin with more equitable educational opportunities or with a more equitable criminal justice system. Working on both will more quickly end the division of American society between a first world country in which White Americans live and the third world country to which now all too many African Americans are confined.

All that it would take to end the enforcement of caste in America is a decision by those enforcing it to stop doing so.

---

[*] Some of the difference between Latino and White rates might be attributable to the tendency of authorities to include Latino's of African origin with African Americans in arrests, charges and sentencing.

Bibliography

ACT. http://www.actstudent.org/scores/norms1.html

ACT. www.act.org/solutions/college-career-readiness/compare-act-sat/

Adams, Vincanne. Markets of Sorrow, Labors of Faith: New Orleans in the Wake of Katrina. Durham & London: Duke University Press, 2013.

Alexander, Michelle. The New Jim Crow Mass Incarceration in the Age of Colorblindness. New York: The New Press, 2012.

Bahchieva, Raisa; Du, Jingqiang; Popkin, Illene; Reilly, Neil; Shultz, Harold. Making Neighborhoods: Understanding New York City Transitions 2000-2010. CHPC New York City.

Baker, Bruce, David Sciarra and Danielle Farrie. Is School Funding Fair? A National Report Card. Education Law Center, New Jersey. Second edition: June 2012.

Beckett, Kathrine. Race and Drug Law Enforcement in Seattle. Report Prepared for the ACLU Drug Law Reform Project and the Defender Association, September 2008. https://www.aclu.org/files/assets/race20and20drug20law20enforcem ent20in20seattle_20081.pdf

Bergad, Laird W. The Concentration of Wealth in New York City: Changes in the Structure of Household Income by Race/Ethnic Groups and Latino Nationalities 1990-2010. CUNY: Latino Data Project, Report 56, January 2014. clacls.gc.cuny.edu/files/2014/01/Household-Income-Concentration-in-NYC-1990-2010.pdf

Bivens, Josh; Gould, Elise; Mishel, Lawrence and Shierholz, Heidi. Raising America's Pay: Why It's Our Central Economic Policy Challenge. Washington, D.C.: Economic Policy Institute, June 4, 2014. http://www.epi.org/publication/raising-americas-pay/

Bivens, Josh; Gould, Elise; Mishel, Lawrence and Shierholz, Heidi. Raising America's Pay: Why It's Our Central Economic Policy

Challenge. Washington, D.C.: Economic Policy Institute, June 4, 2014. http://www.epi.org/publication/raising-americas-pay/

Blackmon, Douglas A. Slavery by Another Name: The Re-Enslavement of Black Americans from the Civil War to World War II. New York: Random House, 2009.

Bostock, Mike and Fessenden, Ford. "Stop-and-Frisk" Is All but Gone from New York. New York Times, September 18, 2014.

Bricker, Jesse; Dettling, Lisa J.; Henriques, Alice; Hsu, Joanne W; Moore, Kevin B.; Sabelhaus, John; Thompson, Jeffrey and Windle, Richard A. Changes in U.S. Family Finances from 2010 to 2013: Evidence from the Survey of Consumer Finances. Federal Reserve Bulletin. file:///Files/Inequality%20and%20Race/U.S.%20Data/FRB%20%20 Federal%20Reserve%20Bulletin%20Inequality%20cf.%20Yellen.ht ml

Caniglia, John. "Cuyahoga County judges sending far fewer felons to prison, marking major shift in Ohio's corrections system." The Plain Dealer, October 25, 2013. http://www.cleveland.com/metro/index.ssf/2013/10/cuyahoga_count y_judges_sending.html

Carson, E. Ann, "Prisoners in 2013, U. S. Department of Justice, Office of Justice Programs, Bureau of Justice Statistics, September 2014, NCJ 247282. http://www.bjs.gov/content/pub/pdf/p13.pdf

Chang, Cindy. "Louisiana is the world's prison capital." The Times-Picayune, May 13, 2012. http://www.nola.com/crime/index.ssf/2012/05/louisiana_is_the_worl ds_prison.html

Chetty, Raj, Hendren, Nathaniel, Kline, Patrick and Saez, Emmanuel. *Where is the Land of Opportunity? The Geography of Intergenerational Mobility in the United States*. NBER, May 2014, pp. 2-3. http://obs.rc.fas.harvard.edu/chetty/mobility_geo.pdf.

Chicago Reader. www.chicagoreader.com/chicago/chicago-marijuana-arrest-statistics/Content?oid=4198958

CIA World Fact Book, 2012.

Cleveland's Plan for Transforming Schools.
http://www.clevelandmetroschools.org/cms/lib05/OH01915844/Cent
ricity/Domain/4/ClevelandPlanExecutiveSummary.pdf

Cohen, Norm. *Long Steel Rail: The Railroad in American Folk Song.*
University of Illinois Press (2nd ed), 2000.

Coleman-Jensen, Alisha, Christian Gregory, and Anita Singh. Household
Food Security in the United States in 2013: Statistical Supplement,
AP-066, U.S. Department of Agriculture, Economic Research
Service, September 2014, table S-1.

Commonwealth Foundation. openPAgov.org.
http://www.openpagov.org/education_revenue_and_expenses.asp

Community Health Needs Assessment; Community Health Improvement
Plan for Hospital Systems Serving Monroe County, New York,
2013. http://www.urmc.rochester.edu/community-
engagement/documents/2013-Monroe-CountyCHNA-and-CHIP.pdf

Cook County Court.
www.cookcountycourt.org/ABOUTTHECOURT/OfficeoftheChiefJu
dge/ProbationDepartments/ProbationforAdults/AdultProbationDepar
tment/Profile.aspx

DeNavas-Walt, Carmen and Bernadette D. Proctor, U.S. Census Bureau,
Current Population Reports, P60-249, Income and Poverty in the
United States: 2013, U.S. Government Printing Office, Washington,
DC, 2014.

Dougherty, Jack. More Than One Struggle: The Evolution of Black
School Reform in Milwaukee. Chapel Hill: The University of North
Carolina Press, 2004, p. 171.

Drellinger, Danielle. "Private school enrollment falls 5% in Louisiana,
even more in New Orleans, Baton Rouge areas." The Times-
Picayune, February 13, 2014.
http://www.nola.com/education/index.ssf/2014/02/private_school_en
rollment_fall.html

Education Law Center, September 14, 2014.

Education Law Center. Abbott v. Burke Overview.
http://www.edlawcenter.org/cases/abbott-v-burke.html

Eichel, Larry. Philadelphia: The State of the City, A 2014 Update. Philadelphia: The Pew Charitable Trusts, April, 2014. http://www.pewtrusts.org/~/media/Assets/2014/04/05/PhiladelphiaSt ateofCityreport2014.pdf?la=en

Evans, Benjamin F., Zimmerman, Emily, Woolf, Steven H., Haley, Amber D. Food Access and Health in Cook County, Illinois. Technical Report. Center on Human Needs, Virginia Commonwealth University, Richmond, Virginia, 2012.

Feeding America. www.feedingamerica.org/hunger-in-america/our-research/map-the-meal-gap/2012/ny_allcdsmmg_2012.pdf

Fitzpatrick, Lauren. Study: Charter schools have worsened school segregation. Chicago Sun-Times, October 13, 2014, citing a recent University of Minnesota Law School Institute on Metropolitan Opportunity study.

Goffman, Alice. On the Run: Fugitive Life in an American City. Chicago: University of Chicago Press, 2014.

Goldring, R., Taie, S., and Riddles, M. (2014). Teacher Attrition and Mobility: Results From the 2012–13 Teacher Follow-up Survey (NCES 2014-077). U.S. Department of Education. Washington, DC: National Center for Education Statistics.

Gottschalck, Alfred, Marina Vornovytsky, and Adam Smith. Household Wealth in the U.S.: 2000 to 2011. U.S. Census. http://www.census.gov/people/wealth/files/Wealth%20Highlights%2 02011.pdf

Haskins, Ron. "Education and Economic Mobility" in Isaacs, Julia B; Sawhill, Isabel V. and Ron Haskins. Getting Ahead or Losing Ground: Economic Mobility in America. The Brookings Institution, 2008. http://www.brookings.edu/~/media/research/files/reports/2008/2/eco nomic%20mobility%20sawhill/02_economic_mobility_sawhill

Heller, Karen. "Another Philadelphia police scandal, right on schedule." Philly.com, The Inquirer, August 7, 2014. http://articles.philly.com/2014-08-07/news/52519336_1_six-narcotics-officers-philadelphia-police-department-narcotics-bureau

Heuer, Ruth and Stephanie Stullich. Comparability of State and Local Expenditures Among Schools Within Districts: A Report from the Study of School-Level Expenditures. U.S. Department of Education, Office of Planning, Evaluation and Policy Development, Policy and Program Studies Service, 2011, p. 29.

http://www.pewstates.org/uploadedFiles/PCS_Assets/2009/PEW_ NEIGHBORHOODS(1).pdf

Illinois Department of Corrections, FY12 Annual Report,

Isaacs, Julia B. "Economic Mobility of Black and White Families" in Isaacs, Julia B; Sawhill, Isabel V. and Ron Haskins. Getting Ahead or Losing Ground: Economic Mobility in America. The Brookings Institution, 2008. http://www.brookings.edu/~/media/research/files/reports/2008/2/eco nomic%20mobility%20sawhill/02_economic_mobility_sawhill

Joint Center or Political and Economic Studies Orleans Parish Place Matters Team. Place Matters for Health in Orleans Parish: Ensuring Opportunities for Good Health for All, June 2012.

Kaiser Family Foundation, State Facts.

Kaiser Family Foundation. Health Coverage by Race and Ethnicity: The Potential Impact of the Affordable Care Act, March 13, 2013. http://kff.org/disparities-policy/issue-brief/health.[*]

Kaiser Family Foundation. New Orleans Five Years After the Storm. 2010. http://kaiserfamilyfoundation.files.wordpress.com/2013/02/8089.pdf

Kane-Willis, Kathleen; Aviles, Giovanni; Bazan, Marcia; Fraguada Narloch, Vilmarie. Patchwork Policy: An Evaluation of Arrests and Tickets for Marijuana Misdemeanors in Illinois. Illinois Consortium on Drug Policy. The Institute for Metropolitan Affairs. Roosevelt University. May 2014, p. 5. Chart: http://www.washingtonpost.com/blogs/wonkblog/wp/2013/06/04/the -blackwhite-marijuana-arrest-gap-in-nine-charts/

Kane-Willis, Kathleen; Aviles, Giovanni; Bazan, Marcia; Fraguada Narloch, Vilmarie. Patchwork Policy: An Evaluation of Arrests and Tickets for Marijuana Misdemeanors in Illinois. Illinois Consortium on Drug Policy. The Institute for Metropolitan Affairs. Roosevelt University. May 2014.

Katz, Michael B. The Undeserving Poor: America's Enduring Confrontation with Poverty. Oxford: Oxford University Press (2nd edition), 2013.

Kochhar, Rakesh; Fry, Richard and Paul Taylor. Wealth Gaps Rise to Record Highs between Whites, Blacks, Hispanics. Pew Research Social and Demographic Trends, Chapter 8. 2011/07/26. http://www.pewsocialtrends.org/2011/07/26/wealth-gaps-rise-to-record-highs-between-whites-blacks-hispanics/

Kornrich, Sabino and Furstenberg, Frank. Investing in Children: Changes in Parental Spending on Children, 1972-2007. Demography (2013) 50:1-23.

Kumar, Sonia. The Maryland War on Marijuana in Black and White. American Civil Liberties Union of Maryland, October 2013.

Kutateladze, Besiki Luka and Nancy R. Andiloro. "Prosecution and Racial Justice in New York County" – Technical Report, Vera Institute Of Justice, January 31, 2014.

Logan, John. US 2010: Discover America in a New Century, Brown University, http://www.s4.brown.edu/us2010/index.htm.

Loprest, Pamela and Mitchell, Josh. Labor Market and Demographic Analysis: A Metro-Level Picture of Short-term Employment Growth by Skill in Philadelphia. The Urban Institute, Washington, D.C., May 2012.

Louisiana State Department of Education, College Going/Enrollment Data for 2011-2012 High School Graduates. http://educatenow.net/wp-content/uploads/2014/05/2011_2012CollegeEnrollmentPersistenceData_NO_only.pdf

Lynch, Mona. "Crack Pipes and Policing: A Case Study of Institutional Racism and Remedial Action in Cleveland," Law & Policy, Vol. 33, No. 2, April 2011.

Lynch, Mona. "Selective Enforcement of Drug Laws in Cuyahoga County, Ohio: A Report on the Racial Effects of Geographic Disparities in Arrest Patterns," ACLU Ohio.

Maryland Department of Public Safety and Correctional Services Quarterly Inmate Characteristics Report, April 2014. http://www.dpscs.state.md.us/publicinfo/pdfs/stats/data-reports/I_and_IStatistics/Inmate_Characteristics/Quarterly_Inmate_Characteristics/FY2014/2014-April_Inmate_Char.pdf

Maryland State Department of Education. 2014 Maryland Report Card.

Massey, Douglas S. and Denton, Nancy A. American Apartheid: Segregation and the Making of the Underclass. Cambridge, MA: Harvard University Press, 1993.

Mauer, Marc. Americans Behind Bars: The International Use of Incarceration, 1992-93.

Mazumder, Bhashkar. "Black-white differences in intergenerational economic mobility in the United States." Economic Perspectives. Federal Reserve Bank of Chicago, 2014. https://www.chicagofed.org/digital_assets/publications/economic_perspectives/2014/1Q2014_part1_mazumder.pdf

Miller, Dana K. (editor). The State of Black Rochester 2013. Rochester, New York: Rochester Area Community Foundation African American Giving Initiative, 2013.

Milwaukee Public Schools. Annual Report, December 2013.

Miner, Barbara J. Lessons from the Heartland: A Turbulent Half-Century of Public Education in an Iconic American City. New York: The New Press, 2013.

National Center for Education Statistics (NCES).

National Center for Health Statistics. Health, United States, 2012: With Special Feature on Emergency Care. Hyattsville, MD. 2013. http://www.cdc.gov/nchs/data/hus/hus12.pdf#018

National Center for Health Statistics. Health, United States, 2012: With Special Feature on Emergency Care. Hyattsville, MD. 2013.

National Research Council of the National Academies. "The Growth of Incarceration in the United States: Exploring Causes and Consequences." Jeremy Travis and Bruce Western, Editors; Washington, D.C., April, 2014.

New York City Department of Health and Mental Hygiene. Epi Research Report, March 2013.

New York City Department of Health and Mental Hygiene. Epi Research Report, April 2013.

New York City Department of Health and Mental Hygiene. Health Disparities in New York City, April 2010, No.1.

New York Post. nypost.com/2014/06/18/4-nyc-neighborhoods-boasting-rentals-for-less-than-2k-a-month/

New York State Board of Regents, June 2012 meeting, p. 11. http://www.regents.nysed.gov/meetings/2012Meetings/June2012/Gra dRate.pdf

New York State Department of Education, "Measuring Student Progress in Grades 3-8 English Language Arts and Mathematics, August, 2014. http://www.p12.nysed.gov/irs/ela-math/2014/2014Grades3-8ELAMath-final8-13-14.pdf

New York State Department of Education, 2012-13 and reportcards.nysed.gov/files/2011-12.

New York State Department of Education, Public School District Total Cohort Aspirational Performance Measure (APM): 2009 Total Cohort as of June 2013, pp. 103-4. http://www.p12.nysed.gov/irs/pressRelease/20140623/District-APM-June-23-2014.pdf

New York State Department of Health. Prevention Agenda 2013-2017. Description of Population Demographics and General Health Status, New York State, 2012. https://www.health.ny.gov/prevention/prevention_agenda/2013-2017/docs/general_description.pdf

New York State Education Department. http://www.p12.nysed.gov/irs/ela-math/2014/2014Grades3-8ELAMath-final8-13-14.pdf.

New York State Office of the Attorney General. A Report on Arrests Arising from the New York City Police Department's Stop-and-Frisk Practices, November 2013.

New York Times, July 22, 2013:
http://www.nytimes.com/2013/07/22/business/in-climbing-income-ladder-location-matters.html?pagewanted=all&_r=2&#map-search

New York Times, June 18, 2014, page B6.

OECD Better Life Index.
http://www.oecdbetterlifeindex.org/topics/income/

Office of Policy, Planning and Assessment (2010). Life Expectancy in Tennessee, 2004-2006. Tennessee Department of Health, Nashville, TN.

Ohio ACLU, "Overcharging, Overspending, Overlooking: Cuyahoga County's Costly War on Drugs." Executive Summary. June 16, 2011.
http://www.acluohio.org/assets/issues/DrugPolicy/DrugPolicyAllianceReport2011_0616.pdf

Ohio Department of Rehabilitation and Correction DRC DataSource Reports - Institution Census Reports.

Ohio Department of Rehabilitation and Correction, 2014 Annual Report.
http://www.drc.ohio.gov/web/Reports/Annual/Annual%20Report%202014.pdf

Oliver, Melvin L. and Thomas M. Shapiro. Black Wealth/White Wealth: A New Perspective on Racial Inequality. Tenth-Anniversary Edition. New York: Routledge, 2006.

Pawasarat, John and Lois M. Quinn, Wisconsin's Mass Incarceration of African American Males: Workforce Challenges for 2013. Employment and Training Institute University of Wisconsin-Milwaukee, 2013, p. 1.
www4.uwm.edu/eti/2013/BlackImprisonment.pdf

Pennsylvania Department of Corrections, Annual Statistical Report, 2011.
file:///Users/mhacls/Downloads/2011%20Annual%20Statitstical%20Report.pdf

Pennsylvania State Coroners Association, Heroin Overdose Death Report, 2009-2013.
http://www.co.westmoreland.pa.us/Archive/ViewFile/Item/495

Perine, Jerilyn; Reilly, Neil; Bahchieva, Raisa. Making Neighborhoods: Study Summary and Highlights. CHPC Citizens Housing Planning Council, November 2014.

Pew Charitable Trusts, 2010. Collateral Costs: Incarceration's Effect on Economic Mobility. Washington, DC: The Pew Charitable Trusts.

Piketty, Thomas. Capital in the Twenty-First Century. Trans. Arthur Goldhammer. Cambridge, MA.: Harvard University Press, 2014.

Pohlmann, Marcus D. Opportunity Lost: Race and Poverty in the Memphis City Schools. Knoxville: The University of Tennessee Press, 2008.

Prince George's County Health Department, Public Health Quick Stats, August 2012. http://www.princegeorgescountymd.gov/sites/Health/Resources/Plan ningHealthStats/Statistics/Documents/Quick+Stats_8-12-1.pdf

Prison Policy Initiative. http://www.prisonpolicy.org/reports/rates.html

Prison Policy. www.prisonpolicy.org/profiles/IL.html

Pudup, Gary, "Rockefeller Drug Laws Create Racial Disparities in Rochester," May 15, 2008. http://www.nyclu.org/content/rockefeller-drug-laws-create-racial-disparities-rochester

Rank, Mark Robert. One Nation, Underprivileged: Why American Poverty Affects Us All. Oxford University Press, 2005.

Reardon, Sean F. and Bischoff, Kendra. Growth in the Residential Segregation of Families by Income, 1970-2009. US2010, November 2011. https://dl.dropboxusercontent.com/u/9108869/RussellSageIncomeSe gregationreport-1.pdf

Reynolds, Arthur J. et al. Association of a Full-Day vs Part-Day Preschool Intervention With School Readiness, Attendance, and Parent Involvement *JAMA.* 2014;312(20):2126-2134.

Rueben, Kim and Murray, Sheila. Racial Disparities in Education Finance: Going Beyond Equal Revenues. Urban Institute Discussion Paper N. 29, November 2008. http://www.urban.org/UploadedPDF/411785_equal_revenues.pdf

Sharkey, Patrick. Neighborhoods and the Black-White Mobility Gap. Philadelphia: The Pew Charitable Trusts, 2009. http://www.pewstates.org/uploadedFiles/PCS_Assets/2009/PEW_N EIGHBORHOODS(1).pdf.

Sharkey, Patrick. Stuck in Place: Urban Neighborhoods and the End of Progress toward Racial Equity.

Shelby County Sheriff's Office. http://www.shelby-sheriff.org/jl/

Sheppard, James M. "Criminal Justice," in Miller, Dana K. (ed.). The State of Black Rochester 2013, Rochester, Rochester Area Community Foundation's African American Giving Initiative, 2013.

Siegel, Loren; Perry, Robert A.; Carey, Corinne. NYCLU, March 2009. The Rockefeller Drug Laws: Unjust, Irrational, Ineffective. http://www.nyclu.org/files/publications/nyclu_pub_rockefeller.pdf

Sims, Patrick and Vaughan, Debra. "The State of Public Education in New Orleans: 2014 Report." New Orleans: The Cowen Institute for Public Education Initiatives at Tulane University, 2014, p. 2. http://www.speno2014.com/wp-content/uploads/2014/08/SPENO-HQ.pdf

Social Science Research Council. Measure of America, 2014. http://www.measureofamerica.org/

Spatig-Amerikaner, Ary. Unequal Education: Federal Loophole Enables Lower Spending on Students of Color. Center for American Progress, August 2012.

Stroud, Matt. "Philadelphia Schools Closing While a New $400 Million Prison is Under Construction: Could It Be Worse Than It Sounds?" Forbes, June 17, 2013. http://www.forbes.com/sites/mattstroud/2013/06/17/philadelphia-schools-closing-while-new-400-million-prison-under-construction/

Substance Abuse and Mental Health Services Administration, Results from the 2012 National Survey on Drug Use and Health: Summary of National Findings, NSDUH Series H-46, HHS Publication No. (SMA) 13-4795. Rockville, MD: Substance Abuse and Mental Health Services Administration, 2013. http://www.samhsa.gov/data/nsduh/2012summnatfinddettables/natio nalfindings/nsduhresults2012.htm#ch2.9

Tennessee Department of Correction, Decision Support: Research & Planning Division, FY 2013 Statistical Abstract, October 2013.

Tennessee Department of Education, Data. http://www.tn.gov/education/data/download_data.shtml

Tennessee Department of Education, State Report Cards. http://edu.reportcard.state.tn.us/pls/apex/f?p=200:20:3966078826724869::NO

Texas Taxpayer & Student Fairness Coalition (TTSFC) v. State, August 28, 2014.

Tippett, Rebecca; Jones-DeWeever, Avis; Rockeymoore, Maya; Hamilton, Darrick and Darity, William, Jr. Beyond Broke: Why Closing the Racial Wealth Gap is a Priority for National Economic Security. Chapel Hill: Center for Global Policy Solutions, May 2014.

U. S. Bureau of the Census 2010 Census Summary File 2, Table DP-1.

U. S. Bureau of the Census, 2012 ACS 1-year survey, tables B19313A&B.

U. S. Bureau of the Census, American Community Survey 2011-2013 3-Year Estimates, table S0201.

U. S. Bureau of the Census, Educational Attainment in the United States: 2007. Population Characteristics, January 2009. http://www.census.gov/prod/2009pubs/p20-560.pdf

U. S. Bureau of the Census, Group Quarters Population by Sex, Age, and Type of Group Quarters 2010, Table QT-P13.

U. S. Bureau of the Census, Selected Economic Characteristics, 2006-2010 American Community Survey, DPO3.

U. S. Bureau of the Census, Selected Economic Characteristics, 2006-2010 American Community Survey Selected Population Tables, DP03.

U. S. Bureau of the Census, Selected Population Profile 2010-2, American Community Survey, S0201.

U. S. Bureau of the Census, Survey of Income and Program Participation, 2008 Panel, Wave 10; Internet Release Date: 3/21/2013, Updated: May 13, 2013.

U. S. Bureau of the Census, Table B19054, ACS 2006-2010.

U. S. Bureau of the Census, U.S. Wealth Tables 2011, Table 1.

U. S. Bureau of the Census, Wealth and Asset Ownership of Households, Table 5. www.census.gov/people/wealth

U. S. Bureau of the Census, Wealth and Asset Ownership. http://www.census.gov/people/wealth/

U. S. Department of Education, National Center for Education Statistics, IPEDS Data Center. http://nces.ed.gov/ipeds/datacenter/Data.aspx

U. S. Department of Education, Office for Civil Rights, 2011 Survey.

U. S. Department of Justice. www.justice.gov/usao/ohn/news/2013/14marcpd.html

U. S. Health and Human Services. www.hhs.gov/healthcare/facts/factsheets/2012/04/aca-and-african-americans04122012a.html

U.S. Bureau of Labor Statistics. http://www.bls.gov/emp/ep_chart_001.htm.

U.S. Department of Commerce, Economics and Statistics Administration, Bureau of the Census. We The Americans: Blacks, September, 1993. http://www.census.gov/prod/cen1990/wepeople/we-1.pdf

U.S. Department of Education Office for Civil Rights. Civil Rights Data Collection. Data Snapshot: School Discipline. Issue Brief No. 1 (March 2014).

U.S. Department of Education, National Center for Education Statistic, The Condition of Education, Status of Rural Education, May, 2013, nces.ed.gov/programs/coe/indicator_tla.asp.

U.S. Department of Education, National Center for Education Statistics, Digest of Education Statistics, 2012, Table 376.

U.S. Department of Education, National Center for Education Statistics, IPEDS.

United States Department of Health and Human Services. Substance Abuse and Mental Health Services Administration. Center for Behavioral Health Statistics and Quality. National Survey on Drug

Use and Health, 2011.
http://www.icpsr.umich.edu/quicktables/quickoptions.do
http://doi.org/10.3886/ICPSR34481.v3

Urahn, Susan K.; Currier, Erin; Elliott, Diana; Wechsler, Lauren, and
Wilson, Denise. Pursuing the American Dream. Philadelphia: Pew
Charitable Trusts, 2012, p. 18.
http://www.pewstates.org/uploadedFiles/PCS_Assets/2012/Pursuing
_American_Dream.pdf

Wakefield, Sara and Wildeman, Christopher. Children of the Prison
Boom: Mass Incarceration and the Future of American Inequality.
Oxford: Oxford University Press, 2014.

Washington Post.
www.washingtonpost.com/blogs/wonkblog/wp/2013/06/04/the-
blackwhite-marijuana-arrest-gap-in-nine-charts/

Wilkes, Rima, and John Iceland. "Hypersegregation." Encyclopedia of
Social Problems. Ed.

Wisconsin State Department of Corrections, Profile of Inmates in Prison
on December 31, 2013, June 2014.

WNYC. Median Income Across the US. http://project.wnyc.org/median-
income-nation/?#11/40.7306/-73.9866

Zimmerman R, Li W, Gambatese M, Madsen A, Lasner-Frater L, Kelley
D, Kennedy J, Maduro G, Sun Y. Summary of Vital Statistics, 2012:
Infant Mortality. New York, NY: New York City Department of
Health and Mental Hygiene, Office of Vital Statistics, 2013.

Index

A

C

233, 238, 242, 243, 244, 255,
256, 260, 261, 262, 265, 266,
267, 268, 273
New York City, ii, 19, 20, 59, 67,
84, 117, 139, 149, 164, 174,
175, 176, 177, 178, 179, 181,
182, 183, 185, 186, 189, 190,
192, 193, 194, 195, 196, 260,
267, 273
New York City Department of
Education, 182, 183, 184, 185,
186, 187, 190, 191, 192
New York City Department of
Health and Mental Hygiene, 176,
195, 273
New York City Police Department,
188, 189
New York Post, 195
New York State, 122, 182, 188, 196,
223, 232, 233, 242, 267
New York State Attorney General,
188
New York State Board of Regents,
196, 267
New York State Department of
Education, 233, 242, 243, 267
New York State Department of
Health, 242, 267
New York State Education
Department, 122, 267
New York State English Language
Arts test, 182
New York State Office of the
Attorney General, 196, 267
New York Times, 48, 66, 67, 152,
184, 196, 242, 261
Nixon, President Richard, 13, 51
nutrition, 71
NYCLU, 238, 243, 270

O

OECD Better Life Index., 242, 268
Office for Civil Rights, U.S.
Department of Education, 66,
104, 116, 122, 152, 173, 197,
219, 255, 272

Ohio, 88, 89, 94, 97, 99, 104, 105,
261, 265, 268
Ohio Department of Rehabilitation
and Correction, 104, 105, 268
Oliver, Melvin, 17, 18, 20, 21, 27,
54, 60, 63, 64, 131, 151, 249,
268
Oliver, Melvin L., 255
Oman, 2
Organisation for Economic Cooperation and Development, 190
Organization for Economic
Cooperation and Development,
197, 227
Orleans Parish, 164, 165, 166, 169,
172, 264
Orleans Parish School Board
(OPSB), 164
out-of-school suspensions, 76, 116,
139, 207
out-school-suspensions, 139

P

parental education, 34, 136, 210
Parents United for Public Education,
219
parole, 53, 81, 86, 98, 144, 167,
168, 213, 238, 239, 259
Pawasarat, John, 144, 145, 146, 149,
153, 268
Pennsylvania Department of
Corrections, 220, 268
Pennsylvania Department of
Education, 219
Pennsylvania Standards School
Assessment, 220
per capita income, 4, 108, 158, 226
per student expenditure, 111
Perine, Jerilyn, 175, 195, 269
Perry, Robert A., 243, 270
Pettit, Betty, 52, 53
Pew Charitable Trusts, 4, 23, 61, 64,
67, 85, 104, 122, 152, 153, 172,
218, 219, 263, 269, 270, 273
Philadelphia, ii, 15, 37, 59, 61, 64,
65, 85, 104, 122, 138, 172, 198,

www.ingramcontent.com/pod-product-compliance
Lightning Source LLC
Chambersburg PA
CBHW072113270326
41931CB00010B/1544